The New

"A century ago, the US had a problem of corporate governance: the separation of ownership (by numerous, weak individual shareholders) from control (by relatively few, powerful corporate managers). Today, corporate shares are now mostly owned and voted not by individual investors, but by a limited group of large institutional investors. These asset managers are supposed to act in the best interests of the ultimate owners, the regular people and small businesses who, frequently through retirement accounts and 401(k)s, are the true suppliers of capital to corporations. But do the asset managers so act? Indeed, can they so act? *The New Power Brokers* elegantly surveys the terrain of this brave new world of asset-manager capitalism, identifying a host of problems and challenges and pointing the way to possible solutions."
—Richard Sylla, Professor Emeritus of Economics, New York University

"New, powerful dynamics shape how institutional shareholders exercise their considerable power over the world's largest corporations. Not only have the shareholders changed, but their investment strategies and objectives have evolved, calling into question whether the traditional model of the large public corporation remains accurate today. *The New Power Brokers* deftly takes the reader inside the black box of institutional share ownership to consider the economic, legal, and technological developments that are shaping this new paradigm."
—Charles Whitehead, Myron C. Taylor Alumni Professor of Business Law, Cornell Law School

"The soft but growing power that large asset managers can exert over public companies has rightly emerged as an important, complicated and increasingly controversial topic in recent years. Investment groups are damned if they do engage more aggressively, and damned if they don't. Sahand Moarefy's book *The New Power Brokers* is an invaluable exploration of the debate surrounding 'asset manager capitalism', and tackles this thorny subject with aplomb."
—Robin Wigglesworth, financial journalist and author, most recently, of *Trillions: How a Band of Wall Street Renegades Invented the Index Fund and Changed Finance Forever*

"Sahand Moarefy's brilliant and compelling analysis of the power of institutional investors today rivals Adolf Berle's response to the power of corporations in the early part of the 20th century. His book demands an equally wide readership so that we can once again generate support for new policies that are urgently needed to build a fairer capitalism."
—Martin Daunton, Emeritus Professor of Economic History, University of Cambridge, and author of *The Economic Government of the World 1933-2023*

"One of the great transformations of corporate ownership in the U.S. is now complete. Institutional investors held 6 percent of corporate equities in 1950 but more than 80 percent now, and from this all else follows. In his tour de force, Sahand Moarefy compellingly demonstrates that the drivers of big business have become the large global asset managers, who determine everything from director independence to environmental progress. To understand why and what the future holds, *The New Power Brokers* is an imperative roadmap."

—Michael Useem, Faculty Director of the McNulty Leadership Program, Wharton School, University of Pennsylvania, and author of *Investor Capitalism: How Money Managers Are Changing the Face of Corporate America*

"For more than a decade, many corporate leaders have declared themselves in favor of a more moral form of capitalism. Some have claimed that institutional fund managers can, simply by their investment choices, solve the planetary challenges we face. With remarkable fluency and expertise, Sahand Moarefy shows instead that asset fund managers and index fund leadership have not been as effective as many claim in implementing the goals of ESG. While some look to business savior figures such as Steve Jobs or Elon Musk as the leaders of capitalism, Moarefy shows instead that we need to be much more focused on the asset managers who are making the decisions that shape our world."

—Jacob Soll, University Professor and Professor of Philosophy, History, and Accounting, University of Southern California, and author, most recently, of *Free Market: The History of an Idea*

"*The New Power Brokers* is an important book, guiding us from the managerial revolution to the shareholder revolution to the passive investing revolution—from a more precise understanding of corporate law to a deeper appreciation of political economy."

—Julius Krein, Editor and Founder, *American Affairs*

Sahand Moarefy

The New Power Brokers

The Rise of Asset Manager Capitalism and the New Economic Order

Sahand Moarefy
New York, NY, USA

ISBN 978-3-031-64732-1   ISBN 978-3-031-64733-8 (eBook)
https://doi.org/10.1007/978-3-031-64733-8

© The Editor(s) (if applicable) and The Author(s), under exclusive license to Springer Nature Switzerland AG 2024

This work is subject to copyright. All rights are solely and exclusively licensed by the Publisher, whether the whole or part of the material is concerned, specifically the rights of translation, reprinting, reuse of illustrations, recitation, broadcasting, reproduction on microfilms or in any other physical way, and transmission or information storage and retrieval, electronic adaptation, computer software, or by similar or dissimilar methodology now known or hereafter developed.
The use of general descriptive names, registered names, trademarks, service marks, etc. in this publication does not imply, even in the absence of a specific statement, that such names are exempt from the relevant protective laws and regulations and therefore free for general use.
The publisher, the authors and the editors are safe to assume that the advice and information in this book are believed to be true and accurate at the date of publication. Neither the publisher nor the authors or the editors give a warranty, expressed or implied, with respect to the material contained herein or for any errors or omissions that may have been made. The publisher remains neutral with regard to jurisdictional claims in published maps and institutional affiliations.

This Palgrave Macmillan imprint is published by the registered company Springer Nature Switzerland AG
The registered company address is: Gewerbestrasse 11, 6330 Cham, Switzerland

If disposing of this product, please recycle the paper.

Preface

The origin story of this book—or, to put it more precisely, the ideas and sentiments that are expressed within it—trace back to a so-called investment stewardship conference I attended as a junior corporate attorney in September 2019. This was the first conference of its kind to which I had been invited and I came expecting that it would be nothing more than a forum to discuss the major corporate and securities law developments of the preceding year. The guest list overwhelmingly consisted of legal professionals, hailing from the law firm world as well as in-house roles at public companies and the world's largest institutional investment firms. I anticipated that the tone and tenor of the discussion would reflect the cerebral temperament characteristic of the corporate bar.

The actual experience of the conference was different. A month prior, the Business Roundtable—a lobbying organization consisting of the CEOs of America's largest public companies—had issued a public statement announcing that it no longer endorsed the view that "corporations exist principally to serve shareholders" and that instead, companies must focus on creating long-term value for all of their stakeholders, such as employees, communities, suppliers, and customers.[1] This proclamation animated the discussion among the conference participants, which ended up assuming an

---

[1] Business Roundtable. 2019. "Business Roundtable Redefines the Purpose of a Corporation to Promote 'an Economy That Serves All Americans.'" *Business Roundtable*. https://www.businessroundtable.org/business-roundtable-redefines-the-purpose-of-a-corporation-to-promote-an-economy-that-serves-all-americans

almost political air—focusing on the responsibilities of companies as *social actors*—rather than the intricacies of new SEC guidance or case law in Delaware's well-established business courts. I was particularly fascinated by the rhetoric of the representatives of the large investment management firms, comprised of investment stewardship personnel who managed the firms' voting decision-making and corporate engagement processes. They were the ones presiding over the conference's panel events and sidebar sessions, and defining the discussion agenda. As the other conference attendees philosophized about the true purpose of the corporation, it was the investment stewardship representatives who steered the conversation and helped guide the participants in thinking about ways to practically enact "stakeholder capitalism"—with respect to traditional corporate governance topics, such as how a company's board of directors should be structured, as well as environmental and social matters, like climate change and diversity. In a sense, these individuals appeared to take on the role of political organizers, who in shaping the discussion agenda among the conference participants imbued the conference with its quasi-political overtone.

The conference left a deep impression on me. As a corporate attorney at one of the nation's leading corporate activism defense law firms, I regularly found myself helping advise America's largest public companies as they contended with a different breed of institutional investor—shareholder activist hedge funds who invested in companies with a view to changing how their businesses were managed and operated. In contrast to the broad-minded, almost idealistic rhetoric I heard from the investment stewardship representatives, these investors were the real Gordon Gekkos of Wall Street, loudly and proudly proclaiming their earthly motivations to do whatever was necessary to maximize share price and financial returns. The differences felt especially pronounced as I left the conference, but the fact that these two types of investment firms seemed focused on changing the companies in which they invested struck me to be an interesting common thread.

In the five years that have elapsed since this conference took place, the world has been rocked by a number of history-altering events, most notably the COVID-19 pandemic and Russia's invasion of Ukraine in 2022. The discourse around the purpose of the corporation has also evolved. The Business Roundtable's 2019 announcement ushered in a cascading wave of calls to transform the governance structure of America's corporations, only to be beaten back in the last two to three years by a torrent of demands to restore the primacy of "shareholder interests" in executive management decisions. What has remained constant through these vicissitudes is the growing power of institutional investors in our economy, which forms the subject matter of this book. This book interchangeably uses a number of terms when discussing these new power brokers in our economy—asset managers, investment firms, institutional investment intermediaries, and the like.

While the Introduction that follows provides a summary of the analyses and arguments set forth in this book, I would like to take the opportunity here to further set the stage by making a few preliminary comments about the book's intended breadth and focus.

This book primarily focuses on the control asset managers have accumulated over America's public companies—that is, companies whose shares are publicly traded on America's major national securities exchanges, like the New York Stock Exchange and NASDAQ, as opposed to privately owned businesses whose stock is held by a limited group of investors. Despite the immense growth that private capital markets have experienced over the last two decades, public markets remain much larger and more significant. As of 2021, the aggregate value of global equity markets was estimated at $124 trillion, compared to $10 trillion for private markets.[2] In addition, as Chapter 7 later details, much of the growth in private markets has been driven by the failures of the public markets. Whatever challenges may be posed by the size of today's private capital markets, they cannot be appropriately dealt with without first engaging with the state of today's public markets and the role institutional investors play therein.

Much of mainstream discourse about the business world fixates on corporations as the central actors in our economy. Indeed, there are important business issues and phenomena—like corporate political spending and market concentration—that cannot be properly evaluated without making the corporation the focal point of the examination. These topics have been extensively written about in the policy literature, and I do not intend to retread that ground here. Instead, this book hopes to broaden the perimeter of the discourse by shedding light on the dominant role that institutional investors play in shaping corporate activity. Over the last few decades, scholars of economics and corporate law have devoted considerable attention to the institutionalization of the investment space, but these discussions have largely been confined to academic journals and are technical in nature and scope. A central objective of this book is to bring this subject matter to a wider readership by providing an account of how our current system of asset manager capitalism has come to function that is at once more fulsome and more accessible to non-experts.

---

[2] SIFMA. 2022. "2022 Capital Markets Fact Book." *Securities Industry and Financial Markets Association*. www.sifma.org/wp-content/uploads/2022/07/CM-Fact-Book-2022-SIFMA.pdf

The topics that are at the heart of this book—corporate governance, proxy voting, and the relationship between shareholders and the companies in which they invest—cannot be understood without engaging with the complex array of legal developments that have shaped today's system of asset manager capitalism. I have made an effort to describe and analyze these developments, while also not getting lost in the weeds and distracting from the larger social and economic themes that are the focus of this book. In that light, I ask for two different forms of dispensation from my readers. To those who are not lawyers, I ask for a measure of patience as we slog through the technical details of the legal and policy changes that have created the world in which we live today. It may be tempting to glaze over this minutia, but I assure the reader that the details are a critical part of the story that merit a close reading. Separately, to those who have a background in corporate law, I ask for some rope as I flesh out the book's bigger picture narrative. Any one of the chapters in this book deals with a multiplicity of legal topics, each of which could be the subject of a hundred-page-plus law journal essay. I have cited a plethora of academic articles and studies that underlie the contentions set forth in this book or that I otherwise think have relevance to the topics discussed herein. At the end of the day, though, my overarching goal in this book is not to provide an exhaustive accounting of each and every work of academic scholarship on the subject of institutional investors, but rather to provide an accurate yet digestible overview of the changes that have transpired in the corporate and investment landscape and my perspective on their larger social implications.

When I first set out to write this book in the Spring of 2022, I did not expect it would take as much time as it did to complete. Alas, the task of undertaking a book project together with a full-time job as a corporate attorney made it inevitable that this book could not be finished in a short, inspired fit of passion. Ultimately, I think the book benefitted from the length of time it took to finalize the manuscript by allowing me to more carefully develop the book's analysis, and enhance the currency of that analysis to reflect a number of the important developments in the investor and corporate governance landscape over the last few years. Top of mind when I had originally begun writing this book were the Big Three index funds—BlackRock, Vanguard, and State Street—whose growing assertiveness as shareholders had begun to draw scrutiny from political talking heads in the late 2010s, particularly with respect to environmental, social, and governance (ESG) issues In the Fall of 2020, I had written an article on the topic for the policy journal *American Affairs* entitled "The New Power Brokers: Index Funds and the Public Interest," and I was looking to use this book as an opportunity to expand on the ideas I had laid out in that article. As I dived into the research and writing process, it became evident that the rise of the Big Three and ESG was just the tip of the iceberg and that the bigger issue that warranted examination was the rise of institutional investors as a group and the wider economic and social effects of their growth in influence. The emergence of large global asset management firms—which include the Big Three index funds but also encompass hundreds of other global asset managers with centibillion or trillion dollar size asset portfolios—became a focal point of attention. Several years later, the popularity of ESG has waned, and so has Big Three advocacy on ESG, mooting some of the partisan controversy surrounding the rise of "Woke Capital". The less politically charged atmosphere that has emerged (at least when it comes to the topic of institutional investors) now provides an opportunity to dispassionately examine the seismic changes that have reshaped our capital markets, with long-lasting consequences that extend beyond the rise of the ESG movement. I hope that this book's expanded scope will contribute to a deeper conversation about the evolution of our system of asset manager capitalism and what the future may look like in our post-ESG world.

Although it would be impossible to thank everyone who helped me as I wrote this book, I must express gratitude to my parents, who first encouraged me to take these ideas and translate them into book form, and my wife, Jeylan, for her patience as this project imposed ever greater demands on a schedule already stretched thin by a demanding legal career. For comments and discussions, this book benefitted from extensive feedback from academics and practitioners in corporate law and finance. I must also thank my friend Sam Safari, who diligently assisted me in proofing, properly formatting, and validating the citations in the manuscript, no small feat given his own busy schedule as a Harvard Law School student. All errors remain my responsibility.

August 2024   Sahand Moarefy

Contents

1	Introduction	1
2	The Early American Corporation	13
3	Adolf Berle and the Modern Corporation	23
4	The Rise of Asset Manager Capitalism	39
5	The Emergence of the Shareholder Primacy Paradigm	55
6	The New Stakeholder Capitalism and ESG	67
7	The ESG Report Card and Rise of Private Markets	87
8	Asset Manager Capitalism and the Energy Industry	105
9	Institutional Setup of Today's Asset Managers	117
10	The Post-ESG World and a Roadmap for the Future	131
11	A New Stewardship Framework	149
Index		161

1

Introduction

On May 26, 2021, oil and gas giant Exxon Mobil reported preliminary vote results from its annual shareholder meeting held earlier that morning. After a grueling six month proxy battle with the hedge fund Engine No. 1, Exxon Mobil announced the election of two of Engine No. 1's nominees and the reelection of eight of Exxon Mobil's incumbent directors. The following week, Exxon Mobil announced an updated vote tally reporting the election of three of Engine No. 1's nominees and the reelection of nine of Exxon Mobil's incumbent directors.

Engine No. 1's victory represented a watershed moment. Owning only a 0.02% stake in Exxon, Engine No. 1 had succeeded in mounting a first-of-its-kind, environmentally focused proxy contest that called on shareholders to vote for its director candidates as part of a corporate overhaul to reduce the company's carbon footprint and accelerate its transition to more sustainable energy alternatives. Despite its diminutive shareholdings, Engine No. 1 managed to get its director candidates elected to Exxon's board by winning the support of Exxon's largest shareholders, including the three largest asset managers in the world—BlackRock, State Street, and Vanguard or the "Big Three"—who had come to support efforts to combat climate change and other Environmental, Social, and Governance causes. The business media immediately seized on the story: "Exxon's Board Defeat Signals the Rise of Social-Good Activists" reported *The New York Times*; the Wall Street research firm Valens Research raved more breathlessly "Engine No.1's victory over Exxon shows that sometimes David can still beat Goliath"; according to

Bloomberg, "Engine No. 1's Win Provides Boost for ESG Advocates."[1] After Engine No. 1's victory, corporate directors needed to prioritize big-picture environmental and social questions, or risk losing their seats. As an executive at one impact investing fund would note: "ESG is now core to investment processes and decisions. Environmental and social issues can now make or break directors in a way that wasn't previously possible."[2]

While Engine No. 1's victory would become arguably the biggest news story for Exxon in 2021, it was not the only hedge fund with which Exxon found itself clashing that year. Almost concurrently with Engine No. 1's launch of its campaign in December 2020, though to less media fanfare, New York-based hedge fund D.E. Shaw began calling on Exxon to cut capital expenditures and operating expenses to maintain its dividend. Unlike Engine No. 1, D.E. Shaw focused on pushing Exxon to take actions to maximize financial returns to shareholders, and to do so quickly. D.E. Shaw also did not run a public proxy contest, instead conducting its pressure campaign primarily through private outreach to the company's board and management. Three months before Exxon's annual meeting, Exxon and D.E. Shaw agreed to bury the hatchet, with Exxon announcing its commitment to realize $6 billion in cost savings and adding two new independent directors to its board with "expertise in capital allocation."[3]

At first glance, Engine No. 1 and D.E. Shaw's campaigns could not appear to be any more different, both in terms of their styles and objectives. On one level, they seem to embody the two competing visions of the public corporation that have been driving much of today's debate about

---

[1] Philips, Matt. 2021. "ExxonExxon's Board Defeat Signals the Rise of Social-Good Activists." The New York Times. https://www.nytimes.com/2021/06/09/business/exxon-mobil-engine-no1-activist.html;

Valens Research. 2021. "Engine No.1's victory over Exxon shows that sometimes David can still beat Goliath." https://www.valens-research.com/investor-essentials-daily/xom-exxon-mobil-engine-no-1s-victory-over-exxon-shows-david-still-beat-goliath/;

Marsh, Alastair and Saijel Kishan. 2021. "Engine No. 1's Exxon Win Provides Boost for ESG Advocates." https://www.bloomberg.com/news/articles/2021-05-27/engine-no-1-s-exxon-win-signals-turning-point-for-esg-investors.

[2] Marsh, "Engine No. 1's Exxon Win Provides Boost for ESG Advocates."

[3] See, e.g., Reuters. 2020. "Hedge fund D.E. Shaw pushes Exxon to make changes, cut costs, boost performance." https://www.reuters.com/article/exxon-deshaw/hedge-fund-d-e-shaw-pushes-exxon-to-make-changes-cut-costs-improve-performance-sources-idUSKBN28J2JQ/;

D.E. Shaw Press Release. 2021. "The D. E. Shaw Group Welcomes ExxonMobil's Announcements." https://www.businesswire.com/news/home/20210301005559/en/The-D.-E.-Shaw-Group-Welcomes-ExxonMobil%E2%80%99s-Announcements;

de la Merced, Michael J. 2021. "How Exxon Lost a Board Battle With a Small Hedge Fund." https://www.nytimes.com/2021/05/28/business/energy-environment/exxon-engine-board.html;

Deveau, Scott. 2021. "Exxon Is Said to Be in Talks With D.E. Shaw on New Directors." https://www.bloomberg.com/news/articles/2021-02-01/exxon-is-said-to-be-in-talks-with-d-e-shaw-over-new-directors.

the future of capitalism, with Engine No. 1's call for greater environmental consciousness signifying a new broader-minded, socially oriented model of corporate purpose, in contrast to D.E. Shaw's narrower emphasis on financial returns. But looking deeper, the success of Engine No.1 and D.E. Shaw's efforts reveal a common thread—the growing power of asset managers over America's public companies. Over the course of the last 70 years, institutional investors—ranging from pension funds to activist hedge funds to the large passive index fund managers—have come to own the substantial majority of corporate equities in the United States and have wielded that ownership to fundamentally reshape corporate America along a variety of dimensions, such as corporate strategy, financial planning, human resources management, and even social and political advocacy. For most of American history, investing was simple: you purchased shares and left the operation of the company to management; if you were dissatisfied with the firm's performance, you sold your shares. With the rise of asset managers, shareholders now attempt to directly change the companies in which they invest.

This book chronicles the economic, legal, and technological developments at the heart of this transformation, and discusses how those developments should inform our thinking about the political economy of capitalism in the twenty-first century.

This book makes three overarching arguments:

First, the rise of asset managers has radically altered the structure of our public markets in ways that call for a reexamination of many of the ideas and assumptions that have long animated discourse about the relationship between shareholders and the companies in which they invest. The conception of shareholder interests as a central focus in corporate governance originally emerged in the early twentieth century as a response to the rise of big business and corporate tycoons who faced relatively limited constraints from shareholders and others in how they operated their businesses. Whether that focus remains sensible today is less clear cut now when, unlike the widely dispersed shareholders of the past, today's shareholders are mostly global asset management firms that are functionally investment intermediaries and whose significant—often controlling—positions in their target companies make it impossible for the latter to ignore their dictates. The nature of investing has also profoundly changed. In conventional thinking, the shareholder is thought of as an individual investor in a single company or limited universe of companies, whereas the underlying providers of capital to the asset management industry are for the most part regular working people investing through 401(k) accounts and retirement plans, the proceeds of which are then deployed by institutional investors in a variety of strategies across a broadly diversified range of assets.

Second, the status quo is suboptimal. Corporate managers regularly face pressure from their institutional investors to prioritize the maximization of short-term financial results over other considerations. Once at the global forefront of research and innovation, American companies today channel more of their earnings towards financing shareholder returns—like dividends and share buybacks—and less capital towards internal investments and organic growth strategies. The Great Financial Crisis ushered in renewed calls for a New Deal-style, stakeholder model of capitalism. But in the absence of the robust civic and regulatory institutional framework that undergirded the New Deal era economic order, new self-styled ESG funds and large global asset management firms have come to fill the vacuum and define the new stakeholder capitalism agenda. Pocketbook economic issues were at the heart of the post-World War II liberal consensus. In the new regime, these types of concerns have fallen by the wayside, with attention becoming increasingly redirected towards social and environmental topics in ways that have proven to be ineffectual and harmful.

Exxon is a case study of the damage that this combination of financial short-termism and new social advocacy can produce. When the war in Ukraine disrupted international energy markets in March 2022, Exxon saw itself struggling to meet increased energy demands as it tried to boost oil production after years of contending with pressure from ESG activists to scale back investments in oil and gas production. At the same time, the constant pressure Exxon faced from more conventionally, financially-focused activist hedge funds and others to cut costs and generate operational savings meant that the energy giant was not in a position to commercialize the clean energy alternatives that it had been exploring at a level that could meaningfully compensate for the reduction in oil and gas output. In 2021, Exxon *decreased* research and development expenses by over $150 million.[4] Almost three years later, questions remain as to what tangible benefits were produced by the activist efforts of Engine No. 1 and D.E. Shaw. Exxon has been able to ramp up energy production to catch up with consumer demand, but that ramp-up has been overwhelmingly driven by renewed investments in the company's traditional oil and gas competencies. According to Danielle Fugere, president and chief counsel of the climate change advocacy group As You Sow, Engine No. 1 "has not made a discernible difference in the way Exxon is addressing climate change." Mark van Baal, founder of the activist group

---

[4] Exxon Mobil Corporation. Annual Report on Form 10-K for the fiscal year ended December 31, 2021. 37.

Follow This, has been even more blunt. The hedge fund, he said in the same May 2023 *New York Times* interview, was "the biggest disappointment in the fight against climate change."[5]

Third, successfully reforming our system of asset manager capitalism requires fresh thinking that does not simply reapprise the policy solutions of the past. The two primary levers for regulating corporate conduct in the United States since the New Deal era—mandatory disclosures and fiduciary duties—emerged as mechanisms to address problems emanating from the relationship between public companies and their shareholders in the first half of the twentieth century. Exclusively relying on these mechanisms to contend with today's predicaments is unlikely to succeed when the identity of the corporation and its shareholders, and the nature of the relationship existing between them, have so dramatically changed.

By focusing on the complexity of historical factors that have shaped the current constellation of power relations among investors, corporations, and everyone else, this book hopes to transcend the siloed nature of how the growing influence of asset managers is often talked about in contemporary policy discourse. In recent years, the Big Three index funds and other large global asset management firms have become the subject of heated attacks by political conservatives who view their advocacy on environmental and social issues as a subterfuge for imposing liberal political values on corporate America. Whether or not the political views that motivate these attacks are substantively correct is beyond the scope of this book, but even under a charitable hearing, conservative critiques miss the forest for the trees by fixating on symptoms of deeper changes in the structure of our financial markets. Root causes must be treated. Attempts to revive an idealized Reagan-era ethos of shareholder primacy are likely to be counterproductive not only on their terms but also in terms of the substantive political objectives of conservatives.

Legal academics and practitioners have exhibited a greater willingness to engage with the more fundamental changes in the structure of our economy. However, their discussions tend to have an insular quality and take for granted the overarching normative assumptions of the legal professional class. Anti-ESG critiques, especially from political conservatives, are dismissed as nothing more than bad-faith partisan attacks by right-wing pundits and talking heads. Again, without engaging in an assessment of whether any particular opinion or policy objective is right or wrong in a metaphysical sense, it would behoove the legal community to forthrightly recognize the essentially political character of the power that institutional investors have

---

[5] Sorkin, Andrew Ross. 2023. "Reassessing Engine No. 1's Fight Against Exxon Mobil." The New York Times. http://www.nytimes.com/2023/05/31/business/dealbook/engine-no-1-exxon-mobil.html.

exerted in our economy and the practical necessity that, in a democracy, the needs and opinions of the wider public must be thoughtfully considered when addressing matters of great public interest. Adolf Berle—one of the key intellectuals who helped mold modern corporate governance theory and to whom we will often refer throughout this book—was a turn of the century Progressive and later New Deal Democrat whose political sensibilities deeply shaped his policy analyses and prescriptions. Berle also appreciated that the legitimacy of the New Deal economic order critically depended on the existence of a robust, broad-based popular consensus. Discussions among today's legal practitioners would benefit from a similar appreciation of public sentiment.

Chapter Overview

Chapter 2 sets the scene for our analysis by describing the evolution of the American corporation through the nineteenth and early twentieth centuries, when many of the characteristics associated with the modern corporation came to form. Throughout much of early American history, corporations could only be created by the affirmative act of legislators, and legislators tended to be relatively parsimonious in their grants of corporate status. Those seeking to organize as corporations had to demonstrate a business purpose that advanced the public interest in order to receive a charter. The provisions of a corporation's organizational documents were hashed out through the legislative process and there were considerable limitations on the ability to amend those provisions without the approval of the state.

The rigidity of the corporate structure gave way as America industrialized in the nineteenth century. State governments faced pressure from business interests and entrepreneurs to take a liberal approach towards granting corporate charters and to provide for a more flexible corporate form that would facilitate the type of risk-taking needed to undertake manufacturing and the other capital-intensive businesses driving the Industrial Revolution. The corporation was a rare form of business organization through the eighteenth century and the early nineteenth century and corporations were often closely held by a few shareholders. By the outset of the twentieth century, the number of corporations in the United States was in the thousands, with medium and large-sized corporations having tens or hundreds of thousands of shareholders.

Chapter 3 reviews the work and thinking of the lawyer Adolf Berle, whose 1932 book *The Modern Corporation and Private Property*, co-authored with economist Gardiner Means, is considered the foundational text of modern corporate governance theory. *The Modern Corporation* is best known for its proposition that the changes that had taken place in corporate law and the American economy over the nineteenth and early twentieth centuries had given rise to a "separation of ownership and control" where management—who now held little or no shares in the companies they ran—exercised unfettered control without accountability to shareholders. Much of how we think about corporate law concepts today evolved in response to this separation of ownership and control problem. The dispersion and relative weakness of shareholders, together with the elimination of traditional legal constraints on the behavior of management, called for the development of new mechanisms to protect shareholders from potential abuses by corporate boards. Directors were conceived as trustees that owed fiduciary duties to their shareholders and the critical question for academics and judges in the domain of corporate law was how to appropriately define those duties. The practical challenges shareholders faced in enforcing those duties made it imperative that corporations provide regular disclosures about their businesses so that shareholders could sell their stock if they became unsatisfied with the performance of their investments or disagreed with management. The centrality of mandatory disclosures in regulating the conduct of public companies in the United States is grounded in this premise.

A deep sense of social responsibility motivated Berle. A New Deal Democrat, he was primarily concerned with the social and economic consequences of unchecked corporate power. The separation of ownership and control was just one part of the problem. It was not enough for corporations to be made accountable to stockholders; they needed to act in the public interest. Berle advocated corporate governance reform as one piece of a larger package of policies aimed at steering corporations to behave as positive social actors. In the decades to come, those policies came to form the legal and institutional basis of the mid-twentieth century New Deal economic order—a period in American history notable for both robust economic growth and relatively broad-based prosperity.

Chapter 4 discusses how the rise of asset managers over the last 50 years has transformed the investment landscape and the investor-corporate power dynamics at the heart of the Berlean model of the public corporation. Institutional investors have emerged as the owners of the substantial majority of corporate equities in the United States, giving rise to what former Delaware Supreme Court Chief Justice Leo Strine calls a "separation of ownership from ownership" in which investment intermediaries—not the ultimate real-world providers of capital—are the direct legal owners of the typical company's stock. An analytical model centered around the relationship between stockholders and corporations misses the need to account for the relationships by and among the institutional investors that legally own any given corporation's stock, the capital providers for which those investors act as custodians and society at large. As institutional ownership of corporate stock has increased, so has common ownership among a smaller number of large and powerful asset managers. The emphasis on defining the fiduciary duties of directors as the paramount problem of corporate law made sense in a world in which shareholders were widely dispersed and faced collective action challenges in holding corporate boards to account. The emergence of large institutional investors owning outsized ownership stakes in America's public corporations has turned this foundational element of the Berlean model on its head.

Equity investing strategies and objectives have evolved. Conventionally, the equity investor was thought of as an individual who invested in a single company or limited set of companies based on an expectation of participating in the long-term growth and profitability of the underlying businesses. The picture has changed with the popularization of new investing strategies among asset managers, such as index investing, algorithmic trading, hedge fund activism, and private equity. Corporate disclosures were critical to the long-term, fundamentals-focused investor of yore. They have less salience in the context of today's wide array of new investing strategies.

As the ownership structure of corporate America has evolved, so too has the corporate shareholder obtained greater centrality in common thinking about the role and purpose of the corporation. Chapter 5 addresses how the shareholder has come to be conceived in mainstream business discourse, and the ways in which asset managers have helped shape that conception. The rise of the ideology of shareholder primacy has its roots in the 1970s with the emergence of the Chicago School of free-market economists, who argued that corporations should operate with only one goal in mind—making shareholders as wealthy as possible. Developments in academia and policy changes created an intellectual and regulatory environment receptive to the ideas of shareholder primacy. The rise of asset managers as corporate shareholders ensured that those ideas acquired practical expression in how corporate managers operated their businesses. Furthermore, while asset managers employ a variety of investing strategies, their market activity is by and large short-term focused, as a result of which the model shareholder has come to signify a shareholder who looks to exit and earn a return from their investment over a short period of time, measured in months or at most a few years. Maximizing shareholder value has been interpreted to mean maximizing shareholder value in the short term, encouraging the implementation of measures that increase market value over a short period of time—such as cutting overhead or implementing financial engineering schemes like share repurchases and dividends—over more long-term strategies that involve increases in research and development or capital expenditure investments that may have a minimal or negative immediate stock price impact. Corporate executives who do not follow the line risk blowback from institutional investors who will not hesitate to replace management teams that fall short of expectations. The short-term-oriented model of the shareholder has also shaped the outlook of asset managers that employ investing strategies in which the corporate governance of an individual company has little or no relevance but that must adopt a workable framework within which to make proxy voting decisions in compliance with their fiduciary duties as investment advisors.

In the aftermath of the Great Financial Crisis, a growing number of academics, policymakers, and business people have called for the revival of a stakeholder-focused paradigm of corporate governance in which companies are encouraged to focus on the interests of not only their shareholders but also other corporate constituencies, such as employees, customers, the environment, and society at large. Chapter 6 discusses this movement and the role played by the Big Three and other large asset management firms, who have been among the most vocal advocates of the new stakeholder capitalism. In the absence of the robust civic and regulatory institutional framework that undergirded the New Deal era economic order, the asset management industry has come to fill the vacuum and define the new stakeholder capitalism agenda. As a consequence, the new stakeholder capitalism paradigm now reflects the institutional outlook of asset managers, and derivatively their incentives and limitations. Rather than explicitly embrace stakeholder capitalism as a system of economic organization, these firms have advocated a vision of stakeholder capitalism grounded in the investment philosophy of ESG, which calls on investors to give greater weight to ESG factors in making investment decisions.

Over the last half of the 2010s and the beginning of the 2020s, ESG activism by the largest asset managers has had a profound impact on the behavior of public companies, particularly with respect to the most common advocacy issues promoted under the ESG banner—gender diversity on corporate boards and climate change. Whether or not that impact has been positive is more questionable. Chapter 7 assesses the economic and social effects of ESG advocacy by institutional investors. There is little evidence that the ESG movement has enhanced any commonly accepted shareholder value metric as envisioned by its leading supporters, a point that has even been acknowledged by those who are sympathetic to the ESG movement's posture on issues like gender diversity and climate change. Public opinion is more fractured than during the New Deal era, with ESG emerging as a lightning rod political issue among Republican politicians and conservative pundits who view ESG activism as a device for forcing liberal values on corporate America. There is scant proof that the ESG-based stakeholder paradigm has changed the dynamics of the financial markets in any way that had led to a decline in the shareholder-centric myopia and economic short-termism that helped usher in the growth of the ESG movement in the years following the Great Financial Crisis. Amidst these pressures, fewer companies find it an attractive proposition to either go or remain public. Particularly among technology and other "innovation economy" businesses, it is difficult to pursue the type of long-term-focused and risky investments necessary to grow and flourish in the public markets. As a result, more than a third of corporate equities in the United States today are managed *outside* of public companies in the private markets, with much of the growth occurring in the years following the Great Financial Crisis.

There is perhaps no area of the U.S. economy that more clearly illustrates the deleterious effects of our current system of asset manager capitalism than the energy industry. Chapter 8 explores this story. As the shale revolution picked up in the early 2010s, depressing oil revenues and profitability for U.S. energy companies, shareholder activist hedge funds took advantage of the resulting shareholder discontent and mounted successful campaigns against energy companies to scrap longer term investments in their businesses and to do everything within their power to juice short-term returns through asset divestitures, share repurchases and dividends. Energy companies also came to face pressure from ESG activists and their supporters within the asset management industry to generally re-orient their businesses away from oil and gas in an attempt to combat climate change. While proponents of ESG have often talked about the potential benefits of renewable and clean energy alternatives, institutional investor advocacy on climate change has in practice had a negative orientation that is almost exclusively fixated on pushing energy companies to scale back emission-producing activities. By focusing their attention on large public corporations, ESG activism has had the effect of encouraging those companies to divest their dirty assets to private actors less susceptible to public scrutiny, enabling the divesting firms to cut their individual emissions, but not necessarily altering overall emission levels. The aggregate impact is that ESG activists have fallen short in achieving their overarching environmental goals, and functioned—hand in hand with traditional activist hedge funds—to foster short-termism and underinvestment in the energy industry.

Chapter 9 probes into the voting decision-making and corporate engagement processes of today's largest asset management firms. Instead of approaching the process as a bottom-up exercise, the big asset managers centralize the authority to engage with individual companies and make voting decisions in "governance" or "stewardship" units that act on behalf of the entire fund complex with respect to any given corporate matter. In turn, how governance units go about making voting decisions is driven by the incentives and limitations faced by the personnel staffing these units. The popularity of ESG has been facilitated by both the ideological inclinations of governance professionals as well as those of the industry's largest clients, which tend to be the country's biggest pension funds. When it comes to formulating views on matters that are traditionally economic in nature or have concrete financial implications, like proxy contests or strategic transactions that require shareholder approval, governance professionals—who overwhelmingly hail from legal and compliance backgrounds—frequently lean on active fund managers and proxy advisors. The result is that, despite the rhetoric among many large asset management firms that they seek to promote "long-term value creation" and the "long-term economic interests" of their investors, there is little evidence that the advent of ESG has translated into any shift in how large asset management firms go about engaging corporations on economic and financial issues since the supposed heyday of shareholder primacy in the 1980s and 1990s.

Over the past several years, the popularity of ESG has dissipated, while the pressures towards short-termism and myopic shareholder-centric thinking appear to be stronger than ever. A reassessment of the ESG paradigm is in order, along with a fresh perspective towards the essential challenges endemic to our system of institutional investor capitalism and how best to overcome them. Chapters 10 and 11 offer a vision for the future. Rather than try to revive the traditional shareholder primacy orthodoxy or double down on ESG, scholars and policymakers should confront the reality that large asset managers have come to function as political actors that wield substantial influence over the economy and society as a whole. With the centralization of the voting decision-making process among the world's largest asset managers, it is incontrovertible that shareholder voting is no longer a straightforward investment exercise based on a bottom-up analysis of a limited universe of companies. A separation of ownership from ownership has emerged, but perhaps more importantly, that separation has birthed a new conception of voting and control that is disconnected from traditional notions of investing. The exercise of shareholder voice has in all practical respects assumed the form of a regulatory power, carried out on the basis of a generalized view of what is "good" for corporate America as a whole, and then applied to America's public companies across the board. Efforts to reform the status quo—whether they are effectuated through formal regulatory measures or the volitional actions of market actors—must begin with an acceptance of this basic fact.

2

The Early American Corporation

Although the term "corporation" is frequently used in common parlance as a synonym for company or to refer to a group of people organizing a business enterprise, the corporate form carries a distinct legal meaning and is generally defined by four characteristics that separate it from other forms of business organization. These characteristics are (1) *a bifurcated ownership and management structure* whereby a corporation's stockholders elect a board of directors that oversees and manages the business on a day-to-day basis, (2) *limited liability*, which means that the liability of stockholders is limited to the amount that each has invested in the corporation and that corporate lenders and other creditors are not able to seek recourse against the personal assets of stockholders, (3) *divisibility and transferability of interests*, referring to the ability of stockholders to transfer their interests to others, and (4) *separate existence*, meaning that a corporation has a separate existence of its own to carry on its business in its own name, including to own property, to enter into contracts, to borrow money, and to sue or be sued.[1]

While human beings have been organizing business enterprises through a variety of legal forms for thousands of years, many of which shared similar characteristics to the corporation, it was not until the seventeenth century that business organizations began to exhibit the full range of modern corporate characteristics. Such companies included the Dutch East India Company and the British East India Company, which have since become

---

[1] Wright, Robert E. 2014. Corporation Nation. Philadelphia: University of Pennsylvania Press, 9–24.

best known for the key role they played in the expansion of the Dutch and British commercial empires during the seventeenth and eighteenth centuries. Both corporations were founded in the seventeenth century, enjoyed limited liability, and were managed by a board of directors that was appointed by a group of stockholders who could transfer their interests.[2]

Corporations became a fixture of American economic life early on in the country's history. Incorporation picked up rapidly following the end of English rule, and by the end of the eighteenth century state legislatures had chartered over 300 corporations. The number of incorporations continued to rise through the Civil War, with slight dips following major economic crises. From 1801 to 1810, state legislatures issued charters for 867 business corporations; in the next decade, 1477; and by the 1850s, almost 8000. While they tended to cluster in the Northeast, corporations appeared everywhere. By the 1830s, even frontier states recorded dozens of incorporations.[3] From 1790 to 1860, the United States chartered over twenty-two thousand corporations, far in excess of the number of corporations created in any other country (and most likely in all other countries combined) during that time.[4]

Nevertheless, in the early part of the antebellum period, corporations were not a common or economically significant device for carrying out business activity. Most early American corporations operated within a state or in a city or town, and were owned by a small group of wealthy and locally based stockholders, who could monitor corporate operations firsthand and often invested with a view to earning their return on investment in the form of regular dividends, rather than capital appreciation, effectively viewing their equity investment as a higher-return, higher-risk fixed income instrument.[5] The ability of a corporation to reliably generate cash figured centrally in the mind of the average equity investor, with virtually all equity returns coming in the form of dividends, not capital gains, and there was often little difference in the returns to stocks relative to bonds. The first "large" corporations—as measured by the size of their operations and their shareholder base—emerged

---

[2] Reamer, Norton, and Jesse Downing. 2016. Investment: A History. New York: Columbia University Press, 64, 66.

[3] Wells, Harwell. 2015. "A Long View of Shareholder Power: From the Antebellum Corporation to the Twenty-First Century." Florida Law Review, 1040–1041. http://www.scholarship.law.ufl.edu/cgi/viewcontent.cgi?article=1236&context=flr.

[4] Gomory, Ralph, and Richard Sylla. 2013. "The American Corporation." Daedalus. Vol. 142. no. 2. 102–118.
http://www.amacad.org/publication/american-corporation.

[5] Ibid.; Sylla, Richard, and Robert E. Wright. 2013. "Corporation Formation in the Antebellum United States in Comparative Context." Business History. Vol. 55. no. 4. 653–669. https://www.tandfonline.com/doi/pdf/10.1080/00076791.2012.74197; Taylor, Bryan. 2020. "GFD Guide to Total Returns." Global Financial Data. http://www.globalfinancialdata.com/gfd-guide-to-total-returns.

in the textile industry in New England in the first two decades of the nineteenth century, though these were tiny enterprises in comparison to the business empires of the Gilded Age. The Boston Manufacturing Company, the first of the large New England textile firms, was organized in 1819 and by 1830 had 76 shareholders, with no individual owning more than 8.5% of all outstanding stock. Twenty years later the company's shareholder base had increased to 123 shareholders. Approximately 51% of the company's outstanding stock was held by 17 individuals while the company's executives owned only 11%. The Merrimack, another textile corporation, reported 390 shareholders in 1842. The rise of the railroad industry in the latter years of the antebellum period facilitated the emergence of larger corporations, but even these companies remained relatively limited business enterprises. The New York Central Railroad, established in 1853 and known as the first railroad conglomerate in the United States, operated exclusively within the State of New York in the first few decades of its operations. The New York Central Railroad's base of shareholders was also fairly circumscribed compared to the national railroad companies that became a fixture in the post-Civil War Era economic order, reporting 2445 investors in various cities in New York after it was formed through a combination of ten smaller companies between Albany and Buffalo.[6]

The corporation was viewed with suspicion in early nineteenth-century America. In the eyes of contemporaries, the combination of limited liability and bifurcated ownership and management that characterized the corporate form made it inherently vulnerable to mismanagement and corruption. Adam Smith, the oft-cited father of modern economics lambasted the structure of joint stock companies in *The Wealth of Nations*. "Negligence and profusion, must always prevail, more or less, in the management of the affairs of such a company," Adam Smith wrote, "the directors of such companies being the managers rather of other people's money than of their own, it cannot well be expected that they should watch over it with the same anxious vigilance with which the partners in private copartner[ship] frequently watch over their own." The United States never went as far in restricting corporate activity as the United Kingdom, which in the early eighteenth century forbade the formation of joint-stock companies unless approved by a royal charter, but Americans shared similar concerns regarding the corporate model. The vast majority of states conferred corporate status in limited circumstances. Prior to 1811, substantially every corporate charter was legislated into the law of the

---

[6] Berle, Adolf A., and Gardiner C. Means. 1932. The Modern Corporation and Private Property. New York: Macmillan Company. 11–14.

state by a separate act.[7] Entrepreneurs would have to petition state legislators for a corporate charter, and legislators would require petitioners to demonstrate that their business activities sufficiently implicated the public interest to justify the grant of corporate privileges. The earliest mentions of corporations made little distinction between for-profit and not-for-profit organizations, because all corporations, even those for-profit, were assumed to provide some public benefit.[8] Businesses structured as corporations included banks, insurance companies, fire brigades, and enterprises involved in the construction of transportation infrastructure, such as turnpikes, bridges, and canals.[9]

The terms of a corporate charter, like any other legislative act, were scrutinized and debated among state legislators, who would have to reach an agreement on the final form of a charter before it came into effect. Given the high financial stakes involved, efforts to unduly pressure legislators were not uncommon, but it was an open and public process that at least nominally aimed to safeguard the public, creditors, and stockholders.[10] Corporations were required to have a clearly defined and limited business purpose, circumscribing the scope of discretion on the part of corporate management to run the business. It was not uncommon for a corporate charter to include limitations on the type and amounts of property the corporation could own, minimum capital and cash requirements in order to operate the business, and specific requirements with respect to how transactions should be conducted.[11] Capital requirements were particularly delineated. The corporation was not allowed to commence business until a certain amount of its shares had been paid-up in cash, and it could not issue additional shares below a fixed minimum rate—called the par value—without running the risk of exposing investors who had acquired shares below par value to potential liability for the balance in the event the corporation later became insolvent. Every shareholder was obligated to contribute a minimum cash amount to acquire shares such that the magnitude of dilution an existing shareholder would experience as a result of future issuances would be constrained by the par value.[12] The terms of a charter could not be easily amended or modified. The adoption of a charter was fundamentally a legislative act, so any change to its terms required action by the state legislator. Subject to very limited exceptions, the rights and obligations of a shareholder could not be altered

---

[7] Ibid., 122.
[8] Wells, "Antebellum." 1042.
[9] Berle, Modern Corporation. 11.
[10] Ibid., 122.
[11] Ibid.
[12] Ibid., 122, 131.

without the affected shareholder's consent. As a matter of law, the position of any individual shareholder in any contractual relationship was viewed to be peculiar to that shareholder, and any law that altered that position without the shareholder's consent was perceived as an unconstitutional impairment of contractual rights.[13]

Courts helped shape a common law for corporations that imposed additional constraints on how corporations could be operated. The common law enshrined within shareholders ultimate control over the corporation. While direct management of the corporation's business was vested in the board of directors, that authority was understood as a limited delegation of enumerated powers—specifically laid out in the charter—with residual control over the corporation residing with shareholders. Shareholders had the right to remove directors at will at any time. Any change in corporate purpose or capital structure had to be approved by shareholders, and in the event of any fundamental change, the shareholder vote had to be unanimous. No shareholder could be bound by the result of any vote which was inconsistent with the object and purpose for which the corporation was formed.[14] Courts fashioned a default presumption of preemptive rights in favor of shareholders, based on the premise that a corporation's initial shareholders had earned a right of priority with respect to future investment opportunities as consideration for the risks and uncertainties they had assumed in participating in the formation of a new business venture.[15]

Finally, corporations were generally only authorized to pay dividends out of the excess profits arising from their ordinary business operations. States required that corporations maintain a minimum amount of capital at all times, providing creditors a baseline level of assets against which they could seek recourse in the event of a default.[16] In certain states, like New York, directors could be held criminally liable if the corporation did not comply with statutory minimum capital requirements.[17]

Because of these protections, the early American corporation was—in the words of Adolf Berle—a "rigid and carefully protected" institution that carried out "a limited enterprise, with participations settled in advance, and safeguarded either by the statutory contract or by the common law in various ways."[18] The picture changed over the course of the nineteenth century as

---

[13] Ibid., 122, 136.
[14] Ibid., 122, 129, 130, 136.
[15] Ibid., 133–134.
[16] Ibid., 122–124.
[17] Ibid., 135.
[18] Ibid., 125.

America transformed from a fledgling commercial outpost to a global industrial power. In 1800, the population of the United States stood at a little over five million; by 1850, it had more than quadrupled to 23 million; by the end of the century, America was home to over 76 million people. While the U.S. economy was primarily agricultural at the outset of the nineteenth century, it rapidly industrialized through the subsequent decades, starting with the rise of textiles to the emergence of railroads and manufacturing industries. With this growth came a significant increase in the demand for corporate charters. The new business enterprises of the industrial era tended to be risky and require sizeable capital investments.[19] The corporate form, which permitted entrepreneurs to quickly raise capital and provided for a limited liability shield that protected them from the possibility of personal ruin, became attractive. Legislatures made efforts to accommodate the greater number of corporate petitions, but the rigidity of the legislative chartering process was ill-equipped to satisfy the rise in demand. America's new class of entrepreneurs did not hesitate to voice their frustration, attacking legislative chartering as an ancient relic that was unsuited to the business necessities of the time and vulnerable to corruption by the rich and powerful.

In the face of these pressures, most states scrapped legislative chartering by the middle of the nineteenth century in favor of a general incorporation regime that permitted entrepreneurs to obtain a charter without legislative intervention. Under the new system, state administrators, rather than legislators, would review applications for corporate status. Rather than scrutinize and recommend modifications to a proposed charter based on a case-by-case evaluation of the interests at stake in any application, state administrators played a purely ministerial role in confirming that the charter complied with generally applicable statutory requirements. General incorporation statutes gave entrepreneurs flexibility to operate their businesses and draft charter provisions as they preferred. Corporations no longer had to limit their activities to a specified purpose, but could operate for any "lawful purpose." The requirement that corporations have a minimum level of paid-in capital was weakened as courts accepted the issuance of stock not only for cash but also for property based on appraisal values determined by corporate boards. Courts watered down the once iron-clad law of preemptive rights by providing for exceptions and restrictions, including limiting the applicability of preemptive rights to increases in authorized share counts and issuances of stock for cash and permitting waivers of preemptive rights by stockholders. The common law prohibition on paying dividends out of capital lost its

---

[19] Wells, "Antebellum." 1042.

bite as courts came to view payments made by shareholders for stock in excess of par value as surplus instead of capital, while certain states amended their corporate statutes to allow dividend payments even in instances when corporate losses had eaten into statutory capital.[20]

Corporate boards and management acquired a greater ability to manage their businesses independently of the influence of shareholders through the right to vote by proxy, which allowed passive and less attentive shareholders to delegate their voting decisions to corporate management. States eliminated the right of shareholders to remove directors at will, thereby empowering directors to effectively do as they saw fit during their term of service.

Jurisdictional competition facilitated the emergence of a more management-friendly system of corporate law. In 1889, the state of New Jersey launched an incorporation race by adopting a series of reforms designed to encourage big businesses to incorporate within its borders, including the removal of unanimous stockholder approval requirements for major corporate transactions (such as charter amendments and the issuance of new securities) and the elimination of restrictions on "anti-competitive and unfair labor practices." Out-of-state corporations could take advantage of these provisions by reincorporating in New Jersey, which many proceeded to do. Other states soon sought to emulate New Jersey's laws and fiscal success, with Delaware eventually pulling ahead in the incorporation race and emerging as the home of the majority of the nation's corporations, a position that it retains to this day. Even states that were not seeking out-of-state incorporators adopted new corporation law statutes that, like those of the "chartermongering" states, empowered boards and management over stockholders in order to retain the incorporation business of firms already located in-state.[21]

By the outset of the twentieth century, corporations carried out large swaths of economic activity in the United States. In 1930, 14 railroad corporations operated over 82% of all road mileage in the United States. More than 86% of mining and quarrying businesses were conducted by corporations in 1902. The percentage had increased to 93% by 1919. That year, 99% of wage earners in the copper industry were employed by corporations, 98% in iron ore, 97% in iron and zinc, and 89% in petroleum and natural gas. By 1899, corporations produced approximately two-thirds of all manufactured products and 87% of all goods produced in 1919. Market concentration among large corporations also increased during this period. At the beginning of 1930, the 200 largest non-banking corporations held $81 billion

---

[20] Berle, Modern Corporation. 135–136.
[21] Wells, "Antebellum." 1060.

in combined assets, representing nearly half of the corporate wealth in the United States.[22]

The nineteenth century and first decades of the twentieth century witnessed significant changes in the size and composition of the corporate shareholder base. Local capital was often insufficient to meet the financing needs of the new capital-intensive enterprises of the industrial era and businesses increasingly looked to a broader base of financing sources to fund their operations. These efforts were aided by technological innovations like the telegraph, and later the telephone, as well as the emergence of stock exchanges with truly national and international reach, enabling corporations to reach a larger universe of individuals and institutions than ever before and giving rise to an active market for corporate equities in which shareholders could quickly value and buy and sell stock. Investor expectations evolved as well. The capital demands of the Industrial era drove corporate enterprises to re-invest a greater proportion of their earnings into operations, rather than make distributions to shareholders, as a result of which equity investments lost their appeal to investors as fixed-income instruments. Many shareholders now invested with the hope of later selling their securities at a greater price based on an appreciation in the underlying value of the business. Equity investments obtained a speculative quality that appealed to a wider pool of potential investors who were not just focused on earning a fixed return.

By 1900, many large corporations had several thousand stockholders each, and at least four—American Sugar, U.S. Steel, and the Pennsylvania and Union Pacific railways—each had over 10,000.[23] The great merger movement, which spanned from 1895 to 1905 and saw over a thousand small and closely held manufacturing firms combine into over a hundred larger industrial giants, further increased the size of the corporate shareholder base. To finance the mergers, corporations needed more cash, which they raised through the issuance of equity securities to the public. Between 1900 and 1917 the three largest American corporations each tripled their number of stockholders. World War I accelerated the trend as public campaigns for Liberty Bonds induced millions of Americans to purchase securities for the first time. After the war, the networks built to sell bonds were repurposed to sell common stock. One study has estimated that the number of stockholders during the 1920s increased from a few hundred thousand before World War

---

[22] Berle, Modern Corporation. 14, 30.
[23] Wells, "Antebellum." 1062; see also Navin, Thomas R., and Marian V. Sears. 1955. "The Rise of a Market for Industrial Securities, 1887–1902." The Business History Review.

I, about 3% of households, to almost eight million at the decade's end, a quarter of all households.[24]

Populist sentiment and suspicion of large financial institutions helped give rise to a regulatory environment that discouraged high ownership concentration among financial intermediaries and widened the dispersion of corporate shareholdings. Through the nineteenth century, U.S. law fragmented intermediaries, their portfolios, and their ability to coordinate among themselves.[25] The United States had a fragmented banking system, as each state chartered and protected its own banks, excluding branches from other states' banks. Despite efforts by the early federalists to establish a sort of central bank in the form of the First Bank of the United States—and later the Second Bank of the United States—these efforts encountered stiff opposition from a range of actors, including state banks who did not want to compete with a central bank, Southerners who feared that a central bank would expand the political and economic control of Northerners at the expense of Southern interests, and anti-Federalists who philosophically opposed centralized power. This pushback culminated in President Andrew Jackson's veto of the rechartering of the Second Bank of the United States in 1832. The United States established "national" banks during the Civil War, but the National Bank Act of 1863 and National Bank Act of 1864 were interpreted as prohibiting the ownership of corporate equities by national banks and restricting the operation of national banks to a single location. In 1895, President Cleveland supported proposals to authorize national banks to branch, but lobbyists for unit banks, which each operated from a single location, killed the proposals. Instead, rural national banks were permitted to conduct business with lower capital requirements, encouraging the growth of the anti-branching banker constituency of small, weak local banks that feared and opposed strong national banking operations. In 1915, the Federal Reserve wanted national banks to branch, but the unit bankers succeeded again. Congress kept banks small and local, largely because its own federal organization tied its members to localities, where small-town bankers were powerful. Large businesses could not rely on a single bank to satisfy their financing needs.[26]

Legislators and regulators also took measures to restrain the power of insurance companies. At the beginning of the twentieth century, several of the largest American financial institutions were insurers, which were not subject to the same geographic and operational limitations as banks. The largest New

---

[24] Wells, "Antebellum." 1066.
[25] Roe, Mark J. 1994. Strong Managers, Weak Owners: The Political Roots of American Corporate Finance. Princeton: Princeton University Press. xiv.
[26] Ibid., 54–59.

York insurers were twice as large as the largest banks and were involved in a wide array of activities beyond underwriting insurance policies, including underwriting securities, buying bank stock, and controlling large banks. In 1905, a series of scandals relating to New York's Equitable Life Assurance Society—one of the nation's three largest insurers—revealed an extensive web of political corruption and nepotism. The New York state legislator responded with a political inquiry, called the Armstrong Investigation, after the state legislator who chaired the investigative committee. By 1906, the State of New York had barred its insurers, whose policies accounted for 6% percent of premiums paid in the entire United States, from owning corporate equities, controlling banks, and underwriting securities. These prohibitions dramatically restricted the scale and scope of the insurance business, limiting insurance companies to their core business of writing insurance and investing in debt, and fostering a corporate culture of investment passivity among issuers.[27]

By the turn of the twentieth century, American capitalism was distinguished by two characteristics—the rise of large, national corporations that dominated the economic life of the country and the dispersion of corporate equity holdings among an ever larger collection of investors.

---

[27] Ibid., 60–93.

3

Adolf Berle and the Modern Corporation

The industrialization and corporatization of the American economy produced immense wealth and transformed the United States into a global economic powerhouse. Just during the last two decades of the nineteenth century, the volume of industrial production, the number of workers employed in industry, and the number of manufacturing plants all more than doubled. By 1899, the aggregate annual value of all manufactured goods in the United States stood at approximately $13 billion, compared to $5.4 billion in 1879. Over the same period, the annual production of steel in the United States increased almost nine-fold, from 1.4 million to more than 11 million tons. Before the end of the century, the United States surpassed Great Britain in the production of iron and steel and was providing more than one-quarter of the world's supply of pig iron. Along with the rise of a new class of exorbitantly wealthy and powerful industrialists captaining the helm of this economic revolution there emerged a larger and more affluent middle class that shared in the prosperity of the era. A series of inventions, including the telephone, typewriter, electric light, refrigerator, and automobile, reshaped the daily life of regular Americans, in addition to facilitating greater commercial activity. The development of a national rail network meant that a cross-country journey that would have taken months to complete earlier in the century could now be done in less than a week and with much less risk and danger.[1]

---

[1] Britannica. 2019. "United States—Industrialization of the U.S. Economy | Britannica." In Encyclopædia Britannica. https://www.britannica.com/place/United-States/Industrialization-of-the-U-S-economy.

© The Author(s), under exclusive license to Springer Nature
Switzerland AG 2024
S. Moarefy, *The New Power Brokers*, https://doi.org/10.1007/978-3-031-64733-8_3

Industrialization also had its costs. Economic inequality skyrocketed. The ranks of the working class significantly expanded, many of whom struggled to make ends meet. Workers were typically unemployed for at least part of the year, and their wages were relatively low when they did work.[2] Conditions in industrial factories were poor and dangerous, with workers having little recourse to challenge their circumstances lest they risk provoking the ire of their employers. Farmers faced hard times as technology and increased agricultural production led to more competition and falling prices for farm products, pushing many young people in the country to move to the city in search of job opportunities and exacerbating the conditions of urban laborers.

Americans quickly recognized the magnitude of the changes reshaping their world. While there was no shortage of business leaders and popular commentators who extolled the technological and economic advancements of the era, many others held deep reservations about the social impact of industrialization. Suspicion of corporate power had been a feature of American political thinking as far back as the days of the founding, and that suspicion became a more pronounced and central force in the political discourse with the emergence of large corporations that exerted market power on a national scale. Supporters of the Progressive movement—which became a major political movement in the late nineteenth century and the first few decades of the twentieth century—made reform of the new corporate and industrial system a linchpin of their political platform, advocating for various regulations on corporate power, such as the abolition of child labor, the establishment of a minimum wage, and the imposition of occupational safety and health standards. A new generation of anti-monopolists, including most prominently lawyer and later Supreme Court Justice Louis Brandeis, attributed a range of social and political ills to rising market concentration and demanded that the government reverse the trend by taking aggressive action to break up the trusts and monopolies dominating the U.S. economy.

It was against this background that the lawyer and academic, Adolf Berle, wrote *The Modern Corporation and Private Property*. Neither the name of the man nor the book may have popular currency, but Berle's analysis of the corporate form in *The Modern Corporation* revolutionized corporate governance theory and underpins much of how we think about the place of the corporation in our society to this day.

---

[2] Library of Congress. 2022. "Overview | Rise of Industrial America, 1876–1900 | U.S. History Primary Source Timeline." https://www.loc.gov/classroom-materials/united-states-history-primary-source-timeline/rise-of-industrial-america-1876-1900/overview/.

The Berlean Corporation[3]

Adolf Berle was born in 1895, the son of Adolf Augustus Berle, a Congregationalist minister. The elder Berle carried a grand conception of his place in the world. While his professional achievements never fully measured up to that conception, he channeled much of that energy to the education of his four children, with a focus on his first son, Adolf Berle. Adolf Berle entered Harvard College at the age of 14, earning a bachelor's degree in 1913 and a master's degree in 1914. He then enrolled in Harvard Law School. In 1916, at age 21, Berle became the second youngest graduate in the school's history, behind only Louis Brandeis. When the United States joined the First World War, Berle enlisted in the army and eventually found a post in the American delegation at the Paris peace talks. Following the war, Berle settled in New York and became a corporate lawyer on Wall Street.

As a young corporate lawyer, Berle saw firsthand the increasing dominance of corporations in American life, and the question of how American society should view the corporation soon became Berle's all-consuming focus. Berle espoused many of the Progressive sensibilities of his contemporaries, actively traveling in Progressive circles, writing for prominent liberal magazines like *The Nation* and *The New Republic,* and participating in social reform organizations. The average lawyer today may perceive a career in corporate law as the safe and predictable path. Berle saw it as a route to better understanding the inner workings of the corporate world and how it could potentially be reformed. In 1927, Berle persuaded a research organization to give him a grant to make a detailed study of the corporation. He hired an economist named Gardiner Means—someone he had known in the Army, who was also a Harvard-educated son of a Congregationalist minister—to work up statistical evidence for the study. In 1932, when Berle was thirty-seven, the study

---

[3] This overview of Adolf Berle's life and scholarship draws heavily from Nicholas Lemann's excellent 2019 book, *Transaction Man: The Rise of the Deal and the Decline of the American Dream*, New York: Farrar, Straus and Giroux. Other scholars have also written extensively about Berle and his legacy, and the reader is encouraged to consult these resources to develop a more complete picture of Berle's views and place in American intellectual history, see, e.g., Mitchell, Dalia Tsuk. 2005. "From Pluralism to Individualism: Berle and Means and 20th-Century American Legal Thought." Law & Social Inquiry. Vol. 30. 179; Bratton, William, and Michael Wachter. 2008. "Shareholder Primacy's Corporatist Origins: Adolf Berle and the Modern Corporation," Journal of Corporation Law. Vol. 34. 99; Wang, Jessica. 2019. "Looking Forward in a Failing World: Adolf A. Berle, Jr., the United States, and Global Order in the Interwar Years." Seattle University Law Review. Vol. 42. 385; Strine, Leo E. Jr. 2008. "Human Freedom and Two Friedmen: Musings on the Implications of Globalization for the Effective Regulation of Corporate Behavior." University of Toronto Law Journal. Vol. 58. 241; Jordan A. Schwartz. 1987. "Liberal: Adolf A. Berle and the Vision of an American Era"; Strine Leo E. Jr., and Michael Klain. 2023. "Stakeholder Capitalism's Greatest Challenge: Reshaping a Public Consensus to Govern a Global Economy." University of Pennsylvania, Institute for Law & Economics, No. 23–24.

was published: *The Modern Corporation and Private Property*, which became a classic almost instantly and still stands as the main intellectual achievement of Berle's life.

In *The Modern Corporation*, Berle charted the changes that had taken place in corporate law and the American economy over the prior century and made two overarching arguments. First, he argued that a small number of corporations had rapidly come to dominate the American economy. Second, Berle contended that the growing dispersion of the corporate shareholder base together with the wide latitude of discretion that the corporate form conferred to management had given rise to a "separation of ownership and control" where management—who now held little or no shares in the average public corporation—exercised unfettered control without accountability to shareholders. "The concentration of economic power separate from ownership has, in fact, created economic empires, and has delivered these empires into the hands of a new form of absolutism, relegating 'owners' to the position of those who supply the means whereby the new princes may exercise their power."[4] The impact extended beyond the "realm of private enterprise," acting as "a tremendous force which can harm or benefit a multitude of individuals, affect whole districts, shift the currents of trade, bring ruin to one community and prosperity to another."[5]

Berle emphasized several key implications arising out of this new state of affairs. The withering away of black-and-white restrictions on the conduct of corporate boards meant that courts had to step in the place of legislators to circumscribe corporate misbehavior and do so on the basis of a generalized framework of fiduciary principles, rather than the more specific legislative dictates of yore. Directors came to be viewed as trustees of their shareholders to whom they owed fiduciary duties with respect to their management of the business. It was not sufficient to assess the "technical correctness" of a board's exercise of its corporate powers by evaluating whether or not conduct ran afoul of specified statutory limitations. The propriety of any corporate action had to be evaluated "in relation to the existing facts with a view toward discovering whether under all the circumstances the result fairly protects the interests of the shareholders."[6] The fiduciary model required judges to rely on their independent sense of fairness and justice to adjudicate corporate disputes, and shareholders would look to courts to fashion "equitable remedies" to address their complaints. "New remedies may be worked out and applied by the courts in each case, depending on the circumstances," wrote

---

[4] Berle, Modern Corporation. 116.
[5] Ibid., 46.
[6] Ibid., 242.

Berle. "No form of words inserted in a corporate charter can deny or defeat this fundamental equitable control. To do so would be to defeat the very object and nature of the corporation itself."[7]

Given the evolving and increasingly complex nature of business activity in the Industrial era, equitable remedies allowed for quicker and more efficient resolution of disputes, but these remedies were by their nature the product of creative judicial decision-making and possessed an inherently unpredictable quality. "[T]he shareholder in the modern corporate situation has surrendered a set of definite rights for a set of indefinite expectations."[8] Lawsuits were expensive and time-consuming, creating a practical obstacle for stockholders—the vast majority of whom were individuals who would have to rely on their own means and resources to finance a legal fight—to hold corporations to account even when they had meritorious claims. "The indefiniteness of [the fiduciary model's] application, and the extreme expense and difficulty of litigation, still leave the stockholder virtually helpless," Berle concluded.[9]

Shareholders only retained one real lever for ensuring they would receive fair treatment—the fact that the vast majority of corporations needed external capital to operate and grow. Even if the law afforded corporate boards wide discretion in how they managed their businesses, they risked scaring away new investors and putting the survival of their companies in jeopardy if they abused that discretion. The emergence of national securities markets on which securities could be freely traded provided investors a mechanism for obtaining up-to-date valuations of their equity positions and exiting their investments if they so desired. "The net result of stripping the stockholder of virtually all his power with the corporation is to throw him upon an agency lying outside the corporation itself—the public market," Berle noted, "[i]t is to the market that most security holders look both for an appraisal of the expectations on their security, and by curious paradox, for their chance of realizing them."[10] It would take another four decades for financial economists to formalize the efficient market hypothesis—which holds that stock prices reflect all available information as of a given time—but one could say Berle assumed a more shorthand version of that theory in drawing a direct nexus between the business performance of a company and the trading price of its stock. As corporations scaled back dividend distributions and re-invested more of their excess profits into their operations, shareholders had to look to

---

[7] Ibid., 243.
[8] Ibid., 244.
[9] Ibid., 243.
[10] Ibid., 247.

securities markets as the primary venue for realizing a return on their investments, which hinged on the value of the underlying business appreciating to an extent such that others would be willing to pay a greater price for the company's stock. "This places the junior security holder still further at the mercy of the management, which can thus retain in the enterprise accumulated profits, and forces him into the public markets to which he is bound to look for realizing his appreciation."[11]

The reliance on the public securities markets—as a source of new capital to growing corporations and a mechanism for realizing investment returns to existing stockholders—made it critical that companies provide regular disclosures about their businesses so that investors could make informed and timely decisions as to whether to buy, hold or sell securities. Stockholders may not have had much practical ability to directly pressure corporate management through the machinery of corporate law, but they could exert that pressure indirectly by selling their securities and depressing a company's stock price when they disagreed with management strategy. In order to effectively exercise that indirect form of pressure, investors needed to have a regular, accurate flow of information from management about the strategic direction and financial condition of their companies. When companies sought to raise capital in the public exchanges, they would work together with their underwriters and attorneys to circulate a brokers' circular to potential investors setting forth the terms of the security offered and a description of the underlying business and its corporate strategy. After completing an offering, investors expected that companies would provide updates on their financial condition and other business developments. By the outset of the twentieth century, investor expectations with respect to corporate disclosures were memorialized in the form of formal listing requirements by the major stock exchanges of the time—such as the New York Stock Exchange and New York Curb—that obligated public issuers to make periodic disclosures in order to maintain their listing status.[12]

Almost a century has elapsed since the original publication of *The Modern Corporation*, and Berle's analysis of the role of director fiduciary duties and mandatory corporate disclosures in regulating corporate behavior continues to possess resonance. The rules governing corporate internal affairs continue to be defined by courts who exercise their equitable discretion to fill in the gaps in corporate law statutes. Delaware, the state in which the majority of U.S. public corporations are incorporated (including approximately 70% of

---

[11] Ibid., 248.
[12] Ibid., 255–285.

Fortune 500 companies), has in place a system of "courts of equity" empowered to adjudicate corporate disputes and whose decisions delineate much of the substantive law regulating the duties of directors, the relationship between corporations and shareholders and significant corporate transactions like mergers and acquisitions.[13] The preponderance of corporations that are not organized in Delaware are incorporated in states that have established a similar system of business courts, many of whose corporate law decisions mirror those of the Delaware Courts of Chancery.[14] Mandatory corporate disclosures remain an essential lever for policing corporate behavior. The Securities Act of 1933 and the Securities Exchange Act of 1934, which are at the heart of our system of regulating securities markets, were enacted shortly after the publication of *The Modern Corporation*. The federal laws authorize an independent agency—the Securities Exchange Commission or the SEC—to enforce securities laws, rather than exclusively relying on the conduct of private actors.[15]

Legal academics and practitioners frequently conceive of problems in corporate governance and management-investor relations as fiduciary duty and disclosure issues and theorize policy solutions through that lens. Policy reform discussions among advocates of stakeholder capitalism and the ESG movement—topics we will cover in greater detail later in this book—revolve around exploring avenues for broadening director fiduciary duties to encompass non-shareholder constituencies and expanding disclosure requirements. Climate change is a prime example. ESG activists have called on directors to give greater consideration to climate change "risks" in the performance of their oversight duties, arguing that the failure to appropriately consider such risks should be grounds for potential breach of fiduciary duty claims. Extensive efforts have been undertaken to push corporations to furnish disclosures concerning the environmental effects of their activities, which in recent years have culminated in new SEC rules mandating companies to provide greater disclosures about their carbon footprint and the measures they are

---

[13] Delaware Division of Corporations. 2022. "Delaware Division of Corporations: 2022 Annual Report." https://corpfiles.delaware.gov/Annual-Reports/Division-of-Corporations-2022-Annual-Report-cy.pdf.

[14] Bach, Mitchell L., and Lee Applebaum. 2004. "A History of the Creation and Jurisdiction of Business Courts in the Last Decade." The Business Lawyer. Vol. 60, No. 1. 147–275.

[15] While Berle did not have a direct hand in crafting federal securities legislation, it is undeniable that the extensive public reporting requirements set out in the statutes and implementing regulations derive from a Berlean perspective on the importance of mandatory disclosures in regulating corporate activity and protecting investors. Indeed, Berle would claim in the 1968 republication of *The Modern Corporation*—three years before his death—that "[t]his book… became the foundation for the Federal legislation begun in 1933 and further developed later, regulating stock markets and the rights of security holders which prevailed in 1968." Berle, Modern Corporation. 253.

adopting to combat climate change.[16] Similar efforts have been undertaken with respect to a range of other ESG topics, like racial and gender diversity and political spending.

New Nationalism Versus New Freedom

The fact that Berle's analytical framework continues to animate mainstream policymaking and corporate governance discourse has imbued *The Modern Corporation* with a timeless quality. Nevertheless, it is necessary to understand the contemporary intellectual and political debates that shaped Berle's overall thinking in order to develop a full appreciation of the ideas and assumptions underlying that framework.

When it came to the question of how the American economy should be organized, early twentieth century Progressives like Berle generally gravitated towards one of two schools of thought, most clearly contrasted in the 1912 presidential campaign, when Berle was a university student. Journalist Nicholas Lemann provides an excellent overview of the competing philosophies in his 2019 book, *Transaction Man: The Rise of the Deal and the Decline of the American Dream*, from which the description below generously borrows. On one side were proponents of Theodore Roosevelt's economic program—the New Nationalism—who called for a strong federal government to check the power of big business. Today Teddy Roosevelt is often remembered as a trustbuster. That reputation is misleading. Roosevelt was not against large economic units per se, only against their excesses. The responsibility of government was to check the excesses, not to break up large companies. Roosevelt increased the power of the federal government to regulate railroads, food, and medicine, but it was his successor, William Howard Taft, who broke up Standard Oil and the steel trust (a decision Roosevelt publicly opposed). Among the leading intellectual advocates of New Nationalism were the three founders of *The New Republic,* Herbert Croly, Walter Lippmann, and Walter Weyl—all friends of Adolf Berle. In 1909 Croly published a Progressive Era manifesto called *The Promise of American Life.* "The net result of the industrial expansion of the United States since the Civil War," Croly wrote, "has been the establishment in the heart of the American economic and social system of certain glaring inequalities of condition and power… The rich men and big corporations have become too wealthy and powerful for their official standing in American life." He argued that

---

[16] Bainbridge, Stephen M. 2021. "Don't Compound the Caremark Mistake by Extending it to ESG Oversight." Business Lawyer, UCLA School of Law, Law-Econ Research Paper No. 21–10.

the only path forward for the United States was to scrap the decentralized and agrarian economic model advocated by the likes of Thomas Jefferson and more forcefully embrace the Hamiltonian tradition of big government and commercialization. In the same spirit, Weyn decried the nation's transformation into a "plutocracy" in his 1913 book *The New Democracy*, asserting that the government had to restore the balance by "enormously increase[ing] the extent of regulation." To Progressives of this ilk, these were challenges of nation-threatening severity, requiring sweeping modernization that would eliminate the vestigial elements of rural nineteenth-century America. Lippmann, in *Drift and Mastery* (1914), argued that William Jennings Bryan ("the true Don Quixote of our politics") and his followers were fruitlessly at war with "the economic conditions which had upset the old life of the prairies, made new demands on democracy, introduced specialization and science, had destroyed village loyalties, frustrated private ambitions, and created the impersonal relationships of the modern world." A bigger federal government, staffed by a new class of technocrats, was the only viable means to fight the dominance of big business.[17]

The other camp of Progressives found their home in Woodrow Wilson's economic program of New Freedom. Supporters of New Freedom—led by Louis Brandeis, who happened to be a friend of the Berle family and an adviser to Wilson during the 1912 presidential campaign—shared the concerns of Rooseveltian liberals towards the rise of big business. But rather than enhance the regulation of large enterprises, Brandeis and his cohorts sought to break them up. The notion of an economic future in which big business clashed with big government did not appeal to them. Instead, adherents of New Freedom were fundamentally opposed to the idea of big business—in Brandeis' words, the "curse of bigness"—preferring an America in which economic power was decentralized and small and medium-sized enterprises dominated the American business landscape. In an attempt to frame the distinction between Wilson and Roosevelt, Brandeis wrote in a private letter to Wilson that Roosevelt "does not fear commercial power, however great, if only methods for regulation are provided," but that "we believe that no methods of regulation ever have been or can be devised to remove the menace inherent in private monopoly and overweening commercial power." During the campaign, Wilson gave speeches that reflected the Brandeisian outlook. He spoke on behalf of "the little man… crushed by the trusts." Trusts, he asserted, were by no means the natural and healthy products of market forces. They had been economically manufactured by underhanded,

---

[17] Lemann, Transaction Man. 29.

albeit legal, means, and they stifled competition. "I take my stand absolutely," Wilson declared, "on the proposition that private monopoly is indefensible and intolerable… And I know how to fight it." As president, Wilson spearheaded the passage of new antitrust legislation, including the Clayton Act and Federal Trade Commission Act, which together with the Sherman Act established the statutory foundation for the modern federal antitrust regime.

Like his Progressive contemporaries, Berle viewed the rising power of big business as a critical social problem. Berle's remonstrances about the diminishing standing of shareholders might suggest to the superficial reader a preoccupation with shareholder rights, but his ultimate concern was the "control power" that had accumulated in the hands of corporate managers. The disenfranchisement of shareholders was just one piece of evidence used to sound the alarm about the growing sway of these individuals, who effectively ran the country.[18] Berle in fact criticized the notion that corporate shareholders should be considered the "owners" of the corporation in the way one would conceive a sole proprietor the owner of his or her business.[19] In the modern corporation, the separation of ownership and control meant that the "two functions of risk and control" were performed by different groups of people, undermining the traditional justification for viewing shareholders as the sole and exclusive beneficiaries of a corporation's profits.[20]

While Berle was a lifelong admirer of Brandeis, he eventually came to reject the anti-monopolist policy prescriptions of the New Freedom movement. Unlike Brandeis, Berle's concerns about the unbridled control exerted by corporate management did not automatically translate into antagonism towards large businesses. Berle saw bigness as an unavoidable aspect of modern life, viewing efforts to turn back the clock to a Jeffersonian economy of small scale proprietorships as a pipe dream. Berle explicitly made the point to Brandeis in a letter following the completion of *The Modern Corporation*:

---

[18] Lemann, Transaction Man. 51.

[19] In the latter case, the entrepreneur managed the day-to-day activities of the business, and in the effort to accumulate profits, satisfy the wants of others by, among other things, providing products and services in demand by the community and employing and providing a livelihood to workers. The allocation of all of the business' profits to the entrepreneur made sense from a social perspective not just "as an inducement to the individual to risk his wealth in enterprise" but also "as a spur, driving him to exercise his skill in making his enterprise profitable." Berle, Modern Corporation. 300.

[20] The "traditional logic of profits" would suggest that a portion of the profits go to those controlling a corporation as "an inducement to the most efficient ultimate management", but Berle cast doubt on the sensibility of this perspective as well given the relatively marginal value of additional income to the captains of industry at the helm of the companies running corporate America. "[I]t is probable that more could be learned regarding [control] by studying the motives of an Alexander the Great, seeking new worlds to conquer, than by considering the motives of a petty tradesman of the days of Adam Smith. Ibid.

The concentration has progressed so far that it seems unlikely to break up even in a period of stress. I can see nothing at the moment but to take this trend as it stands endeavoring to mold it so as to be useful. If the next phase is to be virtually a non-political economic government by mass industrial forces, possibly something can be done to make such government responsible, sensitive and actuated primarily by the necessity of serving the millions of little people whose lives it employs, whose savings it takes in guard, and whose materials of life it apparently has to provide.

In Berle's view, corporations were social institutions that had to be managed for the public interest. "The depersonalization of ownership, the objectification of enterprise, the detachment of property from the possessor, [had led] to a point where enterprise [had become] transformed into an institution which resembles the state in character."[21] The modern corporation called for analysis "not in terms of business enterprise but in terms of social organization," taking into account "a wide diversity of interests—those of the 'owners' who supply capital, those of the workers who 'create,' those of the consumers who give value to the products of enterprise, and above all those of the control who wield power."[22] The structural dynamics of the modern corporation had "cleared the way for the claims of a group far wider than either the owners or the control ... [T]hey have placed the community in a position to demand that the modern corporation serve not alone the owners or the control but all society." "The 'control' of the great corporations should develop into a purely neutral technocracy, balancing a variety of claims by various groups in the community and assigning to each a portion of the income stream on the basis of public policy rather than private cupidity."[23]

Berle and the New Deal Order

Although Berle did not delve into the details of how a "neutral technocracy" would function in *The Modern Corporation*, he backed a range of far-reaching reforms designed to steer corporations to act as positive social actors in other contexts. By the time the book was published, Berle had become a key member of President Franklin Roosevelt's "Brain Trust" and advocated for some of the most aggressive New Deal proposals to reform corporate America. Berle supported the federal chartering of public corporations and

---

[21] Ibid., 309.
[22] Ibid., 310.
[23] Ibid., 312.

hoped that when the SEC was created, it would not only require public informational disclosures by corporations but also directly regulate the financial behavior of issuers—for example, banning margin trading, short selling, and the practice of banks trading stocks for their own accounts rather than those of their customers.[24] Berle enthusiastically championed the National Industrial Recovery Act or NIRA, a law passed during the early days of Roosevelt's presidency that gave the federal government the power to regulate a catalogue of basic decisions made by companies in the ordinary course, such as prices and wages.

Berle's grandest aspirations never came to pass. Berle's draft federal incorporation bill did not gain traction in Congress and failed to make it into federal legislation. Berle had a peripheral role in the creation of the Securities Act and Exchange Act and did not participate in the drafting of the SEC's charter, which established the agency primarily as an administrator of the disclosure regime promulgated by the new federal securities legislation. NIRA was struck down by the Supreme Court as unconstitutional. However, the post-World War II economic order vindicated Berle's vision in other respects. The Nazis and the Italian Fascists had planned economies, and so did the major economies that survived the conflict, not the least being the Soviet Union. Notwithstanding the failure of NIRA, the regulatory power of the federal government radically expanded in other domains. In addition to the SEC, new federal agencies were established for the purpose of regulating big business, such as the National Labor Relations Board, which could require companies to negotiate with unions, and the Social Security Administration, which mandated that corporations set aside funds for their employees' retirement.

As Berle's vision gained ascendancy, Brandeis and other advocates of New Freedom saw their influence diminish in post-war America. Brandesian ideologues like Thurman Arnold, the head of the Antitrust Division of the United States Department of Justice from 1938 to 1943, had freer rein to pursue novel and more aggressive antitrust campaigns than some of his predecessors, but that freedom was not unconstrained as the Roosevelt administration came to view the cooperation of big business as a necessity in resuscitating the economy from the Great Depression. Following the United States' entry into World War II, the military routinely blocked the DOJ Antitrust Division from prosecuting suits that it believed would hamper the war effort. In 1943, Arnold was "kicked upstairs" when President Roosevelt nominated him to an Associate Justice seat on the United States Court of Appeals for the District

---

[24] Lemann, Transaction Man. 51.

of Columbia in order to get him out of the Antitrust Division.[25] Despite the appearance of antitrust crusaders like Graham Morison and Robert Bicks, big business became an even greater economic and social force in the United States through the 1940s and 50s. In 1951, AT&T became the first American company to have one million shareholders, and its stock prices steadily rose throughout the decade. General Motors was the world's largest company, while Du Pont employed one-third more chemists than could be found in all of America's universities. Corporations also merged with increasing frequency during the 1950s.[26] By 1954, 135 corporations owned 45% of the country's industrial assets and 25% of the world's.[27]

The vast resources of these larger corporations allowed them to spend money on research that led to major technological breakthroughs. In 1950, a total of twenty computers could be found in the entire United States; most were part of university or government installations. The next year saw the debut of the UNIVAC 1 computer, produced by Remington-Rand. Then IBM began producing and marketing computers, heralding the dawn of the information age. Among entertainment-based corporations, CBS and NBC initiated color television broadcasts, while in the travel sector, airlines began transporting passengers on jet aircraft.[28] The economy overall grew by 37% during the 1950s and unemployment remained low, at about 4.5%. These gains were fairly evenly distributed, although not necessarily across racial lines.[29] At the end of the decade, the median American family had 30% more purchasing power than at the beginning.[30]

Berle welcomed these developments, which he viewed as a direct outcome of his particular brand of Progressivism. By Berle's account, even the late Brandeis "would be the first to deal with the facts" and to embrace the new way of things.[31] "Its aggregate economic achievement is unsurpassed," Berle wrote about the American economy in 1954, "taking all elements (including human freedom) into account, its system of distributing benefits, though anything but perfect, has nevertheless left every other system

---

[25] Morgan, Ted. 1985. FDR: A Biography (1985). New York: Simon and Schuster. 492, 664–665.
[26] Encyclopedia.com. "The 1950s Business And The Economy: Topics In The News." https://www.encyclopedia.com/social-sciences/culture-magazines/1950s-business-and-economy-topics-news.
[27] Berle, Adolf A. 1954. The Twentieth Century Capitalist Revolution. New York: Harcourt, Brace, and Company.
[28] Encyclopedia.com. "The 1950s Business And The Economy: Topics In The News." https://www.encyclopedia.com/social-sciences/culture-magazines/1950s-business-and-economy-topics-news.
[29] Smith, Noah. 2019. "The 1950s Are Greatly Overrated." Bloomberg. https://www.bloomberg.com/view/articles/2019-11-01/economic-growth-in-the-1950s-left-a-lot-of-americans-behind.
[30] Exploros. "Economy in the 1950s." https://www.exploros.com/summary/Economy-in-the-1950s.
[31] Berle, Adolf. 1959. Power without Property. New York: Harcourt, Brace, and Company. 13.

in human history immeasurably far behind. Its rate of progress shows no sign of slackening."[32] The United States now had a "mixed system of in which governmental and private property are inextricably mingled... not the result of any creeping socialism. Rather it is a direct consequence of galloping capitalism."[33]

Berle was not alone in expressing these sentiments. In the words of historian Godfrey Hodgson, a broad-based "liberal consensus" took shape in American society after the Second World War that embraced the values and institutional architecture of the New Deal order.[34] Liberal economist John Kenneth Galbraith, popularized the concept of "countervailing power", asserting that the prosperity of the New Deal era had been made possible through America's major social institutions—big businesses, big unions and big government—checking and balancing the excesses of one another. David Lilienthal, the former head of the Tennessee Valley Authority and once a fervent Brandeisian, devoted an entire book—*Big Business: A New Era*, published in 1953—extolling the contributions of big business to the shared affluence of the period. The advent of nationwide chain stores constituted "the most spectacular change in the face of everyday American life." "Bigness... served the consumer's interest," improving food quality and hygiene, and even helping Americans achieve "democratic aspirations."[35] Antitrust was viewed as a hammer searching for a nail—according to Richard Hofstadter, another prominent intellectual of the time, "one of the faded passions of American reform." "The steepest rise in mass standards of living has occurred during the period in which the economy has been dominated by the big corporation," he noted. "Whatever else may be said against bigness, the conception of the monopolistic industry as a kind of gigantic, swelling leech on the body of an increasingly deprived and impoverished society has largely disappeared."[36]

The liberal consensus even extended across partisan lines. Dwight Eisenhower, the first Republican president to win the presidency since Herbert Hoover in 1928, governed as a centrist and embraced the central policy programs of the New Deal era, including Social Security, public housing, and the minimum wage. The federal government became a more active player in the economy, expanding the availability of home mortgages through

---

[32] Berle, Capitalist Revolution. 10.
[33] Ibid., 109.
[34] Hodgson, Godfrey. 1976. America in Our Time: From World War II to Nixon—What Happened And Why. Princeton: Princeton University Press.
[35] Lilienthal, David. 1952. Big Business: A New Era. New York: Harper and Brothers.
[36] Hofstadter, Richard. 1964. "What Happened to the Antitrust Movement? Notes on the Evolution of an American Creed." The Business Establishment. 237.

subsidies and making substantial investments in highway construction and public education.[37] Eisenhower's Vice President Richard Nixon, who would become the next Republican president, was similarly supportive of the key tenets of the New Deal economic agenda, endorsing and signing into law the National Environmental Policy Act of 1970 (which established the Environmental Protection Agency to coordinate and enforce federal environmental policy), the Occupational Safety and Health Act of 1970 (which established the Occupational Safety and Health Administration and the National Institute for Occupational Safety and Health) and the Social Security Amendments of 1972 (which expanded Medicare coverage).

By the time Adolf Berle died in 1971, the New Deal order that he helped fashion seemed unshakeable.

---

[37] Cunninghan, Sean P. 2014. American Politics in the Postwar Sunbelt: Conservative Growth in a Battleground Region. New York: Cambridge University Press. 56–69.

4

The Rise of Asset Manager Capitalism

While Berle's model of the corporation lives on in policymaking and corporate governance discourse, the ownership structure of the corporation and investment landscape have profoundly transformed in the half century since Berle's death. Institutions managing money on behalf of others—like index funds, mutual funds, pension funds, and hedge funds—have come to replace individuals and households as the holders of the substantial majority of corporate equities in the United States.[1] In 1950, when Berle was extolling the many virtues of the New Deal economic order, institutional investors held approximately 6% of all corporate equities.[2] By 2019, that percentage had risen to approximately 80%.[3]

---

[1] The corporate law literature includes a number of important articles that the reader is encouraged to review in order to more fully appreciate the variety of scholarly perspectives on the factors and developments that have driven the institutionalization of the investment space. See, e.g., Fisch, Jill, Asaf Hamdani and Steven Davidoff Solomon. 2019. "The New Titans of Wall Street: A Theoretical Framework for Passive Investors." University of Pennsylvania Law Review. Vol. 168; https://scholarship.law.upenn.edu/faculty_scholarship/1983/; Bebchuk, Lucian A., and Scott Hirst. 2019. "The Specter of the Giant Three", University Law Review. Vol. 99B. 721; Coates, John C. IV. 2018. "The Future of Corporate Governance Part I: The Problem of Twelve 13" (Harvard Public Law, Working Paper No. 19–07), https://papers.ssrn.com/sol3/papers.cfm?abstract_id=3247337; Lund, Dorothy S. & Elizabeth Pollman. 2021. "The Corporate Governance Machine," Columbia Law Review. Vol. 121. 2563.

[2] Bebchuk, Lucian, and Scott Hirst. 2019. "The Specter of The Giant Three," Boston University Law Review, Vol. 99.

[3] Greenspon, Jacob. 2019. "How Big a Problem Is It That a Few Shareholders Own Stock in So Many Competing Companies?" Harvard Business Review.

The rise of institutional investors raises important questions about the Berlean paradigm and its continued relevance in understanding the internal workings of corporate America today.

Legislative and Regulatory Changes

A number of developments have driven the sea change in the ownership structure of the typical corporation. For one, legislative and regulatory measures, mostly taking place in the second half of the twentieth century, have encouraged the movement of capital into investment intermediaries. In 1936, Congress passed The Revenue Act, which allowed mutual funds to pass dividends on to investors on an untaxed basis, thereby ensuring that fund shareholders were not disadvantaged relative to direct stock investors.[4] Later, the Taft–Hartley Act of 1947 and the Employment Retirement Income Security Act of 1974 (ERISA) helped encourage the growth of the asset management industry by weakening labor control over retirement assets. The Taft–Hartley Act prohibited employers from contributing to union-controlled pension funds. ERISA subjected private pension promises—hitherto negotiated between employers, unions, and employees—to federal government regulation, with the Department of Labor assuming primary responsibility for interpreting and enforcing the provisions of the statute. ERISA imposed on asset managers a duty to manage investments "with the care, skill, prudence, and diligence under the circumstances then prevailing that a prudent man." In 1979, that duty was expanded to include an obligation to diversify investments consistent with modern portfolio theory—an investment philosophy that gained popularity in the 1980s and held that investors could improve their returns and reduce investment risk by diversifying investments across different assets.[5] State laws governing the fiduciary duties of investment trustees similarly expanded to encourage diversification in investment during this time frame.[6] As a result of these regulatory changes, retirement plan managers began to outsource investment management decisions to professionalized, external asset managers.

---

[4] Braun, Benjamin. 2021. "Asset Manager Capitalism as a Corporate Governance Regime." The American Political Economy: Politics, Markets, and Power, ed. Jacob Hacker, Alexander Hertel-Fernandez, Paul Pierson, Kathleen Thelen. Cambridge: Cambridge University Press. 10.

[5] Title 29 Internal Revenue Code. § 1104.

[6] Schanzenbach, Max M., and Robert H. Sitkoff. 2007. "Did Reform of Prudent Trust Investment Laws Change Trust Portfolio Allocation?" The Journal of Law & Economics. Vol. 50, No. 4. 681–711.

401(k) Plans and IRAs

The trend towards institutionalization accelerated with the emergence of 401(k) plans and individual retirement accounts (or IRAs), which greatly increased the assets under management held by the institutional investors providing these offerings. In 1978, Congress added Section 401(k) to the Internal Revenue Code, which permitted employees to avoid taxes on the portion of income they elected to receive as deferred compensation rather than as direct cash payments. A few years later, the IRS issued regulations on 401(k) plans that sanctioned the use of employee salary reductions as a source of retirement plan contributions. Many employers replaced older, after-tax thrift plans with 401(k) plans and added 401(k) options to profit-sharing and stock bonus plans. Within two years, nearly half of all large firms were already offering a 401(k) plan or considering one. IRAs came into existence with the enactment of ERISA in 1974. Since then, Congress has gradually expanded the menu of potential IRA offerings and relaxed eligibility and contribution criteria.[7] In 1978, Congress established the Simplified Employee Pension (SEP) IRA—an employer-based IRA. Between 1982 and 1986, Congress made the traditional IRA "universal" by allowing all workers under age 70½ to make tax-deductible IRA contributions. Beginning in 1987, Congress eliminated the universality of tax-deductible IRA contributions but permitted workers meeting certain income limits to make such contributions even if they were covered by employer-sponsored retirement plans. After-tax, or nondeductible, contributions were permitted. In 1996, Congress added the Savings Incentive Match Plan for Employees, or SIMPLE IRA, an account targeted at small businesses. Congress expanded the menu of offerings in 1997 with the Roth IRA—a retirement savings account for after-tax contributions—and raised the income limits for IRA contribution deductibility. Congress again raised contribution limits for IRAs in 2001.[8] By the year 2000, there were over $2.6 trillion of retirement assets being managed by institutional investment funds.

---

[7] Employee Benefit Research Institute. 2018. "History of 401(k) Plans: An Update." Employee Benefit Research Institute. https://www.ebri.org/docs/default-source/fast-facts/ff-318-k-40year-5nov18.pdf.

[8] Holden, Sarah, Kathy Ireland, Vicky Leonard-Chambers, and Michael Bogdan. 2005. "The Individual Retirement Account at Age 30: A Retrospective." Investment Company Institute. https://www.idc.org/system/files/attachments/per11-01.pdf.

Investment Strategies

Index Investing

The rise of investment strategies requiring or otherwise involving the direction of asset manager intermediaries has played an important role in the institutionalization of the investment space. First and foremost is the rise of index funds—or investment funds that track the performance of particular market indices, like the S&P 500 or the Dow Jones Industrial Average. The idea of index investing originally gained popularity in the 1960s and 1970s. A group of academics—whose findings were summarized by the economist Burton Maliel in his 1973 book *A Random Walk Down Wall Street*—argued that few investors could "beat the market" and that buying a full array of available stocks could avoid the inefficiencies and costs associated with active investing.[9] During this time, regulators were also escalating pressure on investment companies to reduce the fees paid to their portfolio managers, creating an environment ripe for entrepreneurial asset managers to come up with low-cost investment products.[10] In 1974, investor Jack Bogle founded The Vanguard Group, which launched the first "indexed" fund the same year.[11] Promising the lowest advisory fees in the industry, Vanguard committed to give up on actively selecting stocks, and instead focused on purchasing and holding all the shares in an index of stocks chosen by a third party, until such time as redemptions by its investors required it to sell stocks in the index to generate cash to meet the redemption demand.[12] Since then, the size and significance of index funds in financial markets has steadily increased. In part, this growth has been fueled by the rising popularity of diversification and the emergence of 401(k) and IRA plans that feature index funds as the default investment option. In 2000, indexed funds and ETFs represented $344 billion in domestic equity investments or 2% of total

---

[9] Malkiel, Burton. 2007. A Random Walk down Wall Street: The Time-Tested Strategy for Successful Investing. New York: W.W. Norton. 226–227.

[10] In 1958, in reaction to complaints about the fund industry, the SEC hired academics at the Wharton School of Finance and Commerce to conduct a study of the fund industry. The 1962 Wharton Report concluded that even as fund assets had grown substantially, generating economies of scale, fees remained at 0.5% of assets for most mutual funds, implying weak market competition among fund advisors. Congress responded eight years later by amending the Investment Company Act to require fund advisors act as fiduciaries in regard to their compensation from funds and fund shareholders, and to create a special fund investor private right of action to challenge "excessive" fees. Coates, John C. 2018. The Future of Corporate Governance Part I: The Problem of Twelve. Cambridge, MA: Harvard Law School.

[11] Vanguard. 2023. "Vanguard at a Glance—Facts and Figures." Vanguard. https://corporate.vanguard.com/content/corporatesite/us/en/corp/who-we-are/sets-us-apart/facts-and-figures.html.

[12] Coates, "The Problem of Twelve."

equity market capitalization in the United States. Ten years later, indexed funds and ETFs held $704 billion in domestic equity investments or approximately 7% of total equity market capitalization in the United States. By 2020, the aggregate amount of indexed investments had increased to $3.4 trillion, representing approximately 15% of total U.S. market capitalization, and 20% or more of indexes of large companies, such as the S&P 500 index. These figures, which are based on industry reports, likely understate the scale of index investing given that they exclude assets held by numerous other institutions, such as pension funds and insurance companies, which frequently pursue index strategies. In addition, substantial amounts of assets invested in nominally active funds are in practice indexed, with such funds commonly minimizing management costs by essentially holding an index and selecting a few companies to over- or under-weight.[13]

Alternative Active Investment Strategies: Buyout Funds and Shareholder Activism

Institutional investors have been at the forefront of new alternative active strategies that attempt to generate returns by changing the businesses of the companies in which they invest. Private equity or buyout firms, which acquire controlling stakes in companies with a view to transforming their operations and later selling their interests, have emerged as a major force in financial markets. Buyout firms tend to use significant amounts of debt to finance their acquisitions, which functions to minimize their upfront risk and enhance return multiples when they exit their investments. While investors have employed buyout-style strategies since the dawn of the industrial revolution, they were mostly the domain of wealthy individuals and families and had limited market reach. The growth of the buyout industry accelerated in the latter half of the twentieth century, driven by many of the same legal and economic changes that spurred the growth of the institutional investing industry more generally, as well as a series of other developments. In 1958, Congress passed the Small Business Investment Act, which empowered the U.S. Small Business Administration (SBA) to license private "Small Business Investment Companies" (SBICs) to help the financing and management of small entrepreneurial businesses in the United States. The 1958 Act provided firms structured either as SBICs or Minority Enterprise Small Business Investment Companies (MESBICs) access to federal funds which

---

[13] Coates, John C. 2023. *The Problem of 12: When a Few Financial Institutions Control Everything.* New York: Columbia Global Reports.

could be leveraged at a ratio of up to 4:1 against privately raised investment funds.[14] In 1978, Congress added Chapter 11 to the Bankruptcy Code, allowing bankrupt companies to reorganize their capital structure—rather than requiring them to liquidate—another boon to the buyout industry given that buyout targets are far more likely to file for bankruptcy than comparable non-target companies. Four years later, the SEC adopted Regulation D, providing for various exemptions from federal registrations for securities offerings that allowed for virtually unconstrained capital raising by private equity funds from an unlimited number of moderately wealthy investors. In 1996, Congress passed the National Securities Markets Improvement Act, which permitted regulated funds to raise unlimited capital from an unlimited number of institutions or individuals with $5 million in investments (in contrast to the prior status quo that limited private funds to a hundred investors).

With these barriers to private equity market entry removed, the industry exploded in the 1980s. Over the three years from 1980 to 1982, total commitments to buyout funds were well over twice the total commitments throughout the decade before. The huge increase in high-yield and low-quality debt offerings led to substantial problems in the buyout industry in the latter part of the decade, but the effect was cyclical. As the early 1990s recession led to undervaluation in the public equity markets, institutional buyout firms gained prominence and the industry was once again on an upswing—until, at the turn of the century, the technology bubble burst. This was followed by an upswing that culminated in the 2008 financial crisis. The subsequent decade saw yet another rebound. By 2021, buyout and private equity funds had accumulated global assets of approximately $12 trillion.[15]

Companies owned by private equity firms operate in a "parallel capital universe"—as Harvard Law School professor John Coates calls it—in which their business activities remain largely shrouded to the public, in contrast to publicly traded companies whose shares are traded on the major securities exchanges and which are required to make periodic public disclosures pursuant to the federal securities laws established in the New Deal era. As the private equity industry has grown, so too has this parallel private capital universe. In 2020, private equity managed assets representing 18% of total

---

[14] Mauboussin, Michael J., and Dan Callahan. 2020. "Counterpoint Global Insights—Public to Private Equity in the United States: A Long-Term Look." Morgan Stanley Investment Management. https://www.morganstanley.com/im/publication/insights/articles/articles_publictoprivate equityintheusalongtermlook_us.pdf.
[15] Ibid.

corporate equities, as measured by the Federal Reserve, compared to 4% in 2000.[16]

Shareholder activist investment strategies have also become widespread. Similar to buyout funds, shareholder activists make money by pushing companies to change their corporate strategy, but, unlike buyout firms, shareholder activists do not acquire control stakes. Instead, activists buy up non-controlling interests in publicly traded companies and pressure boards to heed their demands through pressure tactics, from letter writing and other non-public engagement efforts to mounting proxy fights in which activists seek to replace a company's incumbent board of directors with their own slate of director nominees.

Shareholders have pursued activism for as long as stock exchanges have been in existence. In the seventeenth century, Isaac Le Maire, a shareholder and former director on the board of the Dutch East India Company, mounted a highly publicized short-selling campaign designed to bring down the company's share price.[17] In the United States, as the public markets developed and the number and size of corporations increased through the late nineteenth and early twentieth century, so did various contests for control and influence among shareholders.[18] From 1900 to 1950, about 1.22 "offensive" activist initiatives occurred per year, with more occurring in the 1940s and 1950s, spearheaded by renowned investors like Benjamin Graham and J. Paul Getty.[19] In a memorable passage in *The Modern Corporation*, Berle described one of the seminal proxy contests of the 1920s—the battle between Standard Oil and John D. Rockefeller, its most significant shareholder.

The rise of institutional investors in the 1980s and 1990s turbocharged the use of activist strategies. Traditionally passive institutional investors began to exercise their newfound muscle as corporate shareholders to actively influence corporate management. Wharton School professor Michael Useem delved into the then relatively new phenomenon of "investor activism" in his 1996 book *Investor Capitalism: How Money Managers Are Changing the Face of Corporate America*, in which he described the growing trend of blue chip companies, like General Motors and IBM, terminating key members of

---

[16] Coates, The Problem of 12. 54.

[17] Petram, Lodewijk, and Lynne M Richards. 2014. The World's First Stock Exchange. New York: Columbia Business School Publishing.

[18] Cloyd, Mary A. 2015. "Shareholder Activism: Who, What, When, and How?" Harvard Law School Forum on Corporate Governance. https://corpgov.law.harvard.edu/2015/04/07/shareholder-activism-who-what-when-and-how/.

[19] Wright, Robert E., and Richard Sylla. 2011. "Corporate Governance and Stockholder/Stakeholder Activism in the United States, 1790–1860: New Data and Perspectives", Origins of Shareholder Advocacy. New York: Palgrave Macmillan U.S. 231–225.

management and overhauling their strategic direction as a result of pressure from institutional investors.[20] Other investors deployed activism as a more formalized investment strategy, scouring the market for opportunities to make money by pushing public companies to alter strategic course, rather than engaging in activism in an exclusively reactive manner when they became dissatisfied with the management teams of the companies in which they already held investments. Corporate raiders, like Carl Icahn and Nelson Peltz, created investment vehicles for the purpose of acquiring sizeable stakes in companies whose market value they believed could be enhanced if they broke up or divested assets and then pressured those companies to undertake said strategies. By the late 1990s, activist hedge funds entered the fray. These funds would purchase small equity stakes in public companies—often no greater than one to two percent of their market capitalization—in order to push them to take actions to quickly boost their share price and generate financial returns, such as share buybacks, dividends and reducing cash outlays and expenses.

During the past two decades, hedge fund activism has markedly grown. From 2003 through 2014, 275 new activist hedge funds were launched.[21] As of December 31, 2022, assets under management in event-driven activist strategies totaled $168 billion.[22] While much smaller than the size of the index fund and private equity industries, this number does not fully reflect the power of activist funds as that power ultimately derives from their ability to win support from larger institutional investors, rather than the acquisition of direct economic and voting control in their targets. The frequency of activist campaigns has also increased. The number of shareholder activist campaigns reached a record high in 2023, topping the prior record set in 2018, with more than 180 different activists and the greatest number of "first timers" initiating campaigns.[23] Total board seats won by activists increased in 2023 for the third consecutive year, up 13% globally year-over-year, with a record 31% of board seats secured through proxy contests, almost twice the historical mean of 17%.[24]

---

[20] Useem, Michael. 1996. Investor Capitalism: How Money Managers Are Changing the Face of Corporate America. Basis Books: New York.
[21] Cloyd, "Shareholder Activism.".
[22] Williamson, Christine. 2023. "Activist Investment Firms Thriving, But Take Different Tacks on Engagement." Pensions & Investments. https://www.pionline.com/hedge-funds/activist-investment-firms-thriving-take-different-tacks-engagement.
[23] Lazard. 2024. "Annual Review of Shareholder Activism 2023." Lazard. https://www.lazard.com/research-insights/annual-review-of-shareholder-activism-2023/.
[24] Ibid.

Private equity firms and activist hedge funds share several core characteristics that shape their unique brand of active investing. Both are permitted to acquire large block holdings in individual companies, without the minimum diversification requirements that constrain other institutional investors' operations. Investment managers at private equity firms and hedge funds are generally compensated on the basis of a "2 and 20" compensation structure in which they receive only a minor portion of their overall income on a fixed basis (in the form of a management fee equal to 2% of the fund's assets under management), and then a much bigger contingent performance fee equal to 20% of the annual returns generated by the fund. The large contingency fee creates strong incentives on the part of investors to push target companies to do whatever they can to maximize financial returns. These incentives are reinforced by the fact that fund managers often make significant personal investments into the funds.[25]

There are also notable differences. Activist hedge funds tend to take smaller positions in public equities that are relatively easier to liquidate and espouse a shorter time horizon than private equity firms, whose large control stakes in private companies are difficult to exit at a compelling valuation outside of a change of control transaction, which is usually not feasible in any near-term or medium-term horizon. The life of the typical private equity fund today can range from 10 to 15 years, in contrast to that of the typical activist hedge fund, whose fund life is not much longer than five years.[26] The private equity industry consists of approximately 4500 private equity firms in the United States that employ a variety of strategies, including industry-focused funds and funds that invest in particular phases of the corporate lifecycle.[27] This stands in contrast to the several hundred activist hedge funds, the substantial majority of which do not profess particular industry or other operational expertise in the companies in which they invest.[28]

---

[25] Gimigliano, Lorenzo, Pietro Maraldi, and Tommaso Pirozzi. 2021. "Hedge Fund Activism—Our Overview." Bocconi Students Capital Markets. https://www.bscapitalmarkets.com/hedge-fund-activism---our-overview.html.

[26] Pang, Michael. 2023. "A Fund's Life Cycle." Boulder Group. https://boldergroup.com/insights/blogs/the-stages-of-the-fund-life-cycle/#:~:text=Meanwhile%2C%20most%20hedge%20funds%20have,Hedge%20Fund%20Survivorship%202020%20report; The Private Equiteer. 2020. "The Private Equity Fund Life Cycle." The Private Equiteer. https://theprivateequiteer.com/phases-of-the-private-equity-fund-life-cycle/.

[27] Coates, The Problem of 12. 51.

[28] Lazard. 2024. "Annual Review of Shareholder Activism 2023." Lazard. https://www.lazard.com/research-insights/annual-review-of-shareholder-activism-2023/.

Algorithmic Trading Strategies

The growth of institutional investors in the corporate landscape has also been driven by (and contributed to the growth of) new algorithmic trading strategies. Algorithmic trading is computer-determined trading: the algorithm makes important trading decisions, such as with respect to timing, pricing, and execution of a trading order without human interaction.[29] For example, an algorithm could be devised that provides that if X corporation crosses above its 30-day moving average, the fund will automatically purchase Y number of shares of such corporation; and if the stock price of X corporation crosses below its 30-day moving average, the fund should sell the Z number of shares of X corporation.

Technological innovation is most responsible for the ability of traders to execute algorithmic trading strategies. But the mass adoption of algorithmic trading is attributable to the emergence of institutional investors with the technological capabilities to operationalize algorithmic trading strategies, along with broader changes in the architecture of the equity markets over the last fifty years. In 1975, the SEC made fixed commission rates illegal and commission rates dropped significantly. For the first time in almost two centuries, trading fees on stock markets were decided by market competition. Brokers began to compete with one another by offering lower and lower rates and started to innovate and experiment with new trading systems that made the process more efficient. Trading stocks became much easier. Traders could fully access stock markets, and they could do so now at a lower cost from a growing number of brokers, many of which arose during this time period to address demand. The SEC also adopted rules favoring the processing and execution of smaller trades. After the stock market crash of 1987, the SEC adopted the Small Order Entry System (SOES) which required market markets to prioritize the processing of 1000 shares or less over larger orders.[30]

The period witnessed the emergence of electronic communication networks (ECNs) that match buy and sell orders for securities in the market. In 1969, the first ECN—Instinet—was launched. In 1971, the National Association of Securities Dealers (NASD) established the National Association of Securities Dealers Automated Quotation System or, as it is more commonly referred to today, the NASDAQ—a virtual stock exchange on

---

[29] McGowan, Michael J. 2010. "The Rise of Computerized High Frequency Trading: Use and Controversy." Duke Law & Technology Review. https://scholarship.law.duke.edu/cgi/viewcontent.cgi?article=1211&context=dltr.
[30] Hur, Johnson. 2019. "History of Day Trading." BeBusinessed. https://bebusinessed.com/history/history-day-trading/.

which orders were transmitted electronically. Driven by a new era of competitive commission rates, ECNs were able to serve a growing range of clients without the presence of a middleman, driving costs down even further and making automated trading even easier. ECNs like Instinet, SelectNet, and NYSE Arca would all later acquire prominence in the industry.

The ability to trade electronically expanded in the 1990s and 2000s with the emergence of the Internet and high frequency trading systems (HFTs) that enabled traders to analyze market data and signals at high speed and then send large numbers of orders within a very short time period in response to that analysis. HFT algorithms look for signals—such as the movement of interest rates, minuscule economic fluctuations, news, and other subtleties—and generate returns by taking advantage of those signals before anyone else in the market is even aware of them.[31] Today, studies indicate that approximately 10–40% of annual trading volume in equities is attributable to HFT, while on an intraday basis, the proportion of HFT may vary from 0 to 100% of short-term trading volume.[32]

The Separation of Ownership from Ownership and the Evolution of the Model Equity Investor

The rise of institutional investors in corporate America has fundamentally strained the Berlean paradigm. The lengthening of the investment chain has created what former Delaware Supreme Court Chief Justice Leo Strine has dubbed a "separation of ownership from ownership" in which legal ownership over a company's shares—along with the rights associated therewith—no longer sits with the ultimate providers of capital for any given investment, but instead the institutional investment funds that are acting on behalf of those investors. This dynamic carries particular social salience given that the bulk of the capital managed by institutional investors comes from the savings and retirement accounts of regular working people. Asset managers are not just acting as custodians of capital provided by a discrete universe of wealthy individuals. They are in a critical sense custodians of *public capital*. Of the $291 trillion in assets managed by asset managers in 2022, approximately $100 trillion, or 34%, come from pension and insurance assets. That amount jumps to a little over $200 trillion, or approximately 69% of global

---

[31] McGowan, "Rise of Computerized.".
[32] Aldridge, Irene, and Steven Krawciw. 2017. Real-Time Risk: What Investors Should Know about Fintech, High-frequency Trading, and Flash Crashes. New York: John Wiley & Sons.

assets under management, if one also considers the assets of the "mass affluent"—commonly defined as individuals and households with $100 thousand to $1 million of investable assets, which in most Western countries is sufficient to be considered well off or upper middle class, but not independently wealthy.[33]

In addition to the rise in institutional ownership of corporate stock, stock ownership has become concentrated among a smaller number of large and powerful asset managers. A 2017 report by investment advisor Willis Towers Watson found that the top 20 of the largest 500 asset managers controlled 43% of total assets under management, a larger percentage than at any time since 2000. According to another study, more than 75% of U.S. industries have experienced an increase in concentration levels over the past two decades.[34] The increase in common ownership has been driven in significant part by the growth of the "Big Three" index funds—Vanguard, State Street, and BlackRock. Since 1998, the average combined stake in S&P 500 companies held by the Big Three has quadrupled from 5% to more than 20%. During the last ten years, the number of firms in the S&P 500 index in which the Big Three hold 5% or more of the company's equity has increased more than fivefold, with BlackRock and Vanguard each now holding positions of 5% or more of the shares of almost all the companies in the S&P 500. If current trends continue, the combined average ownership stake of the Big Three is estimated to rise to 28% by 2028, and to 33% of S&P 500 equity by 2038.[35]

Equity investing strategies—and how to appropriately conceive of shareholder interests—have also evolved. At the time *The Modern Corporation* was published, the equity investor was conventionally assumed to be an individual who invested in a single company or defined set of companies based on an expectation of participating in the long-term growth and profitability of the underlying businesses. By the turn of the twentieth century, investors increasingly sought out returns in the form of capital gains from the sale and purchase of stock, rather than fixed dividend distributions. In both cases, the prospect of a return was driven by the company's business results. Disclosures

---

[33] PwC. 2023. "Asset and Wealth Management Revolution 2023: The New Context." PriceWaterhouseCoopers. https://www.pwc.com/gx/en/industries/financial-services/asset-management/publications/asset-and-wealth-management-revolution-2023.html.

[34] Eccles, Robert G. 2019. "Concentration in the Asset Management Industry: Implications for Corporate Engagement." Forbes. https://www.forbes.com/sites/bobeccles/2019/04/17/concentration-in-the-asset-management-industry-implications-for-corporate-engagement/?sh=3bc71a38402f.

[35] Fisch, Jill, Asaf Hamdani, Steven Davidoff Solomon. 2019. "The New Titans of Wall Street: A Theoretical Framework for Passive Investors." University of Pennsylvania Law Review. Vol. 168. 17–72. https://scholarship.law.upenn.edu/faculty_scholarship/1983/.

about a company's business performance were essential to the ability of shareholders to make informed investment decisions because business performance went to the heart of what investors cared about in deciding whether or not they wanted to buy, hold, or sell stock.[36]

The investing landscape has changed with the rise of institutional investors and their widespread adoption of new investing strategies. In contrast to the traditional investing model, the index investor invests in a portfolio of stocks tracking a broad market index. Whether any particular company in the index performs well is irrelevant to the inclusion of that company in the index and has a minimal impact on the overall performance of the index. Instead, index funds are *universal owners*. The strategy of diversification underlying index investing means index funds essentially own a slice of the entire economy, or in the case of industry-focused indices, an entire industry, as a result of which risks and returns are measured on an overall portfolio basis. Index fund investments in any given company are functionally subject to an indefinite time horizon as the positions are based on the pre-determined composition of the index and cannot be adjusted on the basis of the fund manager's perspectives concerning the component companies.[37] An individual company's disclosures have no relevance to the ability of an index fund to execute an index investing strategy on behalf of its clients. The sole function of index funds is to channel capital from individuals and institutions who want to invest in an index into a portfolio of stocks that conforms to the specifications of the index.

Buyout firms and activist hedge funds, while distinguished from one another in important ways, both break the traditional investing mold by investing in companies in order to change how they are managed and operated and to generate returns from those changes. How a company has historically performed or is expected to perform based on the execution of current management's business strategy is less important than how the company *could perform* were it to be managed in the manner envisioned by the private equity firm or activist hedge fund. Investors in the past may have occasionally organized collective efforts to replace management or to press the breaks on a corporate initiative, but these actions were by and large sporadic phenomena occurring in response to particular corporate controversies and often involved a sidelined founder or other disgruntled shareholder. Today's

---

[36] This is, of course, not intended as an absolute statement of historical fact. Speculators have always existed and there are notable examples of "voting trusts" and other pooled vehicles as far back as the mid-nineteenth century that sought to amass ownership in a company's stock for the purpose of enacting changes to corporate strategy. But these situations were by and large sporadic phenomena, representing exceptions to the rule.

[37] Irvin, Daniel. 2022. "Universal Owners, Shareholder Primacy, and Stakeholderism." Emory Corporate Governance & Accountability Review. Vol. 10.

activist hedge funds and private equity firms actively seek out companies that they view to be ripe for change and raise capital from their investors with the explicit objective of effecting material changes in the businesses of their investment targets.

Unlike the Berlean model of the long-term fundamentals-focused investor, algorithmic traders do not make trading decisions by analyzing the business performance of individual companies, but instead make money by exploiting statistical patterns and correlations in the market, often with the assistance of HFT systems that enable them to take advantage of trading opportunities faster than other traders. Algorithmic traders rely on corporate disclosures not for what they directly say about a business and its future prospects, but only indirectly and insofar as they pertain to quantitative variables that are susceptible to algorithmic modeling. The reams of disclosures put out by public companies regarding their business activities, management's perspectives on strategy, or the background of a board's deliberations with respect to extraordinary events like mergers and acquisitions, go unnoticed.

Interrogating the New Economic Order

With the locus of power in the corporation now shifted from boards to institutional investors, new questions and issues must be considered.

If management feels like every decision it makes is the subject of a veto from institutional investors, what are the implications for how management ends up running a business—and the economy and society at large? At the core of Berle's analysis was a concern with the costs imposed by the conduct of wayward, unaccountable corporate managers—what economists Michael Jensen and William Meckling (whose work we examine in greater detail in the next chapter) would describe as the agency costs inherent in the separation of ownership and control.[38] Attention must now also be paid to the principal costs that result from asset manager shareholders more intensively molding and regulating the behavior of their portfolio companies, especially to the extent that shareholders have conflicting interests or there are questions regarding their basic competence or business judgment to drive executive decision-making.[39]

---

[38] Jensen, Michael C., and William H. Meckling. 1976. "Theory of the Firm: Managerial Behavior, Agency Costs and Ownership Structure." Journal of Financial Economics. 305–360.

[39] Zohar Goshen and Richard Squire first coined the concept of principal costs in their memorable 2017 law journal article entitled "Principal Costs: A New Theory for Corporate Law and Governance." See Goshen, Zohar and Richard Squire. 2017. "Principal Costs: A New Theory for Corporate

What must one make of the fact that institutional investors are not investing their own wealth, but are functioning as custodians of public capital? The Berlean paradigm assumed as a predicate fact that the corporation's shareholders directly held their economic and voting interests. The intermediary role taken on by institutional investors requires an examination into how the decoupling of these interests and the elongation of the stockholding chain resulting from said intermediation have changed the very nature and social import of shareholder voting. Without the same economic skin in the game, have institutional investors reshaped shareholder voting into an exercise of "empty voting"—or something else—and what if anything should be done about it?[40] An analytical model of corporate governance that focuses on the rights and obligations between stockholders and corporations misses the need to account for the relationships by and among the institutional investors that legally own any given corporation's stock, the capital providers for which those investors act as custodians and society at large.

How should policymakers respond? The focus among academics and lawmakers on director fiduciary duties as the paramount issue of corporate law made sense in a world in which shareholders were widely dispersed and practically unable to fend for themselves. The emergence of large and powerful institutional investment vehicles owning outsized ownership stakes in America's public corporations has turned this foundational premise of the Berlean paradigm on its head. Likewise, the newfound prominence of institutional investing strategies that are not driven by a company's business strategy and performance casts doubt on the sensibility of relying on disclosure as a regulatory panacea. If institutional investors and their real-world providers of capital are not relying on corporate disclosures to guide their investment decision-making, how should one think of the purpose and utility of corporate disclosures? What incentives are there for corporations to produce disclosures of social value, rather than provide an opening for entrepreneurial attorneys to utilize the threat of litigation to extract fees from companies in exchange for meaningless disclosures?[41]

Law and Governance." Columbia Law Review. https://www.columbialawreview.org/content/principal-costs-a-new-theory-for-corporate-law-and-governance/.

[40] The term "empty voting" has been used by a number of scholars in recent years to signify the increasing disconnect between the exercise of shareholder voting and the underlying economic interest associated with the shareholder vote. See, e.g., Hu, Henry T.C. and Bernard Black. 2006. "The New Vote Buying: Empty Voting and Hidden (Morphable) Ownership." Southern California Law Review; Fisch, Jill E. 2021. "Mutual Fund Stewardship and the Empty Voting Problem." Brooklyn Journal of Corporate, Financial & Commercial Law.

[41] While it is neither novel nor inherently problematic to rely on the self-interest of private actors as a mechanism to regulate a market, the utility of that mechanism must be questioned when the end-product of that process is something of little or no social value to its intended audience. A 2015 study

In order to answer these questions, we must develop a deeper understanding of how the rise of institutional investors has shaped the behavior of corporations, together with the wider economic and social context in which they have exerted their influence.

---

by University of Pennsylvania Law School professor Jill Fisch—the most recent one of its kind—sought to answer the question by analyzing the extent to which supplemental disclosures obtained in the context of M&A litigation shape shareholder voting on merger transactions. If such supplemental disclosures had value, the study hypothesized that shareholders would be less inclined to support a transaction following the release of the supplemental disclosures given the likelihood that they would only include negative information that companies would not be inclined to voluntarily publicize in the absence of the threat of litigation. Evaluating data from 453 large public company mergers from 2005 to 2012, the study found no statistically significant relationship between disclosure-only settlements and shareholder voting that suggested that shareholders value the additional information from supplemental disclosures in any way that would affect their vote. To be sure, efforts have been made to reduce the pressure faced by companies to produce frivolous disclosures. The year following the publication of Fisch's study, the Delaware Court of Chancery came out with a ruling in *In re Trulia, Inc. Stockholder Litigation* prohibiting Delaware courts from approving disclosure-only settlements unless the supplemental disclosures addressed material misrepresentations or omissions, and any release obtained by defendants was narrowly tailored to claims relating to the disclosures. While the Delaware decision resulted in greater scrutiny of disclosure-only settlements and higher risk to plaintiff lawyers that they would receive no fees, it fell short in addressing the essential issue. In the years since *Trulia*, plaintiffs have increasingly filed similar cases in federal court, asserting individual disclosure claims under Sects. 10(b) or 14(a) of the Securities Exchange Act in order to acquire federal jurisdiction. Because these cases are brought as individual actions, they do not require court approval of any settlement or payment of fees. *Trulia* made no attempt to address the reality that the prototypical equity investor at the foundation of the modern disclosure regime no longer exists. Whether a disclosure is material depends at least in part on how the target audience of that disclosure views that information, but how can one define such a standard of materiality for an investor base that includes index funds and algorithmic traders who attach little weight to corporate disclosures in making investment decisions? If it were even possible to define such a standard, how can one make such a standard work for the diversity of shareholders that dominate today's corporate landscape? And how can one have confidence that such disclosures would incentivize corporations to act as more positive social actors? Fisch, Jill, Sean Griffith, and Steven Davidoff. 2015. "Confronting the Peppercorn Settlement in Merger Litigation: An Empirical Analysis and a Proposal for Reform." Texas Law Review. January. https://scholarship.law.upenn.edu/faculty_scholarship/775/; Dolan, Matthew J. 2022. "More Pushback to Disclosure-Only Settlements." Sidley Austin LLP. https://ma-litigation.sidley.com/2022/05/more-pushback-to-disclosure-only-settlements/.

5

The Emergence of the Shareholder Primacy Paradigm

As the ownership structure of corporate America has evolved over the last fifty years, so too has the shareholder obtained greater centrality in common thinking about the role and purpose of the corporation. Berle's attention to the interests of shareholders stemmed from their relative weakness in the political economy of early twentieth century American capitalism and reflected more an attempt to curb the perceived excess of power held in the hands of corporate management than an effort to aggrandize the prerogatives of shareholders for their own sake. Today, the ascendency of institutional investors in the corporate landscape has eliminated the separation of ownership and control problem at the core of Berle's analysis, and mainstream corporate governance discourse reflects *an even greater* emphasis on the desires of the shareholder as the animating purpose of the corporation.

The rise of the ideology of "shareholder primacy" has its roots in the 1970s with the emergence of the Chicago School of free-market economists, who argued that corporations should operate with only one goal in mind—making shareholders as wealthy as possible. The late economist Milton Friedman, often considered the leading spokesman of the Chicago School, articulated the philosophy of shareholder primacy in his 1970 essay "The Social Responsibility of Business is to Increase Its Profits." Unlike Berle, who believed that the modern corporation was a social institution and that its relationship to shareholders could not be analogized to that existing between a business and a sole proprietor, Friedman argued that shareholders owned the corporation and that the sole responsibility of the corporate manager was to increase profits. Corporations had to abide by social and legal proscriptions, but in Friedman's view, those proscriptions only functioned to establish the ground rules to be followed in the pursuit of shareholder value maximization, rather than define the substantive purpose of the corporation. "In a free-enterprise, private-property system, a corporate executive is an employee of the owners of the business," wrote Friedman. "He has direct responsibility to his employers [and] [t]hat responsibility is to conduct the business in accordance with their desires, which generally will be to make as much money as possible while conforming to the basic rules of the society, both those embodied in law and those embodied in ethical custom."[1]

In 1976, economists Michael Jensen and William Meckling built on Friedman's analysis in an article for the *Journal of Financial Economics* that is commonly viewed as having established the intellectual foundation for the shareholder primacy worldview, garnering nearly 100,000 citations since its initial publication. In that paper—entitled "Theory of the Firm: Managerial Behavior, Agency Costs and Ownership"—Jensen and Meckling argued that the corporation was "a mere legal fiction" of little analytical import and that instead it should be viewed as a "pure agency relationship" between shareholders and corporate management in which the latter was simply tasked to act on behalf of the interests of the former. Other corporate actors—such as customers, employees, or the environment—had no place in this picture. Jensen and Meckling assumed that shareholder interests equated to shareholder wealth and extrapolated that management should only focus on maximizing financial returns for shareholders as the corporation's residual claimants. Corporate managers who chased any other objective were wayward agents who decreased social wealth by imposing agency costs. Jensen and Meckling called for an examination of potential mechanisms to solidify the obedience of management to shareholders, including modifying "incentive compensation systems for the manager" to address concerns that "large publicly held corporations seem to behave in a risk-averse way to the detriment of the equity holders" and suggesting that "conflicts for control"—like hostile takeovers and proxy fights—should be viewed as a socially valuable outcome of collective action by shareholders.[2]

Inspired by the work of Chicago School economists like Friedman and Jensen, the premises and ideas of shareholder primacy gradually found their way into legal scholarship. Beginning with the work of law professor (and later federal appellate judge) Richard Posner, a new generation of "Law and Economics" scholars emerged who sought to apply economic analysis to

---

[1] Friedman, Milton. 1970. "The Social Responsibility of Business is to Increase its Profits." New York Times Magazine.
[2] Jensen, Michael C., and William H. Meckling. 1976. "Theory of the Firm: Managerial Behavior, Agency Costs and Ownership Structure." Journal of Financial Economics. 305–360.

virtually every area of law, including corporate law. Through the subsequent decades, academics applied the economic theories of the Chicago School in various domains, including in relation to executive compensation,[3] the regulation of hostile takeovers[4] and use of defensive tactics by corporate boards,[5] and the adoption of dual-class shares with differential voting rights.[6]

Regulatory and policy changes followed. Tax cuts in the 1980s encouraged the growth of stock-based compensation plans among executives. In 1981, Reagan's Economic Recovery and Tax Act restored qualified stock options, now renamed incentive stock options, and taxed their profits at the long-term capital gains rate. Reagan also cut the top personal income tax rate to 50% in 1981 and lowered it to 28% by 1986. In 1993, Congress amended the tax code to encourage public corporations to tie executive pay to objective performance metrics. Public corporations began granting their top executives stock options and grants, in lieu of cash, pushing executives to do whatever they could to raise the trading price of their companies' shares. The percentage of CEO compensation coming from stock option grants then rose from 25% in 1994, to over 85% by 2001.[7]

The national securities exchanges, like the New York Stock Exchange and NASDAQ, imposed requirements on listed companies that empowered shareholders, such as mandating boards to include a majority of independent non-management directors, limiting the ability of corporate boards to modify the voting rights of shareholders, requiring shareholder approval to consummate certain extraordinary transactions, and restricting the extent to which companies could "classify" or "stagger" their boards to limit the number of directors who stood for election in any given year.

Developments in academia and policy changes created an intellectual and regulatory environment receptive to the ideas of shareholder primacy. The rise of asset managers as corporate shareholders ensured that those ideas acquired practical expression in how corporate managers operated their businesses. By 1990, institutional holdings represented 46% of corporate stock,

---

[3] Jensen, Michael C., and Kevin J. Murphy. 1990. "Performance Pay and Top-Management Incentives." Journal of Political Economy.

[4] Fischel, Daniel R. 1978. "Efficient Capital Market Theory, the Market for Corporation Control, and the Regulation of Cash Tender Offers." Texas Law Review.

[5] Bebchuk, Lucian. 2002. "The Case against Board Veto in Corporate Takeovers." University of Chicago Law Review; Gilson, Ronald J. 1981. "A Structural Approach to Corporations: The Case against Defensive Tactics in Tender Offers." Stanford Law Review.

[6] Grossman, Sanford J., and Oliver Hart. 1988. "One Share-One Vote and the Market for Corporate Control." Journal of Financial Economics.

[7] Blair, Margaret M. 2003. "Shareholder Value, Corporate Governance and Corporate Performance: A Post-Enron Reassessment of the Conventional Wisdom." Georgetown University. https://ssrn.com/abstract=334240.

compared to 6% in 1950.[8] Whether or not executives personally shared the enthusiasm expressed by the likes of Friedman or Jensen about the virtues of shareholder-centric capitalism, they had limited choice but to heed the calls of their new shareholder base. The greater prominence of institutional investors in the public markets enabled them to overcome the collective action problems faced by the paradigmatic Berlean shareholder and to effectively pressure companies.

The popularization of activist investment strategies and private equity helped fuel this assertiveness among institutional investors. So did other structural limitations and factors. Through the 1980s and 1990s, the assets managed by America's largest investment managers, together with the average investment these firms held in any given company, grew to the point that it became unfeasible for many asset managers to readily dispose theirs positions when they disagreed with management. As the chief investment officer of the California State Teachers' Retirement System would note in an interview in 1990: "[t]he larger public pension funds can't just walk away when companies aren't performing well. There'd be no market. Everybody would be on one side of the trade." Even when a dissatisfied institutional investor was able to identify an acceptable buyer, it faced limited options for reinvestment. With the increasing size of their stock portfolios, the bigger institutional investors often already held positions in the vast majority of the country's largest companies. By the early 1990s, many of the largest asset management firms managed investment portfolios consisting of stocks in hundreds or thousands of companies. In 1991, of the 1,107 institutional investors that had filed a 13F form with the SEC, 119 investors (comprising 52% of the assets managed by all of the 13F filers) each held stock in more than 500 companies, and 33 investors (representing more than 30% of the assets managed by all 13F files) each held stock in more than 1000 firms.[9] Index investing, which was still a relatively young but growing asset class in the 1980s and 1990s, magnified this dynamic by locking capital in a predetermined list of companies. With the lack of flexibility to dispose of their shares, institutional investment firms came to lean more on their ability to exercise voice as shareholders. Institutional investors even formed industry associations and lobbying groups to promote their collective perspectives, like the Council of Institutional Investors, which was created in 1985.

A panoply of policy measures pushed forward by shareholder primacy ideologues—who saw the increasing presence of asset managers in corporate stock ledgers and viewed them as the rightful custodians of shareholder

---

[8] Useem, Investor Capitalism. 25.
[9] Ibid., 30–31.

power—further encouraged activist and activist-like behavior among institutional investors. In 1984, Robert Monks, a corporate lawyer and ardent believer in the Chicago School program, joined the Department of Labor as the administrator of the Office of Pension and Welfare Benefit Programs, where he pushed pension fund managers to take a more proactive—and adversarial—role in exercising voting power as fiduciaries. "[I]t is the duty of the fiduciary of a pension plan under ERISA to scrutinize those actions of management which are put to a shareholder's vote," Mr. Monks noted in one speech. "Sitting on the sidelines, or blindly voting for management would not, in my opinion, discharge the ERISA fiduciary's duty as shareholder."[10] In 1988, a few years after Mr. Monks' departure from the Labor Department, his former colleagues promulgated the so-called *Avon* Letter to establish proxy voting as a fiduciary duty of pension funds.

The SEC took additional steps. In 1992, the SEC comprehensively amended the proxy rules to make it easier for institutional investors to replace corporate boards. The 1992 SEC amendments gave institutional shareholders broad freedom to communicate with each other and the public and to coordinate activist fights; empowered dissident shareholders to mount "short-slate" attacks in which they could nominate a less than full slate of directors (in contrast to the prior status quo that required shareholders to seek the replacement of all of a company's directors up for election in order to mount a campaign); and formally confirmed that communications and recommendations by proxy advisory firms were exempt from proxy solicitation rules, thereby establishing a firm legal footing for the growth of the proxy advisory industry, whose role in the rise of the shareholder primacy worldview we discuss later in this chapter.[11] In 2003, the SEC adopted rules requiring mutual funds to vote their shares and to publicly disclose their voting decisions along with the policies and procedures in accordance with which they made their decisions.[12] Since activist investors were frequently the only actors with the interest to pour over these disclosures and lobby mutual funds as to

---

[10] U.S. Senate. "Department of Labor's Enforcement of the Employee Retirement Income Security Act (ERISA): Hearings Before the Subcommittee on Oversight of Government Management of the Committee on Governmental Affairs." 1985. United States Senate, Ninety-Ninth Congress, First Session. Washington: U.S. Government Publishing Office.

[11] For a detailed exposition on the content of these amendments, see, e.g., Calio, Joseph Evan, and Rafael Xavier Zahralddin. 1994. "The Securities and Exchange Commission' 1992 Proxy Amendments: Questions of Accountability." Pace Law Review.

[12] 17 C.F.R. § 275.204–2(c)(2) (2003). The rule followed a release by the Department of Labor stating that pension funds were required by their fiduciary duties to vote the shares of their portfolio companies. Interpretive Bulletins Relating to the Employee Retirement Income Security Act of 1974, 29 C.F.R. § 2509.94–2 (2002) (explaining that the fiduciary act of managing employee benefit plan assets consisting of equity securities includes voting of those securities).

how they crafted their policies, the practical impact was to incentivize mutual funds to pay more attention to activists and to give greater deference to their adversarial posture toward management.

By the late 1990s, the ideas and assumptions of shareholder primacy had come to enjoy widespread acceptance across corporate America. 1983 was the first year that more than two American public corporations used the term "shareholder value" in their annual reports. In 1989, 30% of public companies were using the phrase.[13] Despite the flexibility boards of directors enjoyed under state corporate law to manage the conduct of their businesses, the rise of assertive institutional investors and regulatory changes at the federal level drove companies to refashion their organizational and governance structures to specifically empower shareholders. Companies created internal mechanisms for soliciting feedback from investors, including establishing investor relations departments and shareholder outreach programs that provided institutional investors a direct outlet for regularly engaging with key members of management.[14] Between 1989 and 1992, the fraction of the top 1,000 firms that had in place confidential shareholder voting more than doubled from 4 to 9%. Companies put in place committees of independent directors—in lieu of management directors—to oversee critical board functions, including with respect to audit matters, compensation and director nominations. Less than one-tenth of the top 1,000 firms operated an independent nominating committee in 1972. Nearly two-thirds did so two decades later. In 1972, 70% maintained a compensation committee. 90% had one by 1992.[15] By 1997, the Business Roundtable, a leading association of CEOs from America's largest public companies, had explicitly come out in support of shareholder primacy as the organizing principle of corporate management, proclaiming that "the principal objective of a business enterprise is to generate economic returns to its owners."[16]

---

[13] Cheffins, Brian R. 2020. "Stop Blaming Milton Friedman!" Washington University Law Review. Vol. 98. 1607.
[14] Useem, Investor Capitalism. 142–144.
[15] Ibid., 160.
[16] Business Roundtable. 2022. "For Long-Term Success, Companies Must Deliver for All Stakeholders." Business Roundtable. www.businessroundtable.org/for-long-term-success-companies-must-deliver-for-all-stakeholders.

The Short-Term Shareholder

As the ideology of shareholder primacy took hold, shareholder time horizons became shorter. In 1960, New York Stock Exchange-listed companies had an annual turnover rate of approximately 12%, implying an average holding period of roughly eight years. By 2000, the annual turnover rate of publicly listed corporate equities was a little less than 200%, implying an average holding period of six months.[17] According to one 1992 quantitative study evaluating a large sample of UK companies, financial markets discounted longer term cash flows at higher rates than shorter term flows, indicating a general predisposition towards short-termism in market valuations.[18] Shareholder primacy was not just about companies listening to their shareholders. It more uniformly came to embody a substantive model of executive decision-making in which the maximization of financial returns over a short period of time, measured in months or at most one or two years, was prioritized over all other considerations. Measures that could reasonably be expected to enhance the market value of a company's stock in the near term—such as streamlining operations, cutting overhead, or implementing financial engineering schemes like share repurchases and dividends or asset sales—became favored over longer term, capital-intensive projects that did not produce results in the short-term (and thus had a minimal or negative immediate stock price impact). In 1995, economists Larry Summers and James Poterba conducted a survey of the CEOs of all firms in the Fortune 1000 that showed that most companies applied investment hurdle rates higher than the cost of capital and forsook profitable investments in order to achieve short-term earnings targets.[19] Another 2006 survey of over 400 corporate finance officers found that 80% were willing to decrease discretionary spending on research and development, advertising, and maintenance to meet quarterly earnings

---

[17] World Bank. 2023. "Stock Market Turnover Ratio (Value Traded/Capitalization) for United States." FRED, Federal Reserve Bank of St. Louis. https://fred.stlouisfed.org/series/DDEM01USA156NWDB; Stout, Lynn A. 2012. The Shareholder Value Myth: How Putting Shareholders First Harms Investors, Corporations, and the Public. San Francisco: Berrett-Koehler; Strine, Leo E. 2010. "One Fundamental Corporate Governance Question We Face: Can Corporations Be Managed for the Long Term Unless Their Powerful Electorates Also Act and Think Long Term?" The Business Lawyer Vol. 66, No. 1. http://www.jstor.org/stable/25758524.

[18] Miles, David, 1993. "Testing for Short Termisn in the UK Stock Market." Royal Economic Society. Vol. 103. 1379–1396. https://www.bankofengland.co.uk/-/media/boe/files/working-paper/1992/testing-for-short-termism-in-the-uk-stock-market.pdf.

[19] Poterba, J. M., and L. H. Summers. 1995. "A CEO Survey of US Companies' Time Horizons and Hurdle Rates." MIT Sloan Management Review. Vol. 37. 43.

targets, even if they knew long-term business performance would suffer as a byproduct.[20]

Deregulation and technological innovation in financial markets facilitated the trend towards short-termism. Up through most of the twentieth century, brokers intermediated the majority of stock transactions, and investors had to pay a fixed commission to trade securities. High transaction costs disincentivized trading at a high frequency. With the elimination of fixed commissions and the emergence of the Internet and high frequency trading systems, the structure of the financial markets transformed. Investors could now analyze market data and signals at high speed and then send large numbers of orders within seconds to exploit the insights ascertained from that analysis.

But regulatory and technological changes were only catalysts. Just as the emergence of institutional investors as corporate shareholders made shareholder primacy an unavoidable feature of twentieth-century American capitalism, it also created immense pressure among executives to pursue short-term strategies. Alternative asset managers, like hedge fund activists, actively sought out investments in companies with a view to inducing changes in their businesses that would translate into quick financial returns. Other institutional investors that purportedly espoused longer term investment horizons also agitated for more short-term-oriented corporate governance and management practices. Private pensions in several key industries—including automobiles, steel, airlines, and tires—encountered worsening conditions during the early 1990s as their parent companies struggled in bitterly competitive environments. The resulting underfunding crisis created tremendous stress on private pension managers to do whatever they could to swiftly pump up returns. While public pensions did not experience a similar deterioration in conditions, they generally faced more underfunding challenges than their private counterparts, which resulted in similar pressure on their managers to quickly produce gains in their investment portfolios. In 1991, 67% of public plans reported underfunding in contrast to only 16% of private plans.[21] Pension plan managers became more focused on generating short-term returns and shifted from lower return, low-risk investments, like

---

[20] Stout, Shareholder Value Myth. 67; Stout, Lynn A. 2003. "The Mechanisms of Market Inefficiency: An Introduction to the New Finance." Cornell Law Faculty Publications. 450; Graham, John R., Campbell R. Harvey, and Shiva Rajgopal. 2006 "Value Destruction and Financial Reporting Decisions." Financial Analysts Journal. Vol. 62. 27–39. http://www.jstor.org/stable/4480788.

[21] Useem, Investor Capitalism. 259–262.

bonds, into higher return, higher risk investment equity strategies, including alternative asset classes, such as private equity and hedge funds.[22]

The increasing size of institutional investors' equity portfolios meant that a growing percentage of corporate equities were being managed by professional investment managers whose job was to generate investment returns and whose performance—like that of any professional—was regularly evaluated by reference to both the manager's prior track record as well as the track record of others in the same industry. As a philosophical matter, an investment manager might sympathize with the idea that business performance should be evaluated over the long term, but practically speaking the manager's ability to maintain his or her job depended on demonstrating results. Sinking money into an investment that was uncertain to yield returns in the near- or medium-term became a riskier and less attractive proposition from the standpoint of job survival and compensation, particularly when investment managers understood that many of their institutional clients were comparing their performance to that of alternative asset managers, like private equity firms and activist funds, who could readily demonstrate the ability to generate (at least nominally) superior returns over a truncated time horizon.

Exacerbating this tendency is the fact that it is easier to evaluate shorter term enhancements to performance (than more impactful operational improvements that take time to produce results). Studies have shown that certain types of information that may be very technical or whose long-term significance is hard to pin down, but which are nonetheless germane to assessing a company's economic health, are often reflected in stock prices more slowly and incompletely than the conventional view of market efficiency would suggest. Investment managers who value business measures designed to enhance short-term returns, such as reducing overhead by terminating employees or scaling back customer service, are more likely to be rewarded by the financial markets, which can readily distinguish their financial benefits but are slower to appreciate the negative long-term consequences of employee disaffection or weakening brand loyalty.[23]

Given the relative simplicity of these types of strategies and the consistency with which they produce immediate and discernible results, short-term-oriented cost-cutting and financial engineering measures came to form a set of best practices that investment professionals—who mostly lacked direct

---

[22] Pew Trusts. 2014. "State Public Pension Investments Shift Over Past 30 Years." Pew Charitable Trusts. www.pewtrusts.org/~/media/assets/2014/06/state_public_pension_investments_shift_over_past_30_years.pdf.

[23] Stout, Shareholder Value Myth. 67; Stout, "Market Inefficiency." 651–659; Graham, "Value Destruction"; Bogle, John C. 2006. "Reflections on the Evolution of Mutual Fund Governance." Journal of Business & Technology Law. Vol. 1. 57.

operational or business experience relevant to the companies in which they invested—could effortlessly apply across the portfolio of their investments. As the growing size of asset manager portfolios placed pressure on institutional investors to exert greater influence over their portfolio companies, it also made it more challenging for investors to develop a sufficiently deep understanding of the companies' businesses on the basis of which they could make actionable voting decisions as shareholders. Short-term financial engineering strategies provided an easy-to-apply heuristic in this context. For similar reasons, many larger asset managers separated their proxy voting function from that of portfolio management by establishing separate investment stewardship or governance units that would uniformly promulgate proxy voting decisions on a company-by-company basis across their complex of funds.[24] In turn, these governance units enlisted the services of "proxy advisory firms" that would provide guidance to institutional investors on how to cast their votes with respect to the gamut of matters up for a shareholder vote in any given year. After Robert Monks concluded his stint at the Department of Labor, in 1986 he proceeded to create the first proxy advisory firm—Institutional Shareholder Services or ISS—which together with Glass Lewis (founded in 2003) would become the nation's leading proxy advisory firms, controlling over 90% of market share in the industry. Proxy advisory firms were another driver of short-termism among large asset managers. These firms often had significant client and other relationships with activist hedge funds and other investors with specific short-term objectives who aggressively lobbied proxy advisory firms to kowtow to their agenda and reflect their perspectives in their proxy advisory recommendations.[25] "If ISS has tended to side with activists, there's a good reason," one former ISS executive has noted. "ISS is not a public institution. It is a private, for-profit company, and they are trying to please their clients. They are issuing recommendations they wish to be well received by their clients. They are not writing this report for the good of society. They're writing for clients who pay them money."[26]

---

[24] Useem, Investor Capitalism. 176–177.

[25] Copland, James, David Larcker, and Brian Tayan. 2018. "The Big Thumb on the Scale: An Overview of the Proxy Advisory Industry." Rock Center for Corporate Governance at Stanford University.

[26] Celarier, Michelle. 2018. "The Mysterious Private Company Controlling Corporate America." Institutional Investor. www.institutionalinvestor.com/article/b16pv90bf0zbj8/the-mysterious-private-company-controlling-corporate-america; Fagan, Matthew. 2018. "Third-Party Institutional Proxy Advisors: Conflicts of Interest and Roads to Reform." University of Michigan Journal of Law Reform. Vol. 51. 621.

The End of History

The apparent omnipresence of the shareholder primacy worldview at the turn of the twenty-first century was neatly summarized by law professors Reinier Kraakman and Henry Hansmann in their 2001 essay for *The Georgetown Law Journal* entitled "The End of History for Corporate Law." Evoking the title of Francis Fukayama's book about the ascendancy of liberal democracy over communism, Hansmann and Kraakman argued that shareholder primacy had prevailed over other models of corporate purpose. "[A]cademic, business and government elites," they wrote, shared a consensus that "ultimate control over the corporation should rest with the shareholder class" and that "the managers of the corporation should be charged with the obligation to manage the corporation in the interests of its shareholders." "Other corporate constituencies, such as creditors, employees, suppliers, and customers, should have their interests protected by contractual and regulatory means rather than through participation in corporate governance." According to Hansmann and Kraakman, the "triumph of the shareholder-oriented model of the corporation over its principal competitors [was] now assured."[27]

---

[27] Hansmann, Henry, and Reinier Kraakman. 2000. "The End of History for Corporate Law." The Georgetown Law Journal. Vol. 89. 439–468.

6

The New Stakeholder Capitalism and ESG

The rise of the shareholder primacy paradigm occurred in the context of a broader political and cultural shift from the tenets of the New Deal liberal consensus towards a new "neoliberal" order in which the government played a significantly reduced role in driving and regulating economic activity.

Milton Friedman and other advocates of the Chicago School program not only embraced the ideology of shareholder primacy but also promoted a laissez-faire philosophy towards government intervention in the economy. The influence of Keynesian economics, which held that fiscal policy could play an important part in maintaining full employment, waned among academics and policymakers as the energy crisis and stagflation in the 1970s pushed many to rethink their assumptions about the federal government's ability to spend its way out of economic crises without spurring inflation or creating other market distortions. Majorities in Congress, with the support of the White House—under both Democratic and Republican governments—oversaw a wave of deregulation across a range of industries, including transportation, energy, finance, communications, and agriculture. These deregulatory measures included the elimination of key pillars of the New Deal economic order, such as the repeal of the Glass-Steagall Act (which prohibited the mixing of investment and commercial banking) in 1999 and a drastic restructuring of the Aid to Families with Dependent Children federal assistance program (which provided financial assistance to children whose families had low or no income) in 1996. Internationally, the system of fixed exchange rates and tight capital controls that underpinned the post-World War II global monetary system collapsed in 1971 when President Nixon suspended the dollar's convertibility into gold. The reduction of tariffs and implementation of new free trade agreements, like the North American Free Trade Agreement (NAFTA), further facilitated the flow of capital, labor, and goods across international borders.

Together, the dwindling role of the government as an economic actor and the ascendancy of the shareholder primacy paradigm reshaped the American economic landscape. Public markets demanded that companies focus on core competencies and divest their non-core competencies, resulting in the proliferation of asset-light organizations that had fewer employees, were less diverse, and were less vertically integrated.[1] The takeover wave of the 1980s accelerated the shift as executive teams were reconstituted to include managers who were predisposed towards shedding labor and divesting physical assets to meet the new financial obligations of their companies and push up share prices.[2] Asset optimization led American corporations to transfer manufacturing functions elsewhere and, in many cases, abroad to foreign countries, where free trade agreements had made it easier for companies to take advantage of lax labor protections cheaper labor. The number of manufacturing plants in America employing more than 5000 employees dropped from 192 in 1977 to 49 in 2007. The number of plants with more than 1000 workers fell by half over the same period.[3] Millions of previously stable and well-paid blue-collar jobs, an outsized proportion of which were unionized, were lost and never subsequently recovered. In 1970, 47.4% of the manufacturing labor force was unionized. By 1994, that percentage had declined to 18.2%.[4]

As executives streamlined and downsized their workforces, they also focused on distributing corporate revenues in ways that supported the price of their companies' stocks, with corporate dividend payout ratios and share buybacks climbing through the 1980s and 1990s.[5] The popularization of management stock plans expanded the wedge between the interests of top management and the interests of other corporate constituencies. Combined with the decline in the quality and security of blue-collar jobs, the emphasis on driving returns towards equity capital intensified income inequality.

---

[1] Boyd, Matthew B. 2022. "The Decline of American Manufacturing and Why Today's Leaders Should Care." Boyd Medical. https://boydbiomedical.com/articles/the-decline-of-american-manufacturing.

[2] Lazonick, William, and Mary O'Sullivan. 2000. "Maximizing Shareholder Value: A New Ideology for Corporate Governance." Economy and Society. 18.

[3] Boyd, Matthew B. 2022. "The Decline of American Manufacturing and Why Today's Leaders Should Care." Boyd Medical. https://boydbiomedical.com/articles/the-decline-of-american-manufacturing.

[4] Lazonick, William, and Mary O'Sullivan. 2000. "Maximizing Shareholder Value: A New Ideology for Corporate Governance." Economy and Society. 19.

[5] Ibid.

According to the Congressional Budget Office, after-tax income (adjusted for inflation) of households in the top 1% of earners grew by 275% during the 1979–2007 period, compared to 65% for the next 19%, just under 40% for the next 60% and 18% for the bottom fifth. The share of after-tax income received by the top 1% more than doubled from about 8% in 1979 to over 17% in 2007. The share received by the other 19% of households in the highest quintile edged up from 35 to 36%.[6]

In this environment, corporate managers came to play in the "expectations market", as former business school dean Roger Martin would later contend in his 2011 book *Fixing the Game*. "Modern capitalism dictates that the job of executive leadership is to maximize shareholder value, as measured by the market value of the company's stock," noted Martin. "To that end, the CEO should always be working to increase the stock price, to raise expectations about the company's stock price ad infinitum… the lesson is that no matter good you are, you cannot bear expectations forever." Fixating on shareholder value gave executives "a task that is ultimately unachievable, in that it requires that they raise other people's expectations continuously and forever." At worst, the constant effort to beat expectations propelled executives to engage in fraudulent or illegal behavior, such as "managing earnings" and other accounting manipulations.[7]

Inflated stock market valuations and the low interest rate environment of the 1990s masked many of the negative effects associated with these changes. With the arrival of the new millennium, the damage became harder to avoid. In May 2000, the Federal Reserve hiked interest rates for the first time in a decade, crashing stock prices. It quickly became apparent that beyond creative financial engineering, a large number of the period's asset-light New Economy businesses had little or nothing to show in the way of real business prospects. In certain cases, the recession revealed rampant fraud. Accounting scandals plunged blue chip companies like Enron, Tyco, and Worldcom into bankruptcy, and landed their senior executives in prison. While the economic situation stabilized over the subsequent years, in 2007 the United States—and the world—found themselves submerged in yet another, more severe financial crisis. Driven by a combination of excessive risk-taking by deregulated global financial institutions and the bursting of the U.S. housing bubble, the Great Financial Crisis was the most significant economic recession since the

---

[6] U.S. Government Congressional Budget Office. 2011. "The Distribution of Household Income and Federal Taxes 2007." http://www.cbo.gov/publication/42729; Pear, Robert. 2011. "Top Earners Doubled Share of Nation's Income, C.B.O. Says." The New York Times. https://www.nytimes.com/2011/10/26/us/politics/top-earners-doubled-share-of-nations-income-cbo-says.html.
[7] Stout, The Shareholder Value Myth. 71.

Great Depression. Over eight million homes were foreclosed over the 2007–2009 period, with home prices declining by 40% on average. Unemployment jumped to 10% by October 2009, resulting in the loss of 8.8 million jobs across the economy. Economists estimate that approximately $17 trillion in household wealth was destroyed as a result of the crisis.[8]

The New Stakeholder Capitalism

The corporate scandals and financial crises of the early 2000s shook the confidence of many in the ethos of shareholder primacy and spurred a chorus of scholars, policymakers, and business executives to call for change. In September 2009, a group of 28 leaders representing business, investment, government, academia, and labor joined the Aspen Institute's Business and Society Program's Corporate Values Strategy Group to release a public statement decrying the rise of short-termism. "Managers, shareholders with varying agendas, and regulators, all, to one degree or another, have allowed short-term considerations to overwhelm the desirable long-term growth and sustainable profit objectives of the corporation," the group asserted. "We believe that short-term objectives have eroded faith in corporations continuing to be the foundation of the American free enterprise system, which has been, in turn, the foundation of our economy."[9] In her 2012 book *The Shareholder Value Myth: How Putting Shareholders First Harms Investors, Corporations and the Public*, Cornell Law School professor Lynn Stout set forth a comprehensive critique of the ideology of shareholder primacy, contending that shareholder value thinking led managers to focus myopically on short-term earnings; discouraged investment and innovation; harmed employees, customers, and communities; and caused companies to indulge in reckless, sociopathic, and irresponsible behaviors.[10] The next year, law professor Pavlos E. Masourous published a sweeping, 400-plus-page survey entitled *Corporate Law and Economic Stagnation: How Shareholder value and Short-termism Contribute to the Decline of the Western Economics* in which he presented empirical data from the prior four decades to demonstrate how the ascendancy of the shareholder primacy worldview and short-termism had depressed GDP growth rates in the United States and Western Europe.

---

[8] Investopedia. 2023. "Lessons From the 2008 Financial Crisis." https://www.investopedia.com/news/10-years-later-lessons-financial-crisis/.

[9] Aspen Institute. 2009. "Overcoming Short-Termism: A Call for a More Responsible Approach to Investment and Business Management." https://www.aspeninstitute.org/wp-content/uploads/files/content/docs/pubs/overcome_short_state0909_0.pdf.

[10] Stout, Shareholder Value Myth.

In the 2010s, these criticisms coalesced into appeals to a broader-minded model of capitalism in which corporations were called on to prioritize long-term results and pay heed to the interests of other non-shareholder stakeholders, such as employees, customers, and the environment. As *The Economist* would note in 2010, the "economic crisis has revived the old debate about whether firms should focus most on their shareholders, their customers or their workers."[11] "We're all stakeholders in the American economy, and many stakeholders have done miserably," former Labor Secretary and Political Pundit Robert Reich noted in a 2014 blog post entitled "The Rebirth of Stakeholder Capitalism." "Maybe a bit more stakeholder capitalism is in order." Business professor Louis Brennan similarly explored the concept in her essay "Is stakeholder capitalism making a comeback?"[12] In August 2018, Senator Elizabeth Warren proposed a federal bill—entitled the Accountable Capitalism Act—obligating companies with over $1 billion in revenue to obtain a federal corporate charter that would require at least 40% of a company's directors to be elected by employees and explicitly mandate that directors consider the interests of all corporate stakeholders, not just shareholders. The same year, Oxford academic Colin Mayer extolled the many virtues of stakeholder capitalism in his book entitled *Prosperity: Better Business Makes the Greater,* contending that corporations should strive to "produc[e] profitable solutions to problems of people and planet." In *Reimagining Capitalism in a World on Fire*, Harvard professor Rebecca Henderson called on companies to "embrac[e] a pro-social purpose beyond profit maximization and tak[e] responsibility for the health of the natural and social systems."[13] In August 2019, the Business Roundtable announced that it no longer endorsed the view that "corporations exist principally to serve shareholders" and that instead companies must focus on creating long-term value for all of their stakeholders, such as employees, communities, suppliers, and customers.[14] Several months later, the World Economic Forum published a manifesto calling on corporate leaders to scrap shareholder-centric thinking

---

[11] The Economist. 2010. "A New Idolatry." The Economist. https://www.economist.com/business/2010/04/22/a-new-idolatry.

[12] Reich, Robert. 2014. "The Rebirth of Stakeholder Capitalism?" Robert Reich (blog). https://robertreich.org/post/94260751620; Brennan, Louis. 2018. "Is Stakeholder Capitalism Making a Comeback?" Trinity College Dublin. https://www.tcd.ie/news_events/articles/is-stakeholder-capitalism-making-a-comeback/.

[13] Mayer, Colin. 2018. Prosperity: Better Business Makes the Greater Good. Oxford, United Kingdom: Oxford University Press; Henderson, Rebecca. 2020. Reimagining Capitalism in a World on Fire. New York: PublicAffairs, a subsidiary of Hachette Book Group, Inc.

[14] Business Roundtable. 2019. "Business Roundtable Redefines the Purpose of a Corporation to Promote 'an Economy That Serves All Americans.'" Business Roundtable. https://www.businessroundtable.org/business-roundtable-redefines-the-purpose-of-a-corporation-to-promote-an-economy-that-serves-all-americans.

and to embrace that "[t]he purpose of a company is to engage all its stakeholders in shared and sustained value creation."[15] In 2020, the World Economic Forum made stakeholder capitalism the theme of its signature annual conference in Davos.

History of Stakeholder Capitalism

Stakeholder capitalism is by no means a novel concept. While Berle never used the term, he concluded *The Modern Corporation* with an invocation of the core principle of stakeholder capitalism, describing the corporation as a fundamentally "social organization" that "involves the interrelation of a wide diversity of interests—those of the 'owners' who supply capital, those of the workers who 'create,' those of the consumers who give value to the products of enterprise, and above all those of the control who wield power."[16] The structural dynamics of the modern corporation had "cleared the way for the claims of a group far wider than either the owners or the control... [T]hey have placed the community in a position to demand that the modern corporation serve not alone the owners or the control but all society."[17]

Since the publication of *The Modern Corporation*, the subject of stakeholderism has generated an extensive body of literature. In 1995, Georgetown University professor Thomas Donaldson and University of Maryland professor Lee Preston examined the varying conceptions of stakeholder capitalism put forward by thinkers in an article that continues to be helpful in unpacking the meaning of stakeholderism. In "The Stakeholder Theory of the Corporation: Concepts, Evidence, and Implications," Donaldson and Preston characterized the stakeholder theory as having three dimensions: (1) a *descriptive* dimension that simply intends to better elucidate the nature of the corporation by modeling its activities as a "constellation of cooperative and competitive intrinsic value"; (2) an *instrumental* dimension that focuses on examining the connections between the practice of stakeholder management and the achievement of various corporate performance goals, such as profitability, stability, and growth; and (3) a *normative* dimension that attaches intrinsic value to the interests of stakeholders and calls on

---

[15] Schwab, Klaus. 2020. "Davos Manifesto 2020: The Universal Purpose of a Company in the Fourth Industrial Revolution." World Economic Forum. https://www.weforum.org/agenda/2019/12/davos-manifesto-2020-the-universal-purpose-of-a-company-in-the-fourth-industrial-revolution/#:~:text=The%20purpose%20of%20a%20company,communities%20and%20society%20at%20large.

[16] Berle, Adolf A., and Gardiner C. Means. 1932. The Modern Corporation and Private Property. New York: Macmillan Company.

[17] Ibid., 312.

corporations to view stakeholders as persons or groups with inherently legitimate interests in procedural and/or substantive aspects of corporate conduct. Donaldson and Preston proceeded then to describe how discussion of stakeholder theory in corporate governance literature often conflated these aspects of stakeholderism, but that ultimately any particular conception of stakeholderism is often driven by a normative perspective on the nature of the relevant stakeholder interests and their relationship to the corporation.

Berle's discussion of stakeholder capitalism in *The Modern Corporation* was predominantly normative in its emphasis. While the book focused on describing the history and evolution of corporate law, his final exhortations about the corporation and its relationship with its stakeholders were centered on the question of how corporations *should be* managed, not how they *were* managed. Berle did not spell out how he envisioned implementing stakeholderism in *The Modern Corporation*, but it is evident from his other work and policy contributions that Berle was most concerned with the *economic* interests of the general public and that he viewed federal regulation as the key instrument by which to protect those interests. By the time *The Modern Corporation* was published, Berle had become a key member of President Roosevelt's "Brain Trust" and advocated for some of the most aggressive New Deal era economic reforms. Berle did not view the public as an abstract idea or seek to narrowly give meaning to the concept of economic interests by fixating on only one dimension of the public's participation in economic life. Berle was focused on the real-world economic impact of corporate conduct and embraced a suite of federal regulations intended to protect the economic wellbeing of individuals and businesses in a holistic sense encompassing their participation in the economy as investors, consumers, and employees.

The post-World War II economic order exemplified the Berlean model of stakeholder capitalism. The assertiveness of the federal government in regulating corporate behavior was a feature of a political economy in which economic activity was shaped by big businesses and other big institutions, such as unions, farmer cooperatives, and consumer advocacy groups. With the diminished influence of Brandeisans, large organizations were seen as part and parcel of the broad-based prosperity of the era. Big businesses, through their greater size and scale, were able to deliver goods and services more cheaply and efficiently and employ a wider segment of the population, while big government and big labor functioned as countervailing forces—to use John Kenneth Galbraith's turn of phrase—that ensured that consumers and workers had effective bargaining power to advocate for their interests.

The success and stability of this system rested on a firm foundation of public support. Berle believed in the capacity of government to effect positive change, but he did not presume such action was legitimate on its face. The New Deal order's legitimacy flowed from the "public consensus" that existed in favor of it, which he defined as "a set of value judgments so widely accepted and deeply held in the United States that public opinion can energize political action when necessary to prevent [economic] power from violating these values."[18] At the core of this consensus was the idea that "capitalism needed to work for the many and that the national government must protect stakeholders like workers and consumers from corporate overreaching."[19] There may have been differences in opinion among Americans on particular policy issues, but the body of "general, unstated premises" that comprised the public consensus embraced the principal tenets of the New Deal order, such that even a staunch conservative like Richard Nixon would readily state in 1971 that "We are all Keynsians now."[20]

The stakeholder model came to reflect the way corporate managers actually approached the management of their businesses. In 1962, Robert Stewart, a corporate planner for Lockheed Martin, put together a team of researchers at the Stanford Research Institute in Menlo Park, California, and established the Theory and Practice of Planning program (TAPP) with a view to helping executives more effectively engage in strategic planning. As part of that effort, Stewart promoted the idea of "stakeholder planning" as a practical framework for making business decisions. Executives were encouraged to examine input on strengths, weaknesses, opportunities, and threats (or "SWOT" variables) from all of the company's stakeholders in order to better understand the impact of their decisions on different groups and how best to address potential conflicting interests. Through the 1960s, the concept of stakeholder planning became popularized in executive management circles. By 1970, TAAP had trained corporate leaders from at least 300 of the largest American companies in its business executive seminars.[21] Business School professors across the country began incorporating TAPP's methodologies in their coursework and Harvard Business School's influential business policy

---

[18] Berle, Power without Property, 22.

[19] Former Delaware Chief Justice Leo Strine provides a helpful review of Berle's theory of public consensus in his article entitled "Stakeholder Capitalism's Greatest Challenge: Reshaping a Public Consensus to Govern a Global Economy." See Strine Jr., Leo E., and Michael Klain. 2023. "Stakeholder Capitalism's Greatest Challenge: Reshaping a Public Consensus to Govern a Global Economy." The University of Pennsylvania, Institute for Law and Economics Research Paper. No. 23–24. 338.

[20] Moore, Marc, and Antoine Rebérioux. 2010. "Corporate Power in the Public Eye: Re-assessing the Implications of Berle's Public Consensus Theory." Seattle University Law Review. Vol. 33. 1109–1139; Murray, John Courtney. 1960. "The Origins and Authority of the Public Consensus." Georgetown University Library. https://library.georgetown.edu/woodstock/murray/whtt_c4_.

[21] Puyt, R.W., Finn Birger Lie, and F.J. de Graaf. 2017. "Contagious Ideas and Cognitive Artefacts: The SWOT Analysis Evolution in Business." BAM 2017 Conference Proceedings. Art 351. 2–19.

textbook—*Business Policy: Text and Cases*—discussed stakeholder planning at length. In a 1974 article entitled "American Finance: Three Views of Strategy" and published in the *Journal of General Management*, Business School professor Isreal Unterman described the widespread application of TAPP's methods across corporate America, including American finance companies like Chase Manhattan.[22]

The Rise of ESG: 2010 to Today

With the rise of the Chicago School and corporate America's espousal of the mantra of shareholder primacy, the concept of stakeholderism as a framework for how to organize economic activity receded from mainstream discourse until the Great Financial Crisis. The new stakeholder capitalism paradigm that has taken shape in the subsequent years differs from that which preceded it in significant ways. The institutional framework within which the New Deal economic order came into being has largely disappeared. In the years immediately following the 2008 financial crisis, Democratic majorities in Congress—with the support of the Obama Administration—ramped up the role of the federal government in a number of areas, including through the passage of the Dodd-Frank Act (which enhanced regulation of the financial services industry), the Affordable Care Act (to expand healthcare coverage), and other legislative and regulatory measures to curb carbon and methane emissions in the fight against climate change. Nevertheless, after four decades of deregulation, the power of the federal regulatory apparatus is much more limited relative to the reach of the federal government in the decades after the Second World War. Policy efforts that have more ambitiously sought to restore the role of the government in facilitating a stakeholder-focused regime of capitalism faltered. Despite the media fanfare it generated, Senator Warren's Accountable Capitalism Act did not find meaningful support in Congress and did not even come to vote. Unions—a key power player in the New Deal economic order—continue to possess less power than they did in mid-twentieth century America. In 2022, the percentage of workers counting themselves as members of unions bottomed out at approximately 10%, compared to 33% in 1957.[23]

---

[22] Soukup, Stephen R. 2021. The Dictatorship of Work Capital: How Political Correctness Captured Big Business. New York: Encounter Books. 53.
[23] Feiveson, Laura. 2023. "Labor Unions and the U.S. Economy." U.S. Department of the Treasury. https://home.treasury.gov/news/featured-stories/labor-unions-and-the-us-economy#:~:text=Over%20the%20subsequent%20decades%2C%20union,20%20percent%20of%20total%20income.

As the institutional architecture of the New Deal order has frayed, globalization has imposed substantial stress on the Berlean notion of public consensus. As Leo Strine and Michael Klain note in their 2023 article revisiting Berle's legacy, "the need for corporations to operate in global markets has... reduced the ability of any chartering nation to hold its corporations accountable to a public consensus of ethical behavior." Corporations now "find themselves subject to the exercise of governmental power by nations that do not share a common set of values, and where there is the opposite of a shared public consensus." "Because American and OECD-domiciled corporations are under pressure to deliver profits, they operate in nations where governments do not adhere to commonly accepted standards of human and civil rights, leaving them vulnerable to pressure to be complicit in oppression and to take stakeholder-unfriendly actions they would never risk at home."[24]

Within this vacuum, a new generation of self-styled socially minded asset management firms has emerged as the institutional vanguard of the stakeholder capitalism revival. Rather than explicitly embrace stakeholder capitalism as a system of economic organization, these firms have advocated a vision of stakeholder capitalism grounded in the investment philosophy of Environmental, Social, and Governance (ESG), which calls on investors to give greater weight to ESG factors in making investment decisions. In the 1970s and 1980s, social activists promoted, with mostly limited success, "socially responsible investing" practices with the express goal of promoting particular political objectives or moral values, like divesting from companies that had operations in Apartheid South Africa or avoiding investments in alcohol or tobacco businesses. The ESG movement makes a different contention—that ESG factors have specific financial relevance to shareholders. ESG advocates accept the premise of shareholder primacy that corporations should prioritize the interests of their shareholders and instead focus on redefining what those interests signify and how best to achieve them. In contrast to more short-term investors, ESG activists claim that they are focused on generating *long-term* value for shareholders, which they argue hinges on corporations considering the interests of their broader base of stakeholders. Shareholders remain at the center of the ESG philosophy; other stakeholders fit into that picture only to the extent their interests serve the needs of shareholders.

The argument was first outlined in a December 2004 white paper authored by a working group of the world's largest institutional investors and financial institutions under the auspices of the United Nations' Financial Sector

---

[24] Strine, "Stakeholder Capitalism's Greatest Challenge," 347.

Initiative. "The institutions endorsing this report are convinced that in a more globalized, interconnected and competitive world the way that environmental, social and corporate governance issues are managed is part of companies' overall management quality needed to compete successfully," the working group emphasized, "[c]ompanies that perform better with regard to these issues can increase shareholder value."[25] The following year, the United Nations Environmental Program commissioned a study from the law firm Freshfields Bruckhaus Deringer, which argued that the financial salience of ESG issues effectively obligated corporate boards to take into account ESG factors in discharging their fiduciary duties.[26] These two reports formed the backbone for the launch of the Principles for Responsible Investment (PRI) at the New York Stock Exchange in 2006 and the launch of the Sustainable Stock Exchange Initiative (SSEI) the following year, each of which became a key organizational pillar for the emerging ESG movement.[27]

In practice, the application of ESG has had two dimensions. One is that it is a stock-picking strategy. Investors identify companies that they deem to be more or less attractive from an ESG perspective and decide whether or not to invest capital in a company on that basis. Another is voting and control. In their capacity as shareholders of their portfolio companies, investors make decisions about whether or not to support certain proposals that come before a shareholder vote based on consideration of ESG factors and, if needed, engage with boards and management to pressure companies to give greater weight to ESG by deploying a range of "activist" tactics, from writing letters to submitting shareholder proposals and mounting a proxy contest (or expressing support for proposals or director slates put forward by a dissident shareholder).

As is evident by the name, the ESG agenda differs from the Berlean stakeholder model by centering environmental and social concerns over issues that are more conventionally understood to have economic import.[28] Climate

---

[25] United Nations. 2004. "Who Cares Wins: Connecting the Financial Markets to a Changing World?" United Nations. The Global Compact. https://www.unglobalcompact.org/docs/issues_doc/Financial_markets/who_cares_who_wins.pdf.

[26] United Nations. 2005. A Legal Framework for the Integration of Environmental, Social and Governance Issues into Institutional Investment. United Nations Environment Programme, Financial Initiative. New York: Freshfields Bruckhaus Deringer.

[27] Kell, Georg. 2018. "The Remarkable Rise of ESG." Forbes. https://www.forbes.com/sites/georgkell/2018/07/11/the-remarkable-rise-of-esg/?sh=d0b035416951.

[28] Mueller, Ronald O., Elizabeth A. Ising, and Thomas J. Kim. 2023. "Shareholder Proposal Developments During the 2023 Proxy Season." Harvard Law School Forum on Corporate Governance. https://corpgov.law.harvard.edu/2023/08/03/shareholder-proposal-developments-during-the-2023-proxy-season/.

change and board diversity represent by and far the most common advocacy issues promoted under the ESG banner, but other common themes include reproductive health, human rights, and animal welfare.[29] Consistent with the ESG movement's acceptance of the foundational premise of shareholder primacy—that the corporation exists to serve shareholders—ESG activists generally promote proposals to enhance the voice of shareholders in the corporate apparatus of the corporation. The consideration of stakeholder interests is considered the best means by which to serve the interests of the "right kind" of shareholders, but it is shareholders nonetheless who call the shots. Virtually all asset managers that embrace ESG principles have adopted voting policies and procedures that seek to empower the power of shareholders in the internal governance machinery of the corporation, including supporting board declassification proposals that require all of a company's directors to stand for annual elections, as well as proposals that make it easier for shareholders to drive corporate action outside of the annual meeting cycle, such as by calling special meetings or acting by written consent in lieu of shareholder meetings.

ESG witnessed tremendous growth in the latter half of the 2010s. In 2020, ESG-related investment funds constituted nearly 25% of new U.S. mutual dollar inflows—double the level in 2019 and up from just 1% in 2014. Overall, the value of assets held in ESG funds invested in U.S. equities nearly doubled from year-end 2019 through year-end 2021, increasing from $276 billion to $550 billion in two years' time.[30] By the end of the decade, most sizeable asset management firms with ownership stakes in public companies had in place proxy voting policies and guidelines that incorporated ESG factors. In 2022, over two-thirds of the 94 largest asset managers in the world had in place proxy voting, engagement, and general stewardship policies expressly setting forth expectations regarding ESG matters, along with a record of engaging companies on ESG issues.[31] The world's largest institutional investors have been at the forefront of the ESG upswing, spearheaded by the Big Three asset management firms—BlackRock, Vanguard, and State Street—whose substantial index funds holdings make them the biggest asset managers on the planet. Most notably, Larry Fink, the founder and CEO of

---

[29] Ibid.
[30] Copland, James R. 2024. "Index Funds Have Too Much Voting Power: A Proposal for Reform." Manhattan Institute for Policy Research. https://manhattan.institute/article/index-funds-have-too-much-voting-power-a-proposal-for-reform.
[31] Alyssa, Hortense Bioy, Lindsey Stewart, Bridget Hughes. 2022. "The Morningstar ESG Commitment Level: Our Assessment of 94 Asset Managers." Morningstar Research. https://investments.metlife.com/content/dam/metlifecom/us/investments/about/sustainability-hub/asset-manager-ecl-2022-landscape-final.pdf.

BlackRock—the largest asset manager in the world—made the ESG vision of stakeholder capitalism a linchpin of BlackRock's corporate governance outlook, describing stakeholder capitalism as the future of capitalism and launching a center for stakeholder capitalism in 2022 to bring together "leading CEOs, investors, policy experts, and academics to share their experience and deliver their insights."[32] While less vocal than the Big Three, other more traditionally active asset management firms have also been important players in the growth of ESG. These include Fidelity, Capital Group, Invesco, T. Rowe Price, and Franklin Templeton, each of which frequently shows up in "top 15" and "top 20" lists of the world's largest asset managers by assets under management.[33]

The role of the asset management industry in pushing forward the ESG agenda has taken multiple forms. They are important providers of ESG investing products to both retail and institutional investors, channeling capital into institutions they deem to be ESG compliant. In 2020 alone, BlackRock raised $68 billion through its ESG products, representing more than 60% of all annual growth.[34] These funds have facilitated the growth of ESG investing not simply by virtue of their size and scale, but also because that platform has enabled them to effectively cross-sell ESG options across their investment platform. Again, in the case of BlackRock, up to at least 2021, a substantial amount of ESG inflows were driven by the firm inserting its primary ESG fund into popular and influential model portfolios offered to

---

[32] Turner, Natasha. 2022. "BlackRock Unveils Stakeholder Capitalism Centre." MA Financial Media. https://future.portfolio-adviser.com/blackrock-unveils-stakeholder-capitalism-centre/; Rubenstein, David. 2020. "Larry Fink Says Stakeholder Capitalism Is the Way Forward." YouTube. https://www.youtube.com/watch?v=1evmygzKF6o; In the same spirit, Bill McNabb and Cyrus Taraporevala, the former CEOs of Vanguard and State Street have lauded the Business Roundtable's 2019 statement in favor of stakeholder capitalism. "By taking a broader, more complete view of corporate purpose, boards can focus on creating long-term value, better serving everyone," noted McNabb. Taraporevala highlighted State Street's support of the stakeholder agenda through its efforts to push "companies to focus on a variety of environmental, social and governance (ESG) issues that impact their ability to generate long-term value." Taraporevala, Cyrus. 2019. "We Need Stakeholder Capitalism to Achieve a Sustainable and Inclusive Future." LinkedIn. https://www.linkedin.com/pulse/we-need-stakeholder-capitalism-achieve-sustainable-cyrus-taraporevala/; Business Roundtable. 2019. "Business Roundtable Redefines the Purpose of a Corporation to Promote 'an Economy That Serves All Americans.'" Business Roundtable. https://www.businessroundtable.org/business-roundtable-redefines-the-purpose-of-a-corporation-to-promote-an-economy-that-serves-all-americans.

[33] Anne Richards of Fidelity, the third biggest asset management firm, echoed the same sentiment, noting that "[i]n the long term, what is good for stakeholders is good for shareholders too" and cautioning against the risks of "alienating non-shareholders - including the customers and employees on whom every business depends." Richards, Anne. 2020. "Sustainability Report 2020: Fidelity CEO Anne Richards on Sustainable Capitalism." Fidelity International. https://www.fidelityinternational.com/editorial/article/sustainability-report-2020-anne-richards-aecdae-en5/.

[34] Wursthorn, Michael. 2021. "Tidal Wave of ESG Funds Brings Profit to Wall Street." The Wall Street Journal. https://www.wsj.com/articles/tidal-wave-of-esg-funds-brings-profit-to-wall-street-11615887004.

investment advisers, who used them with clients across North America. The huge flows from such models meant that many investors got into an ESG vehicle without necessarily choosing one as a specific investment strategy, or even knowing that their money had gone into one.[35]

The more significant channel through which the major asset management firms have driven the popularization of ESG is in their expression of voice as shareholders with significant bloc holdings. The concentration of share ownership among the largest asset management firms has increased over the last two decades, enhancing their ability to exert control over their portfolio companies. The Big Three have been beneficiaries of this trend, with 82% of asset inflows to active and passive mutual funds alike going to the Big Three between 2009 and 2018. By 2017, the Big Three collectively managed approximately 20.5% of equity in the S&P 500 and 16.5% of the Russell 3000 index.[36] According to one study, the Big Three together have the power to cast a majority vote on 49.1% of environmental-focused shareholder proposals, 49.0% of social-focused shareholder proposals, and 65.2% of governance-focused shareholder proposals at Fortune 250 companies.[37]

Gender diversity on boards is the first ESG issue that generated real engagement on the part of asset management firms.[38] Activism on the topic went into high gear in 2017 when State Street launched its Fearless Girl marketing campaign, which led to the placement of a statue of a defiant young girl facing the Charging Bull on Wall Street.[39] In connection with that campaign, State Street announced that it would vote against the chair of the nominating committee at boards that lacked diversity and failed to take appropriate measures to improve it.[40] Over the subsequent five months,

---

[35] Simpson, Cam, and Saijel Kishan. 2021. "How BlackRock Made ESG the Hottest Ticket on Wall Street." Bloomberg. https://www.bloomberg.com/news/articles/2021-12-31/how-blackrock-s-invisible-hand-helped-make-esg-a-hot-ticket?sref=1kJVNqnU&embedded-checkout=true.

[36] Lund, Dorothy S. 2021. "Asset Managers as Regulators." University of Pennsylvania Law Review. Vol. 171. https://scholarship.law.upenn.edu/cgi/viewcontent.cgi?article=9797&context=penn_law_review#:~:text=Asset%20managers%20will%20only%20supply,the%20substance%20of%20their%20rules.

[37] Griffin, Caleb. 2020. "Margins: Estimating the Influence of the Big Three on Shareholder Proposals." SMU Law Review. Vol. 73. https://scholar.smu.edu/smulr/vol73/iss3/6.

[38] The summary below of the ESG activism track record of the Big Three with respect to board diversity and climate change heavily borrows from Dorothy Lund's excellent 2021 article "Asset Managers as Regulators" (in particular, pages 106 to 108 and 113 to 116), which is cited throughout this book together with the underlying source material.

[39] Lublin, Joann S. and Sarah Krouse. 2017. "State Street to Start Voting Against Companies That Don't Have Women Directors." The Wall Street Journal. https://www.wsj.com/articles/state-street-says-it-will-start-voting-against-companies-that-dont-have-women-directors-1488862863.

[40] Baer, Justin. 2017. "State Street Votes Against 400 Companies Citing Gender Diversity." The Wall Street Journal. https://www.wsj.com/articles/state-street-votes-against-400-companies-citing-gender-diversity-1501029490.

State Street had voted against nominating directors at 400 portfolio companies that lacked women directors and had not persuaded State Street they were making enough progress in improving board diversity.[41] Later in 2017, BlackRock and Vanguard joined State Street in its board diversity pressure campaign.[42] In July, BlackRock stated that it planned to vote against directors of nondiverse boards, and in its proxy voting guidelines posted the next year, BlackRock announced that it expected to see companies include at least two women directors on every board.[43] In addition, BlackRock dispatched letters to portfolio companies with less than two woman directors, requesting companies to detail their board diversity practices.[44] In August 2017, the CEO of Vanguard disclosed in an open letter that it would take into account gender diversity in determining whether to vote for directors.[45] State Street went even further, announcing that it would vote against the entire slate of board members on the nominating committee if a company did not have at least one woman on its board, and had not engaged in successful dialogue on State Street's board gender diversity program for three consecutive years.[46]

Climate change also emerged as a banner ESG cause among institutional investors in the mid- to late-2010s, spurred in large part by the adoption of the Paris Climate Accords in 2015, which set forth ambitious goals for reducing global emissions and developing renewable energy solutions.[47] The year after, BlackRock CEO Larry Fink argued that long term investors needed

---

[41] Press Release. 2018. "State St. Glob. Advisors, State Street Global Advisors Reports Fearless Girl's Impact: More than 300 Companies Have Added Female Directors." https://www.businesswire.com/news/home/20180927005518/en/State-Street-Global-Advisors-Reports-Fearless-Girl%E2%80%99s-Impact-More-than-300-Companies-Have-Added-Female-Directors.

[42] Hunnicutt, Trevor. 2017. "BlackRock Supports Effort to Boost Number of Women Board Members." https://www.reuters.com/article/us-blackrock-women/blackrock-supports-effort-to-boost-number-of-women-board-members-idUSKBN19Z09C.

[43] Krouse, Sarah. 2018. "BlackRock: Companies Should Have At Least Two Female Directors." The Wall Street Journal. https://www.wsj.com/articles/blackrock-companies-should-have-at-least-two-female-directors-1517598407.

[44] Gormley, Todd A., Vishal K. Gupta, David A. Matsa, Sandra C. Mortal and Lukai Yang. 2021. "The Big Three and Board Gender Diversity: The Effectiveness of Shareholder Voice." 9.

[45] Open Letter from William McNabb III, Chairman & CEO, Vanguard, to Dirs. of Public Companies Worldwide. 2017. https://www.vanguard.ca/documents/literature/ceo-governance-letter.pdf.

[46] Press Release. 2018. "State St. Glob. Advisors, State Street Global Advisors Reports Fearless Girl's Impact: More than 300 Companies Have Added Female Directors." https://www.businesswire.com/news/home/20180927005518/en/State-Street-Global-Advisors-Reports-Fearless-Girl%E2%80%99s-Impact-More-than-300-Companies-Have-Added-Female-Directors.

[47] Teske, Sven. 2019. Achieving the Paris Climate Agreement Goals. New York: Springer Publishing.

to engage companies on the topic of climate change, issuing a report highlighting the importance of climate change as an issue with significant impact on future portfolios.[48]

When President Trump took office in 2017, his administration promptly proceeded to roll back the vast majority of President Obama's climate change policies, including exiting the Paris Climate Accords in June 2017.[49] Despite these measures, institutional investor activism on climate change continued unabated. In his 2018 letter to CEOs, Fink expressed BlackRock's intention to engage with companies on climate change and the firm's expectation that CEOs "demonstrate the leadership and clarity that will drive not only their own investment returns, but also the prosperity and security of their fellow citizens."[50] In 2019, Fink dedicated the annual CEO letter to climate issues, which he argued would reshape the economy and asset management. In addition to calling for additional disclosure to permit investors to better manage climate-related investment risk, BlackRock announced that it would divest the firm's actively managed portfolios (about $1.8 trillion) from coal stocks.[51] State Street and Vanguard similarly foregrounded their climate change efforts in their annual reports. In September 2019, an alliance of the world's largest pension funds and insurers (representing $2.4 trillion in assets) committed itself at the United Nations' annual climate summit to transitioning its portfolios to net-zero emissions by 2050.[52] In 2020, the Net Zero Asset Managers initiative was launched, which included 220 signatories with over $57 trillion in assets under management, including each of the Big Three. To achieve this objective, each asset management firm committed to use its engagement and voting practices to encourage companies to reduce emissions. That year, Fink dedicated his CEO letter to climate issues, stating that BlackRock was requesting companies to provide detailed disclosures regarding their climate change practices in line with industry-specific guidelines and standards set forth by the Task Force on Climate-related Financial Disclosures.

---

[48] Fink, Larry. 2016. "Larry Fink's 2016 Letter to CEOs." BlackRock. https://www.blackrock.com/corporate/investor-relations/2016-larry-fink-ceo-letter.

[49] Konisky, David M. 2020. Handbook of U.S. Environmental Policy. New York: Edward Elgar Publishing.

[50] Fink, Larry. 2018. "Larry Fink's 2018 Letter to CEOs." BlackRock. https://www.blackrock.com/corporate/investor-relations/2018-larry-fink-ceo-letter.

[51] Fink, Larry. 2019. "Larry Fink's 2019 Letter to CEOs." BlackRock. https://www.blackrock.com/corporate/investor-relations/2019-larry-fink-ceo-letter.

[52] United Nations. 2019. "Investors make unprecedented commitment to net zero emissions." UN Environmental Program.https://www.unep.org/news-and-stories/press-release/investors-make-unprecedented-commitment-net-zero-emissions#:~:text=New%20York%2C%2023%20September%2C%202019%20%E2%80%93%20In%20one,today%20committed%20to%20carbon-neutral%20investment%20portfolios%20by%202050.

The letter then informed CEOs: "[W]e will be increasingly disposed to vote against management and board directors when companies are not making sufficient progress on sustainability-related disclosures and the business practices and plans underlying them."[53] Vanguard and State Street followed suit. Vanguard doubled down on the importance of climate disclosure and emissions reduction in its 2020 investment stewardship annual report, stating: "Where climate change is a material risk, Vanguard encourages companies to set and disclose targets that align with [Paris Agreement] goals, and to both assess and communicate their progress."[54] State Street released a letter in 2020 announcing that it would consider a company's R-Factor (or performance of the company's business and governance across various ESG issues, based on the SASB framework for disclosure) in its voting decisions.[55]

During the 2020 proxy season, BlackRock supported a record number of climate-related shareholder proposals—297 (or 35%), compared to 155 (or 17%) the previous year.[56] The asset management firm voted against the election of 255 directors because of concerns about the performance of their companies on climate issues, up from 55 the previous year.[57] State Street stated that it had voted against entire boards at companies that were "laggards" in terms of their R-Factor score, and backed a record number of shareholder proposals that asked companies to report on the risks of climate change to their business and disclose their plan to address these risks.[58] Vanguard also advocated a gamut of shareholder proposals related to climate disclosure in the 2020 proxy season.[59]

Importantly, despite the Trump Administration's rollback of many of the Obama Administration's climate change-related policies, the Trump White House failed to push back on a lesser-known regulatory change adopted by

---

[53] Fink, Larry. 2020. "Larry Fink's 2020 Letter to CEOs." BlackRock. https://www.blackrock.com/corporate/investor-relations/2020-larry-fink-ceo-letter

[54] Vanguard. 2020. Investment Stewardship 2020 Annual Report. https://about.vanguard.com/investment-stewardship/perspectives-and-commentary/2020_investment_stewardship_annual_report.pdf.

[55] Letter from Cyrus Taraporevala, President and CEO, State St. Glob. Advisors, to Board Members. 2020. https://www.ssga.com/library-content/pdfs/insights/CEOs-letter-on-SSGA-2020-proxy-voting-agenda.pdf.

[56] Posner, Cydney. 2021. "BlackRock Flexes Its Muscles During the 2020-21 Proxy Period." HARV. L. SCH. F. ON CORP. GOVERNANCE. https://corpgov.law.harvard.edu/2021/08/16/blackrock-lexes-its-muscles-during-the-2020-21-proxy-period; see also BlackRock. 2020. Pursuing Long-Term Value for Our Clients, BlackRock Investment Stewardship. https://www.blackrock.com/corporate/literature/publication/2021-voting-spotlight-full-report.pdf.

[57] Posner, BlackRock Flexes Its Muscles During the 2020-21 Proxy Period.

[58] Press Release, State St. Glob. Advisors. 2020. State Street Global Advisors Publishes 2020 Proxy Season Review. https://corporate.vanguard.com/content/dam/corp/advocate/investment-stewardship/pdf/policies-and-reports/2020_investment_stewardship_annual_report.pdf.

[59] Vanguard. 2020. Investment Stewardship 2020 Annual Report.

the Obama Administration pertaining to investment advisors that helped foster the growth of ESG within the asset management industry. Since the passage of ERISA in 1974, any individual or institution that has discretionary authority over worker retirement plans or provides investment advice to a plan for compensation is subject to fiduciary responsibilities. These fiduciary duties largely remained the same in the subsequent 40 years, subject to marginal changes to the flexibility afforded to fiduciaries in the consideration of conventionally non-financial, or non-pecuniary, factors. In 2015, the Obama Administration took action to explicitly permit the consideration of ESG factors among investment advisors by clarifying that ERISA did not prohibit a fiduciary from utilizing ESG factors in investment policy statements or integrating ESG-related tools, metrics, and analyses to evaluate an investment's returns and risks. While prior Department of Labor guidance emphasized the need to document consideration of traditionally non-economic factors, the Obama Department of Labor stated that "consideration of... ESG criteria [does not] presumptively requir[e] additional documentation or evaluation beyond that required by fiduciary standards applicable to plan investments generally[,]" and that a facts and circumstances test applied to determine the appropriate level of documentation.[60] Following the 2016 presidential election, the Trump Administration issued a number of statements suggesting that it would undertake a revamp of the Obama Era Department of Labor guidance, but did not initiate rulemaking procedures until the summer of 2020. When the Trump Department of Labor finally issued the "Financial Factors in Selecting Plan Investments" rule on November 13, 2020, it essentially ratified 90% of the Obama era guidance. The new rule established that ERISA plan fiduciaries could only take into account "pecuniary" considerations, but confirmed that pecuniary returns could be directly impacted by ESG factors and thus could be factored into investment decisions on that basis. In other words, the rule reflected the underlying premise of the ESG worldview that companies should pay greater attention to issues traditionally perceived to be environmental and social issues because of their financial salience to investors.[61]

---

[60] Marsico, Ben. 2021. "Recent Developments In ESG Investing: An Analysis of Securities and Exchange Commission Movement and the Department of Labor's Recent ERISA Fiduciary Rulemaking." University of North Carolina. https://law.unc.edu/wp-content/uploads/2021/04/CE3-MARSICOELPFinal.pdf.

[61] Eccles, Robert, and Daniel F. C. Crowley. 2022. "Turning Down the Heat on the ESG Debate: Separating Material Risk Disclosures from Salient Political Issues." Harvard Law School Forum on Corporate Governance. https://corpgov.law.harvard.edu/2022/09/01/turning-down-the-heat-on-the-esg-debate-separating-material-risk-disclosures-from-salient-political-issues/.

With the inauguration of President Biden in 2021, the climate change movement again found an advocate in the White House. On the day of President Biden's inauguration, the United States re-entered the Paris Climate Accords. Soon thereafter, the Biden administration paused construction of the Keystone XL Pipeline, along with the development of new oil and gas leases on public lands. In 2021, the SEC further catalyzed ESG activism by issuing guidance that expressly empowered shareholders to submit environmental and social proposals without having to demonstrate the economic implications of those proposals. The guidance also permitted shareholders to submit proposals that directed boards to take specific operational actions—such as reducing greenhouse gas emissions—without running afoul of the SEC's long-standing proscription on shareholder proposals that micromanage a board's ordinary course management of a company.[62] In 2022, Democratic majorities in Congress, with the support of the White House, passed the Inflation Reduction Act, providing for the largest investment in climate change mitigation in U.S. history, including approximately $400 billion to climate-related projects, primarily in the form of tax credits for consumers and private businesses.[63]

The Big Three remained at the vanguard of ESG advocacy within the institutional investor community, but other large, more traditionally active investment funds also assumed a greater role. In 2021, Fidelity announced that it would vote against boards with less than 30% female representation.[64] The same year, Invesco updated its proxy voting guidelines to indicate that it would vote against nominating committee chairs at companies where women constituted less than two board members or 25% of the board, whichever was lower, for two or more consecutive years, unless incremental improvements were underway.[65] Although T. Rowe Price did not prescribe a minimum gender diversity requirement in its investment stewardship policy, it updated its policies to provide that it would "generally oppose the re-elections of Governance Committee members if we find no evidence of board diversity" and opposed the reelections of 145 directors across 107 companies during

---

[62] Securities and Exchange Commission. 2021. "Shareholder Proposals: Staff Legal Bulletin No. 14L (CF)." https://www.sec.gov/corpfin/staff-legal-bulletin-14l-shareholder-proposals?

[63] Konisky, "U.S. Environmental Policy." https://en.wikipedia.org/wiki/Climate_change_policy_of_the_United_States.

[64] Turner, Natasha. 2022. "Fidelity Steps Up Scrutiny on Climate and Gender Diversity." MA Financial Media. https://future.portfolio-adviser.com/fidelity-steps-up-scrutiny-on-climate-and-gender-diversity/.

[65] Orowitz, Hannah. 2021. "Invesco Updates 2021 Global Governance and Proxy Voting Policies." Georgeson. https://www.georgeson.com/us/proxy-governance-insights/invesco-updates-2021-global-governance-and-proxy-voting-policies.

the first half of 2022 due to concerns over a lack of gender diversity.[66] Active managers emerged as forceful proponents of climate change activism in the proxy voting process. Almost all of the leading active managers, including Fidelity, T. Rowe Price, Invesco, Capital Group, and Neuberger Berman became members of Net Zero Asset Managers and Climate Action 100+ initiatives. Active managers also revised their proxy voting guidelines to include explicit targets for reductions in carbon emissions, and similar to the Big Three, increasingly put out detailed reports regarding the nature and scope of their climate change "engagements" with portfolio companies.[67] In the first half of the year—when most public companies convene their annual shareholder meetings—of 2022, investors cited climate change as a reason for opposing the election of a management-backed director at 225 U.S. companies, up from 157 in 2021 and 83 in 2020, according to shareholder disclosures.[68]

*****

With the leadership of institutional investors, ESG activism emerged as a sweeping force in the U.S. proxy voting landscape through the latter 2010s and early 2020s. Between 2016 and 2021, activist campaigns with an "Environmental" or "Social" objective doubled as a proportion of all campaigns, from 10 to 20%. In 2021, institutional investors cast a record 40% of their voted shares in favor of environmental and social proposals.[69] Just as the traditional shareholder primacy orthodoxy appeared to have reached its zenith in the early 2000s, by the beginning of 2020s the ESG movement seemed unstoppable.

---

[66] T. Rowe Price. 2023. "Proxy Voting Guidelines." T. Rowe Price Associates, Inc. https://www.troweprice.com/content/dam/trowecorp/Pdfs/proxy-voting-guidelines-TRPA.pdf.

[67] T. Rowe Price. 2021, "ESG Investing Annual Report: How ESG Impacts Our Investment Decisions." T. Rowe Price Associates, Inc. https://www.troweprice.com/content/dam/gdx/pdfs/Annual_ESG_Report.pdf.

[68] Holger, Dieter. 2022. "More Investors Vote Against Corporate Directors Over Climate Change." Wall Street Journal. https://www.wsj.com/articles/more-investors-vote-against-corporate-directors-over-climate-change-11658397600.

[69] Fiske, William P. 2021. "2021 Will Be a Year of ESG Activism." issuu. https://issuu.com/todaysgc/docs/todaysgeneralcounsel_april2021/s/11953134.

7

The ESG Report Card and Rise of Private Markets

Looking back at the growth of ESG over the last decade and a half, what can be said about its achievements and the role that institutional investors have played as ESG advocates?

On the one hand, the ESG movement has undeniably succeeded in influencing corporate behavior. As of 2015, two years prior to State Street's launch of its Fearless Girl marketing campaign, women made up only 20% of corporate directors of S&P 500 companies. Within one year following the announcement of the Fearless Girl campaign, over 300 companies added women to their board. From 2017 to 2020, the number of S&P 1500 firms lacking a woman director dropped from 179 to 30, and by 2020, no S&P 500 company had an all-male board. Empirical research estimates that the Big Three's campaigns led firms to add 2.5 times as many female directors in 2019 as they had in 2016. These interventions instigated governmental authorities to take action. In 2018, the California state legislator adopted S.B. 826, which required any publicly traded company with a principal office in California to include at least one woman on their board by the end of 2019, and two or more by 2021. While the statute was later struck down by the courts, at the time it represented a distinctly ambitious legislative measure to promote gender diversity that would have been inconceivable without the activism of major institutional investors.[1]

---

[1] Lund, "Asset Managers", 108; see also Gormley, Todd A., Vishal K. Gupta, David A. Matsa, Sandra C. Mortal, and Lukai Yang. 2021. "The Big Three and Board Gender Diversity: The Effectiveness of Shareholder Voice." European Corporate Governance Institute, Finance Working Paper No. 714/2020. https://papers.ssrn.com/sol3/papers.cfm?abstract_id=3724653.

ESG activists have made a dent as climate change activists. One study of over 900 climate change shareholder proposals from 2009 to 2022 found that on average a company's environmental performance (measured by Bloomberg's environmental performance ratings) improved by approximately 20% after receipt of a proposal than before compared to the matched sample.[2] Companies have markedly expanded their climate-related disclosures over the last decade, providing greater visibility to investors and the general public about their climate change efforts. Many companies have stated that they have expanded their disclosures as a response to ESG activism among large asset managers like the Big Three.[3] Another study has found a strong negative association between Big Three ownership and subsequent firm-level carbon emissions.[4]

As Professor Dorothy Lund of the USC Gould School of Law has noted, institutional investors have effectively taken on the role of regulators in their advocacy on gender diversity and climate change. Asset managers have adopted "rules" (from demands to enhance disclosures to more concrete requirements, like diversity quotas or emission cutback targets), and enforced them with consequences (votes against directors). By comparison, formal regulatory remedies seem to lack potency.[5] California's S.B. 826 imposed only up to $300,000 for violations of its gender diversity mandate, which for most public companies is far a more palatable penalty than losing a director seat.[6] In the same spirit, Fink has characterized BlackRock's ESG activism as a response to "government[] failing." In his 2020 CEO letter, Fink noted that BlackRock would push companies to abide by the mandates set forth in the 2015 Paris Climate Agreement, even after former President Trump withdrew from it, and underscored the need for enhanced disclosures on climate change practices as the SEC grappled with legal and other roadblocks in implementing new disclosure requirements.[7] "Because better sustainability disclosures are in companies' as well as investors' own interests," Fink noted

---

[2] Diaz-Rainey, Ivan, Paul A. Griffin, David H. Lon, Antonio J. Mateo-Márquez, and Constancio Zamora-Ramírez. 2023. "Shareholder Activism on Climate Change: Evolution, Determinants, and Consequences." Journal of Business Ethics. https://link.springer.com/article/10.1007/s10551-023-05486-x#auth-Ivan-Diaz_Rainey-Aff1.

[3] Azar, Jose, Miguel Duro, Igor Kadach, and Gaizka Ormazabal. 2020. "The Big Three and Corporate Carbon Emissions around the World." Centre for Economic Policy Research. https://papers.ssrn.com/sol3/papers.cfm?abstract_id=3753922.

[4] Ibid.

[5] Lund, "Asset Managers", 109.

[6] Ibid.

[7] Ibid, 117.

in 2021, "I urge companies to move quickly to issue them rather than waiting for regulators to impose them."[8]

On the other hand, when one holistically considers the influence of the ESG movement—both in terms of its overarching objectives, as well as its wider social and economic impact—the results appear to be mixed. It is unclear whether progress on the ESG front has enhanced any commonly accepted shareholder value metric in a statistically meaningful manner, a point that has even been acknowledged by those who are sympathetic to the ESG movement's posture on issues like gender diversity and climate change.[9] Although numerous consulting firms and public advocacy groups have released white papers touting the financial benefits of board diversity, statistical support for that contention is harder to come by in academic, peer-reviewed studies.[10] When academics have tried to replicate the findings of pro-diversity consulting reports, they have failed, finding no or little linkage between profitability and executive diversity.[11] A recent study published by the University of Western Ontario found that increased gender and ethnic diversity in board positions had a positive effect on shareholder value (as measured by earnings per share), but determined that the relationship was statistically insignificant. At the same time, the study found that corporate social responsibility-related diversity initiatives had a negative effect on shareholder value.[12] The record for climate change is more ambiguous. While ESG advocacy may have resulted in certain firms cutting back their individual emissions, overall emissions have not declined. Greenhouse gas emissions from fossil fuels reached a record high of 36.8 billion metric tons in 2023. At current rates of emissions, scientists calculate there is a 50% chance

---

[8] Ibid.

[9] Oriane, and Aneeta Rattan. 2022. "Stop Making the Business Case for Diversity." Harvard Business Review. https://hbr.org/2022/06/stop-making-the-business-case-for-diversity.

[10] See, e.g., Klein, Catherine. 2017. "Does Gender Diversity on Boards Really Boost Company Performance?" Knowledge at Wharton. https://knowledge.wharton.upenn.edu/article/will-gender-diversity-boards-really-boost-company-performance/; Terjesen, Siri. 2023. "The Case Against Board Diversity Mandates." Club for Growth Foundation. https://clubforgrowthfoundation.org/the-case-against-board-diversity-mandates/; Shabbir, Urwah. 2020. "The Effect of Diversity on Shareholder Value: Do Gender, Ethnic and CSR Diversity Initiatives Influence Shareholder Value?" University of Western Ontario. https://papers.ssrn.com/sol3/papers.cfm?abstract_id=3833073.

[11] Mackintosh, James. 2024. "Diversity Was Supposed to Make Us Rich. Not So Much." The Wall Street Journal. https://www.wsj.com/finance/investing/diversity-was-supposed-to-make-us-rich-not-so-much-39da6a23.

[12] Shabbir, Urwah. 2020. "The Effect of Diversity on Shareholder Value: Do Gender, Ethnic and CSR Diversity Initiatives Influence Shareholder Value?" SSRN. https://deliverypdf.ssrn.com/delivery.php?ID=8140971030980910790221120270700730290170560720920620360000960891080960180301250270270430290220610450070550020097065085025113069029094032037017028120098064076081007019070003023124083104015095094003073100073101114118101094002099067088109012097124001093094&EXT=pdf&INDEX=TRUE.

that within seven years global temperatures will regularly exceed the 1.5 degrees Celsius above pre-industrial levels identified in the Paris Agreement as a threshold beyond which worsening and potentially irreversible effects of global warming are likely to emerge.[13] As we will discuss more extensively in the next chapter, the focused attention among ESG advocates on large public companies has encouraged some firms to divest their emission-producing assets to less scrupulous parties who are not subject to the same level of public scrutiny and oversight, thereby worsening emissions on an economy-wide level.[14]

Public sentiment also warrants consideration. As Berle acknowledged, the legitimacy of the New Deal paradigm flowed from the broad-based public support it commanded. A New Deal Democrat, Berle was certainly not above the fray of partisan politics, but he understood that the stability and durability of the post-World War II order depended on the existence of a general bipartisan consensus that supported the fundamental tenets and values embodied in that order. The wider population—not just Berle or other New Deal boosters like him—needed to buy into the idea that the system as it operated was good in a deeper, normative sense.

ESG causes like board diversity and climate change do not enjoy a similar level of widespread public support. In recent years, ESG has become a political lightning rod, with Republican politicians and conservative pundits claiming that the movement is a ploy for forcing "liberal" values on businesses—and derivatively, the general populace—outside of traditional political processes. Conservative commentators like Tucker Carlson and Glenn Beck have publicly lambasted the ESG agenda on their media programs. Former Vice President Mike Pence has excoriated the ESG movement as a partisan left-wing cause, warning that "[t]he woke left is poised to conquer corporate America," and Senator Tom Cotton has publicly demanded answers

---

[13] NOAA. 2023. "Record carbon dioxide emissions impeding progress on meeting climate goals." National Oceanic and Atmospheric Administration. https://research.noaa.gov/2023/12/05/record-fossil-carbon-dioxide-emissions-impeding-progress-on-meeting-climate-goals-report/; Jackson, Rob. 2023. "Global carbon emissions from fossil fuels reached record high in 2023." Stanford Doerr School of Sustainability. https://sustainability.stanford.edu/news/global-carbon-emissions-fossil-fuels-reached-record-high-2023.

[14] See also Schwartz, Jeff. 2022. "Stewardship Theater." 100 WASHINGTON UNIVERSITY LAW REVIEW, 416 ("[T]he case for profitability [resulting from climate change activism on the part of asset managers] is highly theoretical. It assumes that the proposals lead to changes in corporate behavior, that climate-change risk is priced into the market, and that any loss to a company from the disclosure of questionable practices, or from adopting more sustainable practices, is made up by the market-wide gain and the gain to other firms. There is no empirical evidence suggesting that these assumptions hold true").

from BlackRock about its involvement with Climate Action + 100, threatening an antitrust action of some kind in retaliation.[15] Florida Governor and former 2024 Republican Presidential candidate Ron DeSantis has perhaps been the most aggressive anti-ESG voice among Republicans. In 2022, DeSantis worked with the trustees of the Florida State Board of Administration to pass a resolution prohibiting the State of Florida's fund managers from considering ESG factors in making investment decisions. The next year, DeSantis helped push a legislative effort to bar the consideration of ESG criteria by financial institutions in Florida.[16] The bill was signed into law in May 2023, following the enactment of similar legislation in Indiana and Kansas that forbade state retirement accounts from investing in ESG-related funds.[17] One may disagree with anti-ESG activists or have reason to question their motives, but no one can dispute the fact that there is substantial controversy and lack of bipartisan consensus when opposition to ESG has become a visible aspect of how one of the country's two main political factions defines itself.

More generally, there is little evidence that the ESG movement's priorities align with those of the wider population, irrespective of partisan affiliation. It is hard to find any level of popular support or fixation on the topic of board diversity that approximates the amount of fanfare the subject has generated among institutional investors. Polling data consistently shows that less than 5% of the public view any environmental issue as the "most important problem" facing the United States.[18] Particularly in the case of ESG-driven climate change activism, asset manager advocacy has a propensity to produce regressive impacts. In a working paper for the European Corporate Governance Institute, law professors Zohar Goshen and Assaf Hamdani point out that government policies that reduce carbon emissions tend to have disproportionately adverse effects on low-income households and the working population. For example, a carbon tax leads to higher energy prices, which affect low-income households the most, as these households allocate a larger portion of their income towards energy-related expenses and are less likely to afford

---

[15] Coates, The Power of 12. 123; Pence, Mike. 2022. "Republicans Can Stop ESG Political Bias." Wall Street Journal Opinion. https://www.wsj.com/articles/only-republicans-can-stop-the-esg-madness-woke-musk-consumer-demand-free-speech-corporate-america-11653574189.
[16] Hood, David. 2023. "DeSantis Signs Sweeping Anti-ESG Bill Targeting Funds, Banks." Bloomberg Law. https://news.bloomberglaw.com/esg/desantis-signs-sweeping-anti-esg-bill-targeting-funds-banks.
[17] Zahn, Max. 2023. "What is ESG Investing and Why are Some Republicans Criticizing It? A Divide has Emerged Over Investing that Takes into Account Social Issues." ABC News. https://abcnews.go.com/Business/esg-investing-republicans-criticizing/story?id=97035891.
[18] Gallup. 2023–2024. "Most Important Problem." In Gallup Historical Trends. https://news.gallup.com/poll/1675/Most-Important-Problem.aspx.

energy-efficient alternatives. However, government actors—like Congress—can mitigate the regressive effects of their climate change regulations through redistributive policies, which the private sector is ill-equipped to replicate. In fact, private ESG initiatives provide governmental bodies like Congress with a pretext not only to avoid implementing their own climate-saving measures but to ignore the regressive effects of ESG policies as someone else's problem, given that regulators typically have greater incentives to provide compensating adjustments when their own actions impose new burdens on the poor.[19]

In the meantime, pocketbook issues that are behind much of the unease regular Americans feel about the economy—the offshoring of jobs and supply chains, inflation, economic inequality—have received minimal attention within the ESG framework. There is scant proof that the ESG-based stakeholder paradigm has changed the dynamics of the financial markets in any way that had led to a decline in the shareholder-centric myopia and economic short-termism that set the stage for the growth of the ESG movement in the years following the Great Financial Crisis. The ESG agenda as it has been embraced by asset management firms does not claim to challenge the core premise of shareholder primacy that corporations exist to serve the interests of shareholders. With the increasing amount of corporate control that has accumulated in the hands of the largest asset managers over the last two decades, the continued support among asset managers of pro-shareholder primacy corporate governance procedures and practices has translated into the governance architecture of corporate America becoming even more shareholder-centric. Before 2000, most public companies did not permit shareholders to either convene a special meeting or take action by written consent without a meeting. By 2017, approximately 70% of companies provided shareholders with at least one of these rights.[20] Classified board structures—in which only a subset of a company's directors stand for election in any given year—were fairly common for much of the twentieth century. At most companies, shareholders would have to mount multiple proxy contests in order to effect a change of control of the board. Almost 60% of S&P 1500 firms had a classified board in the decade from 1990 to 2000.[21] By

---

[19] Goshen, Zahar, Assaf Hamdani and Alex Raskolnikov. 2024. "Poor ESG: Regressive Effects of Climate Stewardship." European Corporate Governance Institute—Law Working Paper No. 764/2024. SSRN: https://ssrn.com/abstract=4771137.

[20] Catan, Emiliano M., and Marcel Kahan. 2019. "The Never-Ending Quest for Shareholder Rights: Special Meetings and Written Consent." BU Law Review. Vol. 99.

[21] Field, Laura, and Michelle Lowry. 2022. "Bucking the Trend: Why Do IPOs Choose Controversial Governance Structures and Why Do Investors Let Them?" Journal of Financial Economics. Vol. 146.

2023, that percentage had dropped to 11%.[22] The percentage of independent directors on large U.S. public company boards increased from approximately 75% in 2005 to 85% in 2023.[23] In 2001, 301 S&P 500 companies had a poison plan in place—which make it more difficult for bidders to mount hostile takeovers of target companies—compared to six S&P 500 companies by the end of 2021.[24] At the end of 2010, 73.5% of S&P 500 companies and 26.5% of Russell 3000 companies required that directors who did not receive a majority of votes cast by their shareholders tender their resignation, regardless of whether or not the incumbent directors faced a competing slate. Eleven years later, those percentages had increased to 89.77% and 45.97%, respectively.[25]

Helping fuel these changes has been the adoption by the SEC of a panoply of rules and regulations that have given greater voice to asset managers in the proxy voting process. In 2007, the SEC put in place rules allowing companies and other soliciting persons the option of delivering proxy materials via the Internet in lieu of paper materials, which increased the ease with which more cost-sensitive institutional investors could pursue activist campaigns. In 2009, the SEC eliminated the ability of brokers—which typically vote in accordance with management recommendations—to engage in discretionary voting in uncontested director elections, thereby enhancing the influence of activists and proxy advisory firms in director elections (including through "vote no" and "withhold vote" campaigns where company directors did not face a competing slate of directors). In 2021, the SEC adopted final rules that became effective the following year requiring that participants in contested director elections use "universal proxy cards," or proxy cards naming all director nominees presented for election, including those of the company and the dissident shareholder, making it easier for dissident shareholders to garner votes for their director nominees.

Although the large global asset managers have been at the forefront of ESG advocacy, with respect to economic matters the key activist players in the investment world remain short-term-focused activist hedge funds. Today, these funds are as active and influential as they have ever been. In 2023, activist funds launched 229 campaigns globally, in line with 2022's 235

---

[22] Spencer Stuart. 2023. "2023 U.S. Board Index." Spencer Stuart. https://www.spencerstuart.com/-/media/2023/september/usbi/2023_us_spencer_stuart_board_index.pdf?sc_trk=BDB9A48933CA433C9DDD7D4E85D62A38.

[23] Gordon, Jeffrey N. 2007. "The Rise of Independent Directors in the United States, 1950–2005: Of Shareholder Value and Stock Market Prices." Stanford Law Review. Vol. 59.

[24] Poison Pills in Force Year over Year Profile Report, FACTSET RSCH. SYS. (retrieved Sept. 28, 2022).

[25] Takeover Defense Trend Analysis, FACTSET RSCH. SYS. (retrieved Sept. 28, 2022).

campaigns, representing the busiest two-year span on record. The substantial majority of these campaigns centered around conventional economic activist themes, like mergers and acquisitions (49% of all campaigns, an all-time high and well above the trailing four-year average of 42%), strategy and operations (31%), and capital return demands (18%). Activists won 134 board seats in 2023—more than the number of board seats in any of the prior four years—representing a 13% increase in board seats won via settlements relative to 2022 and a record number of seats won via final proxy votes at annual shareholder meetings. Virtually all of the activists spearheading these contests were traditional short-term-oriented hedge fund activist players, with Elliott Management and Starboard—two archetypical activist hedge funds—being 2023's leading activists.[26]

The clout of activist hedge funds only appears to have strengthened with the conclusion of the most recent proxy season prior to the publication of this book. Activist funds have increasingly succeeded in demanding corporate boards form special committees including activist directors to evaluate key corporate items like strategic alternatives, operating portfolios and capital allocation policies. In 2024, ten special committees were formed as part of settlements—the largest number in the past decade. Eight of these were part of private settlements, and special committee formation was a criterion in over 30% of private pacts. Activists are also winning their contests faster than ever before, with the average span between public demand and settlement for the 2024 proxy season plunging to 34 days, falling by half vs. 2023 and down from 77 days in 2022.[27]

While the Big Three and other large asset managers frequently justify their ESG advocacy in terms of a larger effort to promote "long-term value creation" and the "long-term interests" of their investors, their growing power in the proxy voting landscape has actually facilitated the success of short-term-focused, hedge funds activists. By definition, the ability of activist hedge funds, who typically do not own more than a few percentage points of a company's outstanding shares, to mount successful contests turns on winning support from the larger asset managers. The increasing frequency and success of hedge fund activist campaigns in recent years cannot be explained without accounting for that fact. From 2012 to 2018, support for activist board slates among the ten largest institutional investors rose by more than 21%, with

---

[26] Barclays. 2023. "Barclays 2023 Review of Shareholder Activism." Barclays. https://corpgov.law.harvard.edu/wp-content/uploads/2023/07/Barclays-H1-2023-Review-of-Shareholder-Activism-002-1.pdf.

[27] Tucker, Pat, Garrett Muzikowski, and Sean Lange. 2024. "What Settlement Data Says About the Evolution of Activism." FTI Consulting. https://corpgov.law.harvard.edu/2024/07/15/what-settlement-data-says-about-the-evolution-of-activism/?utm_source=rss&utm_medium=rss&utm_campaign=what-settlement-data-says-about-the-evolution-of-activism.

the bulk of the increase being driven by the voting activities of the Big Three, whose support for activist funds rose by more than 94% over the same period.[28] There is evidence that the growing concentration of voting power among index funds has contributed to a rise in the number of campaigns initiated by activists. In a 2019 study of 466 activist campaigns over a six-year time frame, researchers found that an increase of 3 or 4 percentage points in passive ownership at any given company made it 30% more likely to face a campaign to oust directors and 150% more likely to face an actual proxy fight. The same amount of additional passive ownership made a company 16% more likely to settle a proxy fight—which usually results in the activist getting a board seat—and 11% more likely to be sold to a third party.[29]

Zohar Goshen and University of Washington Business Economics Professor Doron Levit have put forward a more formalized model of this symbiotic relationship between activist hedge funds and large asset management firms in their June 2024 research paper "Common Ownership and Hedge Fund Activism: An Unholy Alliance?" Goshen and Levit contend that, by promoting shareholder-friendly governance policies in their portfolio firms, the big asset managers make companies more vulnerable to activist hedge funds attacks than they otherwise would be, thereby pushing companies to take greater measures to quickly enhance returns to their institutional shareholders, including by paring down investments in their businesses and reducing wages.[30]

The continued vitality of the activist hedge fund industry has made it ever more challenging for public companies to manage their businesses on a long-term basis. According to a 2020 HEC Paris analysis of data from over 2600 publicly owned U.S. firms during the 2000–2016 period, the targets of activist hedge fund campaigns consistently came to prioritize short-term returns over long-term performance. While many companies assailed by activist hedge funds initially experienced an uptick in market value, that uptick quickly evaporated over time, with companies frequently finding themselves in a worse position than they were before the activists' entry into their stock. On average, the market value of targeted firms increased 7.66% one year after activist ownership, but decreased by 4.92 and 9.71%

---

[28] Kovler, Harkins. 2019. "Recent Institutional Investor Voting Trends in Contested Board Elections," HKL & Co. https://hklco.com/research-1/recent-institutional-investor-voting-in-contested-board-elections-2019-p6mtt.

[29] Appel, Ian R., Todd A Gormley, Donald B Keim. 2019. "Standing on the Shoulders of Giants: The Effect of Passive Investors on Activism." The Review of Financial Studies. 10.1093/rfs/hhy106.

[30] Goshen, Zohar and Levit, Doron, 2024. "Common Ownership and Hedge Fund Activism: An Unholy Alliance?". European Corporate Governance Institute—Finance Working Paper No. 982/2024, Available at SSRN: https://ssrn.com/abstract=4835079 or https://doi.org/10.2139/ssrn.4835079

in years four and five. Similarly, the profitability of targeted firms increased between 1.10 and 1.50 percentage points in the first and second years after activist ownership, but operating cash flow decreased by 15.82% in year two to 27.12% in year five. Accounting for changes in asset allocation, such as mergers or divestitures, firms in the sample set decreased the size of their workforces, operating expenses, R&D spending, and capital expenditures during the one- to five-year period after being targeted. In year one, these spending cutbacks increased investing cash flow more than the decreases in operating cash flow, resulting in targeted firms having an average cash surplus of $53 million. Yet, after year one, investing cash flow did not increase to an extent that offset losses in operating cash flow, climaxing in an average cash deficit of $61 million by year three.[31]

The proliferation of short-term hedge fund activism has produced perverse effects beyond depressing market valuations and long-term profitability. Multiple academic studies over the last decade have demonstrated negative impacts on financial solvency and corporate credit profiles resulting from activist hedge fund attacks.[32] A 2019 paper by Columbia Law School professors John Coffee and Joshua Mitts found that hedge fund activism frequently imposes "agency costs" on other stockholders by increasing the likelihood that target companies will experience informed trading in their stock in the wake of a successful activist engagement. Based on a review of public filings from 7,799 public companies from 2000 to 2016, Coffee and Mitts determined that, once an activist fund-nominated director joined a corporate

---

[31] Des Jardine, M. R., and Rodolphe Durand. 2020. "Disentangling the Effects of Hedge Fund Activism on Firm Financial and Social Performance." Strategic Management Journal, Vol. 41. See also K.J. Martijn Cremers et al. 2018. "Hedge Fund Activism and Long-Term Value." https://ssrn.com/abstract=2693231; deHaan, Ed, David F. Larcker, and Charles McClure. 2018. "Long Term Economic Consequences of Hedge Fund Activist Interventions." https://ssrn.com/abstract=3260095 (the "long-term returns [from activism] insignificantly differ from zero"); Coffee, Jr., John C., and Darius Palia. 2016. "The Wolf at the Door: The Impact of Hedge Fund Activism on Corporate Governance." 41 J. CORP. L.; Strine, Jr., Leo E. 2017. "Who Bleeds When the Wolves Bite?: A Flesh-and-Blood Perspective on Hedge Fund Activism and Our Strange Corporate Governance System," 126 YALE L.J. 1870, 1870.

[32] See, e.g., Zhiyu Feng, Felix, Qiping Xu and Heqing Zhu. 2018. "Caught in the Crossfire: How the Threat of Hedge Fund Activism Affects Creditors." http://papers.ssrn.com/sol3/papers.cfm?abstract_id=271 (noting firms with an ex ante high likelihood of hedge fund activism experience substantial losses in bondholder wealth); Jory, Surendranath, Thanh Ngo and Jurica Susnjara. 2017. "The Effect of Shareholder Activism on Bondholders and Stockholders." 66 Q. REV. ECON. & FIN. 328, 328 (observing that "activists' demands cause a significant decline in bond returns, and affect long-term bonds the most"); Klein, April and Emanuel Zur. 2011. "The Impact of Hedge Fund Activism on the Target Firm's Existing Bondholders." 24 REV. FIN. STUD. 1735, 1735 (noting that the bond returns from ten days before to one day after the filing of a Schedule 13D are negative (−3.9%), that the average abnormal bond returns for one year after the filing date are an additional −4.5%, and that the abnormal stock returns are negatively related to the abnormal bond returns at both the short-term and long-term intervals).

board, the target company experienced an abrupt increase in information leakage in which stock prices began to more closely anticipate future public disclosures, with a difference-in-differences increase in leakage of approximately twenty-five to twenty-seven percentage points. From this fact, the study inferred "some activist engagements may be motivated (at least on the margin) not simply by efficiency considerations, but by the knowledge that the appointment of a director will give them access to material, nonpublic information" and that accordingly this "subsidy" should "logically cause an increase in the number of activist engagements, even if these engagements did not produce value for the other shareholders"—on either a short-term or long-term basis.[33]

Other direct indicators reveal the persistence of short-termism in financial markets and corporate decision-making. Stock turnover rates have not meaningfully changed over the last decade, and continue to be considerably higher than pre-1990 levels. As of 2019, the annual turnover rate of publicly listed corporate equities was approximately 70% (implying an average holding period of a little over a year).[34] Share buybacks and dividends remain popular capital allocation strategies. From 2000 to 2017, the U.S. stock market facilitated negative net equity issuance of almost $5.4 trillion, effectively functioning as a mechanism to channel capital out of—rather than into—corporations on an unprecedented scale.[35] Based on one 2016 analysis, the propensity towards deploying capital towards dividends and share buybacks, in lieu of internal investment to innovate and grow, has accelerated among public companies over the last two decades. As a percentage of assets, total investment was approximately 17.5% in 2000; by 2015, that percentage had dropped to 11.6%.[36] During the same time period, the equally weighted ratio of cash to assets increased from 9.2% to 21.6%. With these record levels of cash, public corporations ramped up dividends and share repurchases. The equally weighted average of total payouts in the form of both dividends and repurchases as a percentage of net income was 27.1% in 1975. Although the ratio declined to 20.5% in 1995, the rate gradually increased to 49.9% of net income in 2007, decreased slightly during the Great Financial Crisis, and

---

[33] Coffee, Jr., John C., Robert J. Jackson, Jr., Joshua R. Mitts and Robert E. Bishop. 2019. "Activist Directors and Agency Costs: What Happens When An Activist Director Goes on the Board?" 104 CORNELL L. REV. J.
[34] World Bank. 2023. "Stock Market Turnover Ratio (Value Traded/Capitalization) for United States." FRED, Federal Reserve Bank of St. Louis. https://fred.stlouisfed.org/series/DDEM01USA156NWDB.
[35] Fichtner, Jan. 2020. "The Rise of Institutional Investors." International Handbook of Financialization. London: Routledge.
[36] Kahle, Kathleen M., and René M. Stulz. 2017. "Is the US Public Corporation in Trouble?" Journal of Economic Perspectives. Vol 31.

then rebounded to 47.0% in 2015.[37] More recent data appears to substantiate the persistence of this trend. Annual share buybacks and dividends among S&P 500 companies surged to record levels in 2022, representing a total 7% increase relative to 2021 levels and a total 18% increase relative to 2018 levels.[38] While buybacks dropped in 2023, that shortfall was more than made up by the amount of dividends paid out by companies that same year.[39]

The rising concentration of equity ownership among institutional investors has produced negative effects in labor markets. A 2022 study by José Azar of the University of Navarra, Yue Qiu of Temple University, and Aaron Sojourner of the Upjohn Institute examined the effects of institutional ownership on labor market outcomes from 2000 through 2017 and concluded that greater common ownership in a labor market was associated with both lower wages and a lower employment-to-population ratio.[40] Another working paper by Antono Falato of the Federal Reserve Board looked at data from the U.S. Census Bureau Longitudinal Business Database for the 1982 to 2015 period and determined that firms that experience an increase in ownership by larger and more concentrated institutional shareholders tend to have lower employment and wages. Based on Falato's analysis, the labor losses were accompanied by higher shareholder returns but no improvements in labor productivity, suggesting that the growing influence of institutional investors simply functioned to reallocate rents away from workers. The rise in concentrated institutional ownership during the last four decades potentially explained up to a quarter of the decline in the ratio of total wages and salaries to Gross Domestic Income over the same time period.[41]

---

[37] Ibid.
[38] Chisholm, Jamie. 2023. "Global Buybacks Surged to Record $1.3 Trillion in 2022, Almost Eclipsing Dividends." MarketWatch. https://www.marketwatch.com/story/global-buybacks-surged-to-record-1-3-trillion-in-2022-almost-eclipsing-dividends-d18be151.
[39] Pisani, Bob. 2024. "Good News, Bad News. Record Dividends Paid to Investors in 2023, but Buybacks Plunged." CNBC. https://www.cnbc.com/2024/01/04/good-news-bad-news-record-dividends-paid-to-investors-in-2023-but-buybacks-plunged.html.
[40] Azar, José, Yue Qiu, and Aaron Sojourner. 2022. "Common Ownership in Labor Markets." Upjohn Institute. Kalamazoo: W.E. Upjohn Institute for Employment Research. 10.17848/wp22-368.
[41] Bahn, Kate, and Carmen Sanchez Cumming. 2022. "How Corporate Governance Strategies Hurt Worker Power in the United States." Washington Center for Equitable Growth. https://equitablegrowth.org/how-corporate-governance-strategies-hurt-worker-power-in-the-united-states/; Falato, Antonio, Hyunseob Kim and Till Von Wachter. 2022. "Shareholder Power and the Decline of Labor." National Bureau of Economic Research. https://www.nber.org/system/files/working_papers/w30203/w30203.pdf.

The Rise of Private Markets

In considering the impact of institutional investors on corporate America—whether by virtue of their ESG advocacy or their more direct effects on economic activity—it is not sufficient to examine how asset managers have shaped the behavior of companies in a vacuum. One must consider more specifically the impact on the relationship between corporations and public markets—that is, the major national securities exchanges like the New York Stock Exchange and NASDAQ on which the securities of the nation's largest companies trade and the center of gravity in our modern system of regulating corporate governance and securities markets. It is worthwhile to remember that the public markets (and in particular, the increasing dominance of large publicly owned corporations in the U.S. economy) were at the heart of Berle's analysis in *The Modern Corporation.* In the decade preceding the publication of the book, retail investment in stocks and bonds had grown dramatically, and the number of shareholders doubled from 2.4 million in 1924 to 5 million in 1927, doubling again to 10 million in 1930. By then, 44% of the largest 200 corporations were under effective management control, with no single entity holding more than 5% of any given company's voting stock.[42] It was in this context that Berle came to view corporate disclosures as a means by which to check and protect against misbehavior by corporate management. As long as investors had a fair and accurate picture as to how executives were managing their businesses, they could express their dissatisfaction by exiting a company's stock. Likewise, companies who misbehaved risked starving themselves of access to capital. The establishment of the Securities and Exchange Commission and imposition of mandatory periodic disclosures on publicly listed corporations reflected the centrality of this premise in the thinking of Berle and contemporary policymakers.

By contrast, over a third of corporate equities in the United States today are managed *outside* of public companies in the private markets, with much of the growth occurring in the years following the Great Financial Crisis.[43] In 2010, global public equity issuances were worth more than twice the funds raised in private markets. In the years that followed, private markets fundraising gradually increased relative to public offerings until, in 2016, private markets fundraising overtook equity issuances in public markets. Since 2017, annual global fundraising in private markets has approached,

---

[42] Mizruchi, Mark. 2004. "Berle and Means Revisited: The Governance and Power of Large U.S. Corporations." Theory and Society. https://www.jstor.org/stable/4144886.
[43] Coates, The Problem of 12. 55.

and often exceeded, $1 trillion.[44] Even in 2020, when the global pandemic prompted many private markets players to pause investing, fundraising still nudged the $1 trillion mark and exceeded the $800 billion or so raised in public markets, with private market assets under management rising to $10 trillion in the aggregate. As the pandemic waned, private markets surged again, and private equity fundraising reached another all-time high in 2021. In the challenging macroeconomic environment of 2022, private equity fundraising dipped by an estimated 21.5%, but still exhibited greater resilience than public markets equity issuance.[45] Based on current trends, private markets assets under management are expected to triple to $30 trillion during the next market cycle.[46] As a result, the public markets have become a smaller universe. While the aggregate market capitalization of public corporations in 2023 was larger than it has ever been, the number of publicly listed corporations is at a historic low. In 1975, there were 4819 publicly listed U.S. corporations, increasing through the subsequent decades to a peak of 7507 firms in 1997, and then precipitously declining to 3768 corporations by 2023.[47]

Legal and technological changes have facilitated the emergence of private markets during the last half century, but these changes alone do not explain the growing prominence of private market capital as an alternative to public market capital, particularly over the course of the last decade. The reality is that fewer companies find it an attractive proposition to go or remain public.

Among technology businesses, it has become progressively more difficult to pursue the type of long-term-focused and risky investments that are required to successfully innovate within the confines of the public markets. Shai Bernstein of Harvard Business School has written extensively on this topic. In a 2022 article for *Annual Review of Financial Economics*, Bernstein concluded that, while publicly traded companies enjoyed greater access to inexpensive capital, the empirical evidence overwhelmingly showed that they struggled with deploying that capital towards innovation and instead frequently focused their efforts on commercialization and short-term projects. On the other hand, private firms had a more limited menu of financing options, but their invulnerability to the pressures of the stock market made it easier for

---

[44] Meister, Steffen. 2023. "The New Traditional Asset Class." Partner's Group. https://www.partnersgroup.com/-/media/Files/P/Partnersgroup/Universal/videos-document/2023-partners-group-white-paper-the-new-traditional-asset-class.pdf.
[45] Ibid.
[46] Ibid.
[47] Kahle, "Corporation Trouble"; CRSP. 2023. "U.S. Market Update." Center for Research in Security Prices, University of Chicago Booth School of Business. https://www.crsp.org/wp-content/uploads/2023/10/CRSP_Market_Update_-_August_2023.pdf.

them to pursue innovative, yet riskier, investments.[48] In another article for the think tank *Third Way*, Bernstein provided direct evidence of the greater stresses faced by public companies in pursuing innovation by comparing the quality of patents put out by firms that went public with firms that were about to go public but held back because of market volatility and evaluating whether the underlying ideas were subsequently used as building blocks for new inventions. The study found that going public meant a 40% decline in quality innovations for newly public companies in the five years immediately following listing, while the companies that flirted with an IPO but stayed private innovated at an accelerated rate. Innovation among newly public companies tended to be pursued through external acquisitions, versus in-house research and development. In the first year after going public, there was a 10% chance of acquiring an external patent compared to 2% for companies that stayed private. In the first five years after the IPO, roughly 30% of the patent portfolio of the public company firms was composed of patents attained through acquisitions.[49]

Not surprisingly, it is not uncommon to hear executives in the tech world gripe about the challenges of pursuing innovation as a public company. The complaint is why, in response to inquiries as to his unwillingness to take Facebook public, Mark Zuckerberg stated in 2010 that "being private is better for us now because some of the big risks we want to take in developing new products" and that "it would be even more difficult if we had a public stock price bounding." Facebook ended up going public two years later, primarily because its shareholder base crossed the maximum threshold for avoiding the SEC's public filing requirements as a private company. Elon Musk has also been a vocal critic of the public markets, notably arguing in 2018 that he wanted to make Tesla a private company because "being public… subjects us to the quarterly earnings cycle that puts enormous pressure on Tesla to make decisions that may be right for a given quarter, but not necessarily right for the long-term."[50]

---

[48] Bernstein, Shai. 2022. "The Effects of Public and Private Equity Markets on Firm Behavior." Annual Review of Financial Economics. https://doi.org/10.1146/annurev-financial-052021-072939.

[49] Bernstein, Shai. 2017. "Innovator's Dilemma: IPO or No?" Third Way. https://www.thirdway.org/report/innovators-dilemma-ipo-or-no.

[50] Glover, George. 2023. "Elon Musk Really, Really Hates Running a Public Company." Business Insider. https://www.businessinsider.com/elon-musk-tesla-ceo-funding-secured-x-spacex-cathie-wood-2023-12; Krisher, Tom. 2018. "Musk Says Investors Convinced Him Tesla Should Stay Public." Associated Press. https://apnews.com/general-news-1357ed7e3d214f5880f36404fd3591bb; Musk, Elon. 2018. "Taking Tesla Private." Tesla.com. https://www.tesla.com/blog/taking-tesla-private. Spector, Bert. 2022. "Elon Musk Argues Twitter would be Better Off in Private Rather than Public Hands—Corporate Governance Scholars would Disagree." The Conversation. https://theconversation.com/elon-musk-argues-twitter-would-be-better-off-in-private-rather-than-public-hands-corporate-governance-scholars-would-disagree-181382.

Technology enterprises are not the only types of businesses that have been reticent about subjecting themselves to the travails of the public markets. "Take-private" transactions—in which public companies go private by means of a sale to management and/or a third-party—have acquired greater popularity in recent years, accounting for over 80% of value in all M&A transactions in 2023.[51] Take-private targets are frequently mature companies contending with tough times who view going private as an opportunity to escape short-term public market pressures to restructure and make operational improvements.[52] IPO listings have declined over the last 30 years, but take-private transactions are the primary driver behind the fall in the number of public companies in the United States, accounting for over 60% of public company delistings during the time frame.[53]

To be sure, the reluctance among many companies to go public is not solely driven by the short-term pressures they face from institutional investors. Public companies are subject to elevated regulatory costs. However, there is no evidence that regulatory costs account for the considerable *decrease* in initial public offerings over the last two decades. During this time, the disclosure burden has both increased and decreased for public companies. Legislation like the 2002 Sarbanes–Oxley Act has created new reporting obligations for public corporations, while other reforms such as the JOBS Act and FAST Act have reduced disclosure requirements. According to a 2021 study by Michael Ewens of the California Institute of Technology and Kairong Xiao of Columbia University that examined the effects of regulatory costs across a sample of 21,066 public firms, regulatory costs were associated with a 7% decrease in IPO likelihood, but the major regulatory changes of the 2000s had no statistically significant impact on IPO volume. Removing the Sarbanes–Oxley Act only increased the average IPO likelihood after 2000 from 0.95% to 0.96% because many potential IPO candidates were small enough to be exempted from the new regulations. Removing all estimated regulatory costs increased the average IPO likelihood after 2000 from 0.95%

---

[51] Obregon, Roberto, and Frank Benham. 2019. "Decreasing Number of Public Companies." Meketa Investment Group. https://meketa.com/wp-content/uploads/2012/10/Decreasing-Number-of-Public-Companies-FINAL.pdf; Wilson, Drew. 2023. "Private Equity Take-private Deals Hit 16-year High." S&P Global. https://www.spglobal.com/marketintelligence/en/news-insights/latest-news-headlines/private-equity-take-private-deals-hit-16-year-high-78173569; Zhang, Hannah. 2023. "Take-Private Dealmaking Continues at a Record Pace." Institutional Investor. https://www.institutionalinvestor.com/article/2bstr1aauoiex26hff668/portfolio/take-private-dealmaking-continues-at-a-record-pace; Indap, Sujeet. 2023. "The Appeal for Executives of having Private Equity Owners." Financial Times. https://www.ft.com/content/bef7391b-b4a5-49cb-b07d-984c666f9ab1.

[52] Gaither, Kate. 2021. "Why Going Private Can Be an Attractive Option for Struggling Companies." Johnston Clem Gifford PLLC. https://www.johnstonclem.com/news-insights/why-going-private-can-be-an-attractive-option-for-struggling-companies/.

[53] Obregon, "Decreasing Numbers."

to 1.4%, which explained only 7.4% of the decline in IPO likelihood from pre-2000 to post-2000.[54] Ewens and Xiao also observed that regulatory costs played little to no role in the upswing in take-private activity, a finding they attributed to the fact that regulatory costs are mostly upfront and irreversible, factoring into the decision to go public but not so much the decision to go private.[55]

Another important point to acknowledge is that private markets are not completely impervious to the sway of institutional investors. A significant driver of the growth in private markets over the last 30 to 40 years has been the rise of private equity, which has drawn its own chorus of scrutiny from scholars and policymakers. These critics argue that, similar to shareholder activist hedge funds, private equity funds hurt the economy and society at large by pushing companies to prioritize the maximization of short-term financial returns, and have done so in a "shadow economy" free from public oversight. In the words of federal prosecutor and former Department of Justice attorney Brendan Ballou, "private equity has reshaped American business by raising prices, reducing quality, cutting jobs, and shifting resources from productive to unproductive parts of the economy."[56]

Although critiques of the private equity industry are not hard to come by, the evidence underlying these critiques is tentative and disputed. Relative to shareholder activist hedge funds, private equity firms have longer time horizons and deeper industry and life cycle specialization relevant to the companies in which they invest, making them less prone to adopt the abusive practices pushed by many activist hedge funds. Private equity portfolio companies are not subject to the same pressure to hit quarterly earnings targets that overhang public company management teams, affording corporate managers greater flexibility to undertake operational and other improvements that take time to produce results. Furthermore, even if one were to give critics of the private equity industry the benefit of the doubt, they overlook an essential point. The growth of private equity is not an endogenous phenomenon that can be exclusively attributed to regulatory and technological changes but is a function of the failures of the public markets that have reduced the attractiveness of public market capital as a financing option for many corporations. Management teams often look to private equity as a last resort for financing. The cost of private market capital is materially higher than the cost of public market capital, and private equity

---

[54] Ewans, Michael, Kairong Xiao, and Ting Xu. 2022. "The Regulatory Costs of Being Public." Cato Institute. https://www.cato.org/research-briefs-economic-policy/regulatory-costs-being-public.
[55] Ibid.
[56] Brendan. 2023. Plunder: Private Equity's Plan to Pillage America. New York: Public Affairs.

firms have a reputation—rightly or wrongly—for overhauling management teams that does not predispose executives to be solicitous of private equity solutions.[57] That the private equity industry has flourished despite these inherent structural disadvantages speaks more to the shortcomings of our public markets than anything else. Whatever the negative economic and social effects of private equity, they are symptoms of the deeper challenges endemic to the public markets and any effort to remedy those negative effects must start with reform of the public market dynamics that have driven companies to seek out capital alternatives in the first place.

---

[57] Gompers, Paul A., Steven N. Kaplan, and Vladimir Mukharlyamov. 2023. "The Market for CEOs: Evidence from Private Equity." National Bureau of Economic Research. https://www.nber.org/papers/w30899.

8

Asset Manager Capitalism and the Energy Industry

There is perhaps no area of the U.S. economy that more clearly illustrates the deleterious effects of our current system of asset manager capitalism than the energy industry. During the 2010s, investment in oil and gas production markedly decreased. After booming during the so-called shale revolution, capital expenditures in oil and gas exploration and production peaked at over $700 billion in 2014, representing 3.6% percent of global investment that year. Thereafter, oil production declined to $350 to $450 billion per year from 2015 to 2021.[1] The cyclical reversal disproportionately affected publicly traded companies, which cut oil and gas investment more than national oil companies—consistent with investment declining more notably in the Americas and Africa, as opposed to the Middle East and Russia. While swings in capital expenditure are not unusual in the oil and gas industry, declines in oil and gas expenditure during this period far exceeded investment declines in prior periods with comparable decreases in oil and gas prices.[2]

Activist hedge funds played a key role in fostering this dynamic. As the shale revolution picked up in the early 2010s, depressing oil revenues and profitability for U.S. energy companies, shareholder activist hedge funds took advantage of the resulting shareholder discontent and mounted successful campaigns against energy companies to scrap longer-term investments in their businesses and do everything within their power to juice up short-term

---

[1] Ramaswamy, Vivek. 2022. "Our Letter to Chevron." Strive Capital Management. https://www.strive.com/strive-asset-management-letter-to-chevron.
[2] Ibid.

returns through asset divestitures, share repurchases, and dividends. Energy companies are long-term businesses requiring large capital investments that may not be realized for several years. At the time, many upstream exploration and production companies were increasing capital spending in order to transition their portfolios away from low-priced natural gas in North America to higher-return oil plays. With greater pressure on the bottom line and share prices, shareholders became less willing to accept these longer-term investments, a sentiment that activist hedge funds did not hesitate to exploit.[3]

When oil prices further collapsed in 2014–2016—from approximately $135 per barrel in June 2014 to a little over $43 per barrel in January 2016—the pressure on energy companies intensified. In 2013, there were over 270 reported hedge fund activist campaigns targeting energy companies; in 2014, over 340 reported activist campaigns; and in 2015, over 370 activist campaigns.[4] A sampling of these campaigns reveals the common underlying themes.[5]

In May 2012, shareholder activist Carl Icahn disclosed a 7.6% ownership stake in Chesapeake Energy, then the nation's second-biggest natural gas producer after Exxon Mobil, lambasting the company's capital management and investment strategy. Shortly after Icahn's announcement, Chesapeake's CEO stepped down from his position as board chairman and the company's board agreed to replace four of its nine members with appointees chosen by Icahn and another significant shareholder, Southeastern Asset Management.[6] In the years that followed, the company scaled back investment activity and ramped up asset divestitures. In September 2012, Chesapeake announced the sale of $6.9 billion in land comprising its shale operations.[7] In 2013, Chesapeake Energy sold 162,000 acres in northeastern Pennsylvania

---

[3] Plath, Chris. 2014. "Shareholder Activism: Impact on North American Corporate Sector." Moody's Ratings. http://www.law.harvard.edu/programs/corp_gov/activist-interventions-roundtable-2014-materials/2014_03_shareholder-activism-impact-on-na-corporates.pdf.

[4] Latham & Watkins. 2016. "Energy-Focused Activism." Latham & Watkins LLP. https://www.lw.com/admin/Upload/Documents/OilAndGasMandA/Governance/An_Overview_of_Energy_Focused_Activism.pdf.

[5] Law360. 2014. "Spotlight On Shareholder Activism in the Energy Industry." Law360. https://www.law360.com/articles/500481/spotlight-on-shareholder-activism-in-the-energy-industry.

[6] Dezember, Ryan and Daniel Gilbert. 2012. "Icahn Takes Chesapeake Energy Stake." The Wall Street Journal. https://www.wsj.com/articles/SB10001424052702304840904577426622973904532; New York Times. "Chesapeake Agrees to Revamp Its Board." New York Times. https://www.nytimes.com/2012/06/05/business/chesapeake-agrees-to-new-board.html.

[7] Mufson, Steven. 2012. "Debt-plagued Chesapeake Energy to sell $6.9 billion worth of its holdings." Washington Post. https://www.washingtonpost.com/business/economy/debt-plagued-chesapeake-energy-to-sell-69-billion-worth-of-its-holdings/2012/09/12/6b973420-fd0e-11e1-b153-218509a954e1_story.html.

to Southwestern Energy for around $93 million. Later in May 2013, Chesapeake sold approximately 99,000 acres in southwestern Pennsylvania to EQT Corporation for $113 million. In July 2014, the company sold an additional 22,000 acres in southwestern Pennsylvania to Canonsburg-based Rice Energy for $336 million.[8] In December 2014, Chesapeake closed a sale of assets in the Southern Marcellus Shale and a portion of the Eastern Utica Shale to Southwestern for net proceeds of $5 billion, followed by the announcement of a $1 billion common stock repurchase program.[9]

In October 2012, hedge fund Third Point disclosed in an investor letter that it had acquired a significant stake in Murphy Oil and called on the company to streamline operations and dispose of a litany of assets, including its Canadian natural gas assets, UK refining business, and its interest in an oil sands project valued at approximately $2.6 billion, all for the purpose of generating cash proceeds for shareholders.[10] Less than two weeks later, Murphy Oil announced plans to break itself apart and return cash to shareholders, approving a special dividend worth $500 million and a share buyback program worth $1 billion over the next year.[11]

In November 2012, TPG-Axon, a 4.5% shareholder in SandRidge Energy, sent a letter to the board decrying management's "reckless spending and lack of financial discipline" and the company's lackluster stock price performance.[12] Over the following weeks, TPG-Axon continued writing ever more aggressive letters and increasing its equity stake in SandRidge.[13] By the beginning of December, TPG-Axon had initiated a campaign to solicit written consents from SandRidge shareholders to remove and replace all of its incumbent directors.[14] In March 2013, the company settled its fight with TPG-Axon by agreeing to fire its chief executive and form a strategy

---

[8] Summerfield, Richard. 2014. "Southwestern Energy to acquire Chesapeake assets." Financier Worldwide. https://www.financierworldwide.com/southwestern-energy-to-acquire-chesapeake-assets#:~:text=In%20May%202013%2C%20Chesapeake%20sold,Rice%20Energy%20for%20%24336m.

[9] Chesapeake Energy. 2014. Chesapeake Energy Corporation Closes Southern Marcellus and Utica Shale Sale, Announces $1 Billion Common Stock Repurchase Authorization. Chesapeake Energy Corporation. https://investors.chk.com/2014-12-22-chesapeake-energy-corporation-closes-southern-marcellus-and-utica-shale-sale-announces-1-billion-common-stock-repurchase-authorization.

[10] Third Point. 2012. "Third Quarter 2012 Investor Letter." Third Point LLC. https://www.scribd.com/document/108887940/Third-Point-Q3-2012-Investor-Letter-TPOI.

[11] Gelles, David, Dan McCrum and Ed Crooks. 2012. "Murphy Oil activist investor scores win." Financial Times. https://www.ft.com/content/e1f3b540-17cf-11e2-9530-00144feabdc0.

[12] SandRidge Energy, Inc. 2012. "Schedule 13D." Securities and Exchange Commission. https://www.sec.gov/Archives/edgar/data/1349436/000090266412001410/p12-1844sc13d.htm.

[13] Alison Sider. 2013. "SandRidge Gives In, Settling Proxy Fight." Wall Street Journal. https://www.wsj.com/articles/SB10001424127887324392804578358801077322418.

[14] Ibid.

and planning committee "for the purpose of long term strategy and planning, including the undertaking of a comprehensive strategic review of the [SandRidge's] general and administrative expenses for the purpose of reducing such expense."[15] In January 2014, SandRidge agreed to sell off its drilling fields in the Gulf of Mexico to Fieldwood Energy for $750 million.[16] In September, the SandRidge board approved a program to repurchase up to $200 million of the company's common stock.[17] Through the rest of the year, 27.4 million shares were repurchased under the program for approximately $111.3 million.[18] SandRidge also began cutting its capital investment levels, announcing in January 2015 a 56% lower annual capital budget followed the next year by another announced cutback of 60% in capital spending.[19]

In January 2013, Elliott Management—one of the largest and oldest activist hedge funds—announced its intention to run a proxy contest against oil and gas giant Hess Corp. to replace five of the company's 14 incumbent directors. Elliott attacked Hess for its capital investment strategy, stating that the company had "squandered billions on adventures around the globe" and bemoaned the "immaterial return of cash to shareholders" generated over the prior decade.[20] In an effort to win institutional investors to its side, Hess authorized a $4 billion share repurchase program and a 150% increase in its annual dividend.[21] After a lengthy and bruising proxy fight, Elliott and Hess entered into a settlement agreement hours before shareholders began arriving for the company's annual investor meeting in May 2013.[22] As part of the

---

[15] SandRidge Energy, Inc. 2013. "Schedule 13D." Securities and Exchange Commission. https://www.sec.gov/Archives/edgar/data/1349436/000090266413001567/p13-0963sc13da.htm.

[16] SandRidge Energy Sells Gulf of Mexico Business to Fieldwood Energy—WSJ; activist hedge funds Wounded by Former Shale-Boom Star—WSJ.

[17] SandRidge Energy. 2014. "SandRidge Energy, Inc. Announces Share Repurchase Program." PR Newswire. https://www.prnewswire.com/news-releases/sandridge-energy-inc-announces-share-repurchase-program-274001841.html.

[18] SandRidge Energy, Inc. 2012. "Form 10-K." Securities and Exchange Commission. https://www.annualreports.com/HostedData/AnnualReportArchive/s/NYSE_SD_2015.pdf.

[19] Pramanick, Anannya. 2015. "SandRidge Energy Halves 2015 Capex, Cuts Rig Count." Reuters. https://www.reuters.com/article/sandridge-results/update-1-sandridge-energy-halves-2015-capex-cuts-rig-count-idUSL4N0W064920150226/.; SandRidge Energy. 2016. "SandRidge Energy, Inc. Updates Shareholders on Operations and Reports Financial Results for Fourth Quarter and Fiscal Year 2015." PR Newswire. https://www.prnewswire.com/news-releases/sandridge-energy-inc-updates-shareholders-on-operations-and-reports-financial-results-for-fourth-quarter-and-fiscal-year-2015-300242794.html.

[20] Eliot Management. 2013. "Elliott Management's Perspectives on Hess." Securities and Exchange Commission. https://www.sec.gov/Archives/edgar/data/4447/000110465913005512/a13-3887_2ex1.pdf.

[21] Hess Corporation. 2013. "Form 10-Q." Securities and Exchange Commission. https://www.sec.gov/Archives/edgar/data/4447/000119312513326860/d561628d10q.htm.

[22] De La Merced, Michael J. 2013. "How Elliott and Hess Settled a Bitter Proxy Battle." New York Times. https://archive.nytimes.com/dealbook.nytimes.com/2013/05/16/hess-and-elliott-settle-fight-over-companys-board/.

settlement, Hess agreed to give Elliott three board seats and split the roles of chairman and CEO. Hess also pushed forward with its new capital return initiatives. By March of the next year, Hess had purchased a cumulative 31.9 million shares of common stock at a total cost of approximately $2.54 billion, representing about 9% of its fully diluted shares as of the date its purchase program began. Hess then announced in May 2014 that it had agreed to sell its retail business to Marathon Petroleum for $2.6 billion in cash. The company earmarked proceeds from the sale for additional share repurchases. By June 2014, almost a year after Elliott's activist victory, Hess reported asset sales of more than $12.0 billion.[23]

On January 25, 2013, Carl Icahn filed a Schedule 13D reporting a 5.6% ownership position in deepwater driller Transocean, stating that the company "should return capital to shareholders and…. declare a dividend of at least $4.00 per Share" and that he planned to have discussions with the company regarding "the possible addition of shareholder selected nominees to the Board of Directors."[24] Following a number of discussions between Icahn and the Transocean senior management team, Transocean announced on March 3, 2013, that its board of directors would recommend that shareholders approve a dividend of $2.24 per share, to which Icahn responded the next day with a press release restating its recommendation in favor of a $4.00 per share dividend and his intention to nominate at least three alternative director nominees for the company's 2013 annual shareholder meeting.[25] Despite failing to win support at the annual meeting, Icahn continued his pressure campaign until Transocean finally relented in November and agreed to raise its dividend to $3.00 per share (amounting to a total $1.1 billion dividend) in connection with a settlement agreement with Icahn's fund. As part of the settlement, the company also announced an $800 million cost-cutting program.[26]

In October 2013, hedge fund JANA Partners disclosed a 7.5% stake in QEP Resources and called on the board to divest its midstream business

---

[23] Levitt, Aaron. 2013. "Hess the Latest Target of Increasingly Energy-Focused Activist Investors." InvestorPlace Media. https://investorplace.com/2013/03/hess-the-latest-target-of-increasingly-energy-focused-activist-investors/.

[24] Transocean Ltd. 2013. "Proxy Statement." Securities and Exchange Commission. https://www.sec.gov/Archives/edgar/data/921669/000092846413000069/rigdefc14a041713.htm.

[25] Ibid.

[26] Prasad, Sakthi. 2013. "Transocean Reaches Deal with Icahn to Resolve Proxy Battle." Reuters. https://www.reuters.com/article/idUSBRE9AA05M/.

and deploy the proceeds to "pursue a significant return of capital to shareholders."[27] JANA Partners restated these demands in a more pointed letter in November, accusing the then-CEO of "standing in the way of maximum value creation."[28] The next month, the QEP board announced that it had decided to pursue a separation of its midstream business.[29] In February, QEP provided an update on the status of its review process and announced four new initiatives: (i) the preparation and filing of documents to effectuate a spin-off of the midstream business, (ii) the commencement of a sale process of the company's non-core Midcontinent upstream assets, (iii) the approval of a $500 million share repurchase program, and (iv) an agreement to appoint two new directors to the board.[30] Shortly thereafter, JANA Partners and QEP Resources entered into a cooperation agreement, with JANA Partners agreeing to support QEP Resources' slate of directors for that year's annual shareholder meeting.

In pushing companies to prioritize short-term financial returns over longer-term investments, hedge fund activism produced a number of second- and third-order negative effects that sapped the strength of the domestic energy industry. As a response to activist pressure, energy businesses restructured their incentive and compensation plans to reward executives based on achieving near-term profitability benchmarks, rather than by reference to production of specified volumes of oil and gas, exacerbating the pressure on management teams to focus on short-term results.[31] In the case of many activist targets, asset dispositions were not sufficient to fund share repurchase and dividends, pushing companies to incur debt to fund shareholder returns, and thereby increasing the overall risk and leverage profile of the energy industry. Enhanced use of debt to fund shareholder rewards was credit

---

[27] Rosenstein, Barry. 2013. "Letter to the QEP Board of Directors." Securities and Exchange Commission. www.sec.gov/Archives/edgar/data/1108827/000090266413003475/p13-1861exhibitb.htm.

[28] Rosenstein, Barry. 2013. "Letter to the QEP Board of Directors." Securities and Exchange Commission. sec.gov/Archives/edgar/data/1108827/000090266413003683/p13-1989exhibit_c.htm.

[29] QEP Resources. 2013. "QEP Resources Announces Decision to Pursue a Seperation of its Midstream Business." Securities and Exchange Commission. https://www.sec.gov/Archives/edgar/data/1108827/000110882713000033/exhibit991.htm.

[30] QEP Resources. 2014. "Resources Provides Update On Strategic Iniatives." Securities and Exchange Commission. https://www.sec.gov/Archives/edgar/data/1108827/000110882714000007/a2314exhibit991.htm.

[31] Dezember, Ryan, and Matt Grossman. 2022. "Why Shale Drillers Are Pumping Out Dividends Instead of More Oil and Gas." The Wall Street Journal. https://www.wsj.com/articles/why-shale-drillers-are-pumping-out-dividends-instead-of-more-oil-and-gas-11653274423?mod=article_inline.

negative at Murphy Oil (Baa3 negative), as was the adoption of a large dividend at Transocean (Baa3 negative).[32] The outcome was more dramatic with SandRidge, which filed Chapter 11 bankruptcy in 2016.[33]

The ESG/TSR Activist Pincer Attack[34]

As energy companies became the target of activist hedge funds, they also faced greater pressure from ESG activists to re-orient their businesses away from oil and gas in an effort to combat climate change. The climate change movement has a long-standing history, with support from a range of actors, including governments, national and international non-governmental organizations, and public interest activist groups. The movement obtained further wind in its sails during the second term of the Obama Administration when the United States and over 190 other countries entered into the Paris Climate Accords in 2015. In the time since institutional investors have been able to exercise a unique influence in advancing the climate change agenda. Asset managers are one of the few institutions that have the power to directly shape corporate behavior while also having the international reach and scale required to confront a global challenge like climate change. With the increasing popularity of ESG, asset management firms have been a critical force in pushing companies to take specific measures to combat climate change even when shifts in the political landscape have made governments less supportive of the cause.

Notwithstanding these characteristics, a deeper examination of institutional investor advocacy efforts reveals the difficulties of shoehorning a global challenge like climate change—involving a complexity of considerations and

---

[32] French, Gretchen. 2014. "Armed with More Cash, Activists Are Casting a Wider Net: Energy." Moody's Ratings. http://www.law.harvard.edu/programs/corp_gov/activist-interventions-roundtable-2014-materials/2014_03_shareholder-activism-impact-on-na-corporates.pdf; SandRidge Energy. 2016. "SandRidge Energy Files "Pre-Arranged" Reorganization Under Chapter 11, Announcing Restructuring Support Agreement with Creditors Holding Over Two-Thirds of its $4.1 Billion in Funded Debt Obligations." PR Newswire. https://www.prnewswire.com/news-releases/sandridge-energy-files-pre-arranged-reorganization-under-chapter-11-announcing-restructuring-support-agreement-with-creditors-holding-over-two-thirds-of-its-41-billion-in-funded-debt-obligations-300268813.html.

[33] Dezember, Ryan. 2016. "Activist Hedge Funds Wounded by Former Shale-Boom Star." Wall Street Journal. https://www.wsj.com/articles/activist-hedge-funds-wounded-by-former-shale-boom-star-1460712782.

[34] The title of this section is inspired by a 2021 memorandum published by the law firm Wachtell, Lipton, Rosen & Katz entitled "The ESG/TSR Activist "Pincer Attack." Harvard Law School Forum on Corporate Governance. https://corpgov.law.harvard.edu/2021/01/26/the-esg-tsr-activist-pincer-attack/.

trade-offs—into an ESG-based analytic framework that evaluates environmental and social factors in terms of their salience to the ability of individual companies to deliver financial returns to shareholders. In the context of the energy business, ESG activism has had the practical effect of exacerbating the worst tendencies promoted by traditional hedge fund activism, while failing to meaningfully move the needle in the fight against climate change.

Historically, ESG activism has had a negative orientation that is almost exclusively focused on pushing energy companies to scale back emission-producing activities. While many ESG advocates have expressed enthusiasm about the potential benefits of clean energy and renewable alternatives, experts have been unable to demonstrate the economic viability of deploying these strategies at any level of scale that would come close to filling the gap that would arise from achieving net-zero emissions. In shareholder speak, there is no evidence-based case that investments in clean energy alternatives are conducive to enhancing profitability, however long the time frame, when assessed in light of the significant capital outlays and costs that would be required to operationalize such alternatives. Climate change has been reduced to a "risk" to the capacity of companies to generate financial returns. The content of shareholder proposals on climate change, which are often filed by public interest groups but whose success depends on the support of institutional investors and other substantial shareholders, reflects this focus. These proposals have generally demanded that firms provide greater disclosures concerning the risks and costs of climate change to their businesses, and in recent years, included more aggressive demands to cut back emissions (such as requests that firms report on their plans to cut emissions in compliance with the Paris Accords, and others directly mandating companies adopt net-zero greenhouse gas reduction targets across their full value chain, including "Scope 3" emissions produced by third parties that only have an indirect association with the subject company).[35] By contrast, it is challenging to find examples of shareholder proposals or other shareholder efforts aimed at animating companies to take positive steps to fill the void introduced by cutting back their emission-producing activities.

Another feature of ESG activism, and to a large degree a function of ESG's negative thrust, is that companies have been encouraged to divest their dirty assets to other companies, enabling the divesting firms to cut their individual emissions, but not necessarily altering overall emissions levels in the economy. By increasing the cost of capital associated with operating emission-producing businesses, climate change activists have encouraged their targets—mostly big

---

[35] Ramaswamy, "Chevron Letter."

public companies that easily catch the attention of public interest groups and large asset managers—to divest those assets at a discount to private actors who are not subject to the same public scrutiny and enjoy a lower cost of capital that enables them to continue or even expand their polluting, profit-generating operations.[36] In 2021, Anglo American Plc, one of the world's most powerful mining companies, became "a case study in unintended consequences" after climate activists and investors urged it to stop digging up coal. In previous years, in an attempt to assuage activists, Anglo American had divested its coal mines in Rio Tinto and formulated a plan to gradually shut down its mining operations in South Africa. But this was not enough for ESG advocates, so Anglo American decided to spin-off another company called Thungela that would retain all of its coal operations, after which investors could then "decide for themselves" if they wanted to hold or sell shares of the spun-off entity. Once the spin-off was underway, Thungela's Chief Executive Officer, July Ndlovu reversed course, announcing they were looking to *grow* their coal production, not shrink it. "I didn't take up this role to close these mines, to close this business," Ndlovu said. The company's South African mines had the potential to add a decade or more of mining, producing more than 10 million tons of coal per year.[37]

Likewise facing pressure from institutional investors to quickly and dramatically cut emissions, international oil and gas giant BP announced the sale of its Alaska oilfields in September 2019 as part of a series of transactions aimed at wiping off at least a sixth of the company's carbon emissions. The Alaska divestiture was consummated the subsequent year and appeared to have helped BP reduce its Scope 1 and 2 production-based emissions by 16%, but the effect on overall emission levels in the area is debatable. The acquirer of BP's Alaska oilfields was a privately held energy exploration and production company that, according to a Bloomberg investigation, had "made a name buying oil and gas assets no one else wants" and, based on an examination of state data, had by 2021 already increased emissions beyond 2019 levels, more than offsetting BP's emission reductions attributable to the sale.[38]

---

[36] Levine, Matt. 2021. "Someone Is Going to Drill the Oil." Bloomberg. https://www.bloomberg.com/opinion/articles/2021-07-08/someone-is-going-to-drill-the-oil?embedded-checkout=true; Schupp, Brandon. 2021. "Putting the "green" in green investing." Norton Rose Fulbright LLP. https://www.specialsituationslaw.com/2021/11/19/putting-the-green-in-green-investing/.

[37] Price. 2021. "Activist Investor Push To End Coal Mining Is Backfiring." Business Insider. https://markets.businessinsider.com/news/stocks/activist-investor-push-to-end-coal-mining-is-backfiring-1030971440.

[38] Adams-Heard, Rachel. 2021. "What Happens When an Oil Giant Walks Away." Bloomberg. https://www.bloomberg.com/graphics/2021-tracking-carbon-emissions-BP-hilcorp/.

Anglo-American and BP are not one-off examples.[39] A 2023 Environmental Defense Fund study entitled *Transferred Emissions: How Risks in Oil and Gas M&A Could Hamper the Energy Transition*, notes that the number of public-to-private transfers of oil and gas assets—that is, sale transactions in which public companies divest oil and gas businesses to non-public acquirors—exceeded the number of private-to-public transfers by 64% over the 2017 to 2021 period. In other words, M&A activity in the energy industry was pushing more dirty energy businesses into the hands of private operators, who were not subject to the same level of oversight and transparency as public companies. The study also noted that assets were increasingly moving away from companies with environmental commitments. In 2018, deals that shifted assets away from companies with environmental commitments accounted for only 10% of transactions. By 2021, these deals accounted for 15% of transactions. From 2018 through 2021, more than twice as many deals moved assets away from operators with net-zero commitments than the reverse.[40]

The focus among ESG activists on scaling back operations and pushing companies to divest assets or break up their businesses has found them allies among activist hedge funds with more conventional financial objectives who see the congruency between their strategies and those deployed by ESG practitioners and perceive an opportunity to justify their campaigns in more politically palatable language. In May 2021, Elliott Management mounted a public campaign to pressure Duke Energy to break itself up into three companies so that Duke Energy could refocus itself as a "cleaner, more reliable energy" company.[41] Later that year, Elliott deployed similar rhetoric in its demand that UK-based energy company, SSE, separate its renewable energy

---

[39] See, e.g., Lund, "Asset Managers", 144 ("Not only that, there are major limits on the Big Three's regulatory reach: their penalties are unlikely to affect a private company or company with a controlling shareholder, to take two examples. In addition, public companies can escape the reach of their rules by going private or divesting high externality assets."); Mahoney, Paul and Julia Mahoney. 2021. "The New Separation of Ownership and Control: Institutional Investors and ESG." COLUM. BUS. L. REV. 840, 856 ("When it comes to carbon production and use and climate-sensitive assets, an S&P 500 index fund does not own the market ...."); Dharmapala, Dhammika and Vikramaditya Khanna. 2021. "Controlling Externalities: Ownership Structure and Cross-Firm Externalities." 33–34 (Eur. Corp. Governance Inst., Working Paper No. 603/2021), https://papers.ssrn.com/sol3/papers.cfm?abstract_id=3904310 [https://perma.cc/4VRC-TYJF] (claiming that companies with controlling stockholders are less likely to act in ways that minimize cross-firm externalities).

[40] Malek, Gabriel. 2022. "Transferred Emissions: How Risks in Oil and Gas M&A Could Hamper the Energy Transition." Environmental Defense Fund. https://business.edf.org/wp-content/blogs.dir/90/files/Transferred-Emissions-How-Oil-Gas-MA-Hamper-Energy-Transition.pdf.

[41] Elliott Investment Management. 2021. "Elliott Investment Management Sends Letter to Board of Directors of Duke Energy Corporation." PR Newswire. https://www.prnewswire.com/news-releases/elliott-investment-management-sends-letter-to-board-of-directors-of-duke-energy-corporation-301292688.html.

business.[42] Other smaller hedge funds in the activist space have also deployed the ESG mantra, such as London-based Bluebell Capital Partners, which publicly urged mining and commodity trading firm Glencore in November 2021 to separate its thermal coal operations on the basis that those businesses rendered it "not an investible company for investors who place sustainability at the heart of their investment process."[43]

The aggregate impact is that ESG activists have fallen short in achieving their overarching environmental goals, and also functioned—hand in hand with more traditional activist hedge funds—to encourage short-termism and underinvestment in the energy industry. By February 2022, arguably at the peak of ESG's popularity within the asset management industry, energy companies in the West found themselves completely unprepared to meet the demands of consumers when Russian energy access was suddenly terminated following Putin's invasion of Ukraine. The substantial reductions in oil and gas production over the prior years far exceeded any enhancements in clean energy capabilities during that time. In Europe, in particular, households and businesses had become dependent on energy supplies from Russian national oil and gas companies that did not have to contend with the same pressures from ESG and hedge fund activists to which Western energy firms found themselves subject.

In the more than two years that have followed Russia's invasion, the worst of the energy crisis has passed, but the fundamental dynamics of our public markets have not changed.[44] The 2022 energy shortage dissipated not only as a result of ramped-up oil and gas production but also because of extraordinary government efforts to address the energy shortage, like President Biden's authorization of the release of over 200 million barrels of crude oil from the Strategic Petroleum Reserve that year. Many of the smaller, private operators that have driven the growth in oil and gas production over the last few years have been acquired by larger public companies, who, at the continued pressure of their asset manager shareholders, have favored distributing cash

---

[42] Rosenbaum, Jeff, and Nabeel Bhanji. 2021. "Elliott Publishes Letter on SSE Calling for Immediate Action to Enhance Governance and Value." Businesswire. https://www.businesswire.com/news/home/20211206005885/en/Elliott-Publishes-Letter-on-SSE-Calling-for-Immediate-Action-to-Enhance-Governance-and-Value#:~:text=The%20letter%2C%20sent%20in%20the,in%20shareholder%20value%20become%20permanent.

[43] Koilparambil, Aby Jose, Clara Denina and Zandi Shabalala. 2021. "Activist Investor Bluebell Urges Glencore to Separate its Thermal Coal Unit." Reuters. https://www.reuters.com/markets/europe/activist-investor-bluebell-urges-glencore-separate-its-thermal-coal-unit-2021-11-30/.

[44] Krauss, Clifford, and Michael D. Shear. 2022 "Biden will Tap Oil Reserve, Hoping to Push Gasoline Prices Down." New York Times. https://www.nytimes.com/2022/03/31/business/energy-environment/biden-oil-strategic-petroleum-reserve.html; Geman, Ben, and Erin Doherty. 2022. "Biden Ordering Massive Release of Oil in Bid to Curb Gas Prices." Axios. https://www.axios.com/2022/03/31/biden-strategic-petroleum-reserve-oil-release.

back to investors over drilling new wells.[45] In significant part because of this dynamic, growth is expected to slow dramatically in the near- to medium-term. A renewed trend of deal-making and asset divestitures has encouraged sellers to accelerate fracking of previously drilled wells to boost output and appear more attractive to buyers, depleting the country's supply of untapped well, while the focus on acquiring and integrating new businesses and assets has distracted buyers from making investments in the development of their long-term production capabilities.[46] The fight against climate change seems as daunting as it ever was. Greenhouse gas emissions from fossil fuels reached a record high of 36.8 billion metric tons in 2023. At current rates of emissions, scientists calculate there is a 50% chance that within seven years global temperatures will regularly exceed the 1.5 degrees Celsius above pre-industrial levels identified in the 2015 Paris Agreement as a threshold beyond which worsening and potentially irreversible effects of global warming are likely to emerge.[47] Barring deeper changes to the structure of the financial markets, the future of the energy industry—and the fight against climate change—remains uncertain.

---

[45] Henderson, Bob. 2024. "America's Oil Power Might Be Near its Peak." The Wall Street Journal. https://www.wsj.com/business/energy-oil/americas-oil-power-might-be-near-its-peak-5d956a24; Uberti, David. 2023. "Big Oil Has $150 Billion in Cash and Investors Want a Share." The Wall Street Journal. https://www.wsj.com/articles/big-oil-has-150-billion-in-cash-and-investors-want-a-share-b5cdea35.

[46] Henderson, "Oil Peak."

[47] NOAA. 2023. "Record Carbon Dioxide Emissions Impeding Progress on Meeting Climate Goals." National Oceanic and Atmospheric Administration. https://research.noaa.gov/2023/12/05/record-fossil-carbon-dioxide-emissions-impeding-progress-on-meeting-climate-goals-report/; Jackson, Rob. 2023. "Global Carbon Emissions from Fossil Fuels Reached Record High in 2023." Stanford Doerr School of Sustainability. https://sustainability.stanford.edu/news/global-carbon-emissions-fossil-fuels-reached-record-high-2023.

9

Institutional Setup of Today's Asset Managers

In order to understand how today's asset management firms have exerted their voice with respect to ESG and other matters—and why they have exerted that voice in the manner they have—it is critical to understand the incentives and limitations that have shaped their behavior.

Arguably the most notable development in the asset management industry of the last two decades is the dramatic growth in index investing and the concomitant increase in the size of the portfolios of today's largest asset management firms. The big asset managers find it ever more challenging to express their sentiments as to any given company's performance or strategic direction by adjusting their equity position. The ability to assert voice as an investor has emerged as the only practical lever of influence among the largest institutional investors. The sizeable equity stakes these firms hold in any given company means it is very difficult to readily dispose of shares in the event of a disagreement with management, and the bigger portfolios—that often comprise virtually all if not all public-traded equities—limit opportunities for reinvestment. Due to the increased prominence of index investing, a significant amount of the capital managed by asset managers is locked into indices with pre-specified allocations across the firms comprising the relevant index that cannot be altered when an asset manager's views with respect to a particular company evolve.[1]

---

[1] As Jeff Schwartz of the University of Utah notes: "In theory, managers of index funds have the most to gain from stewardship. Active managers primarily try to improve performance through their stock picking. But index-fund managers cannot choose their investments. Thus, the only way to improve performance and generate the increased profits that come with it is through monitoring their portfolio companies. Since the Big 3 specialize in managing index funds, this might suggest

The rise of indexing and the increasing size of today's largest asset managers has not only created pressure on asset managers to exert influence in the boardroom but also further destabilized the traditional assumptions and ideas underlying the concept of making voting decisions and engaging with a company as a shareholder. Today's biggest asset managers are universal owners who effectively own a slice of the overall economy. A substantial portion of the capital managed by these firms flows from individuals and businesses who are also diversified investors. In the case of most working people, these equity investments are funded via a 401(k) or pension plan that deploys index and other diversified investing strategies that contemplate investments across a wide range of companies. The conventional notion of a shareholder myopically making investment-related decisions with respect to an individual company in which he or she has invested based on views about the performance of the company is no longer appropriate. As a universal owner, it seems fitting that any concept of shareholder value by which asset managers are guided in formulating investment and voting decisions make room for the fact that their ultimate beneficiaries are frequently diversified investors and consider on a more aggregate basis the performance of the wider portfolio of an asset manager's equity investments (as opposed to focusing on individual companies). By way of example, Jeffrey Gordon of Columbia Law School has suggested that it would be more sensible for index funds and other large asset managers with extensively diversified portfolios to focus their stewardship efforts on addressing the "systematic" risk elements that impact companies across their portfolios rather than idiosyncratic, firm-specific risks that should be eliminated as a result of diversification.[2]

While the prototypical model of the shareholder assumes that an investor can always liquidate his or her stake in a company in the event of a disagreement with management, the practical limitations faced by asset management firms in adjusting their equity positions means they should theoretically make

---

an inclination towards stewardship." "Stewardship Theater." 411. Needless to say, we also delve into these trends and dynamics in greater detail earlier in this book (see Chapter 5 and "Investment Strategies– Index Investing" and "The Separation of Ownership from Ownership and the Evolution of the Model Equity Investor" in Chapter 4).

[2] Gordon, Jeffrey N. 2022. "Systematic Stewardship." 47 J. CORP. L. 627 (2022).
https://scholarship.law.columbia.edu/faculty_scholarship/3799. See also Condon, Madison. "Externalities and the Common Owner". 2020. 95 WASH. L. REV. 1 (asserting that "diversified investors should be rationally motivated to internalize intra-portfolio negative externalities"); Coffee, John C. 2021. "The Coming Shift in Shareholder Activism: From 'Firm Specific' to 'Systematic Risk' Proxy Campaigns (and How to Enable Them)." 16 BROOK. J. CORP. FINANCE & COM. L. 45 (distinguishing between two types of shareholder activism—(1) firm-specific activism, which has a long history and focuses on changes at a specific target company, and (2) system risk activism, which seeks to reduce the systematic risk in a portfolio and thereby benefit diversified investors).

investments with a longer term investment horizon than smaller, undiversified investors who are able to quickly trade in and out of their stock positions. In the case of indexing, that time horizon is indefinite given the investor's inability to adjust its position in an individual company absent a change to the composition of the overall index. It is not sufficient to judge whether or not a particular corporate action is beneficial to investors by assessing its impact over a few months or years. Rather, the question becomes whether any given corporate decision or strategy will drive growth and profitability on a more sustainable basis, theoretically in perpetuity.

At the same time that these changes in the structure of institutional investment vehicles and the public markets suggest the need for a more ambitious re-imagination of the ways in which investor voice should be asserted, there are several characteristics of how the asset management industry operates that in practice have militated against such a broader minded re-imagination.

First, by virtue of their business model, the large asset management firms have limited incentives to expend resources to monitor and evaluate companies on an individual basis. A key value proposition of diversification and indexing is that they represent low cost investing strategies and that they offer the opportunity to enhance risk-adjusted returns by allowing investors to invest across a wide variety of companies and reduce firm-specific risk along with the need to expend energy to monitor the performance of individual companies. Conventional equity index fund expense ratios are six-hundredths of a percent. By comparison, the median equity mutual fund charges more than fifteen times the rate that index funds charge.[3] Even if firm-specific interventions might enhance value in the stock of the applicable company, the associated expenses will likely outweigh the benefits to be obtained from any enhancements, particularly when one considers the negligible impact of any firm-specific improvement on a larger portfolio of investments and in the context of a large asset manager's indefinite time horizon.

The pressure among big asset management firms to minimize costs does not just apply to their indexed offerings. The rising popularity of index investing over the last two decades has meant that institutional investors as a class—including active funds—have found themselves under strain to trim fees in order to retain investors lest they lose investors to passive funds.[4] Other structural factors have made cost an important value differentiator in the competition for customers and assets. Due to their economies of scale, large asset management firms are able to spread out their fixed costs across a

---

[3] Coates, The Problem of 12. 33.
[4] IG Prime. "What Is Fee Compression & How Does It Affect assET Managers?" IG Bank. https://www.ig.com/en-ch/prime/insights/articles/fee-compression-asset-managers-220826.

larger consumer base and outcompete smaller investment companies. Beyond limited niche alternative strategies, the offerings of the large asset managers are virtually identical, placing greater stress on firms to try to distinguish themselves on the basis of cost.[5] Over the last decade or so, many fund companies have been engaged in a price war, aggressively cutting fees in an attempt to compete with one another and maintain, or gain, market share.[6] According to one 2019 study, from 2014 through 2019, asset managers voluntarily gave up nearly $16 billion in fees by reducing the expense ratios they charged for their investment products. During the same time frame, products with expense ratios less than 5bps grew 20 times faster than products with expense ratios greater than 20bps over the prior five years.[7]

Cost is not the only aspect of the large asset manager business model that dissuades firms from undertaking a broader minded approach towards "investment stewardship." Even if index stewardship efforts could be reasonably anticipated to improve returns in a sufficiently reliable and meaningful way to offset associated costs, funds would still only be incentivized to implement such efforts if those improved returns could be expected to provide a competitive advantage relative to their peers. As Jeff Schwartz of the University of Utah notes:

> Funds are only at a competitive advantage when their return exceeds their competitors' returns after fees. The problem with stewardship as a competitive tool is that competing mutual funds own many of the same firms. If an asset manager engineers an increase at one of the firms in one of its funds, it shares the gains pro rata with competing funds. Because of this overlapping ownership, there is only a competitive advantage for stewardship when funds own proportionally more shares in the target firm than its competitors. If it owns proportionally fewer, then the intervention actually worsens the fund's competitive position. For index funds, there is no hope for competitive advantage through stewardship. Since index funds own the same firms in the same proportions as other index funds, they cannot outcompete other index funds by improving the performance of their portfolio firms. Beyond that, there is no reliable way to know exactly what competitor funds own. Mutual funds must publicly disclose their holdings every quarter, but they file these reports up to sixty days from quarter end. The holdings information is, therefore, out of date. And even if this information were obtainable, it would not be useful. The

---

[5] Steele, Graham. 2020. "The New Money Trust: How Large Money Managers Control Our Economy and What We Can Do About It." American Economic Liberties Project. https://www.economiclibe rties.us/wp-content/uploads/2020/11/Working-Paper-Series-on-Corporate-Power_8_FINAL.pdf.
[6] Ibid.
[7] Miller, Warren. 2019. "The Game Theory of Fund Price Wars." Flowspring. https://www.flowsp ring.com/research/The-Game-Theory-of-Fund-Price-Wars.

competitive landscape at the asset-manager level is enormously complex. The different funds that they oversee have different portfolio mixes and different competitors. Stewardship would inevitably advance the competitive interests of some of their funds and hurt others. Thus, any competitive gains at one fund would be offset by diminished competitiveness at others.[8]

Secondly—and in tension with the trend towards indexing and the desire to minimize costs—many of the dynamics that we described in Chapter 5 that pre-dispose large asset managers to act in a short-termist fashion continue to exist. Pension underfunding is even a worse problem than it was in the 1990s, further inducing pension managers to seek out aggressive investment strategies that will quickly generate returns.[9] Asset management firms typically consist of an umbrella of various funds, including both passive and active funds. There is no evidence that how the job performance of active portfolio managers is evaluated, or that the factors that otherwise shape the decision-making of active portfolio managers, have evolved.[10] The rise of passive investing and the cost dynamics of the asset management industry means that large asset managers are cautious about incurring expenses, but the emergence of event-driven funds that purport to deliver above-market returns within a short time also continues to motivate active fund managers to search for more avenues to generate compelling returns.

What has been the practical outcome of this confluence of varying incentives and limitations in terms of how large asset management firms actually approach the process of expressing their voice as investors? While there are differences, even among the Big Three, several shared characteristics predominate:

(1) The big asset management firms do not approach the process of expressing voice as a bottom-up exercise. By and large, these firms centralize the authority to engage with individual companies and make voting decisions in "governance" or "stewardship" units that act on behalf of the entire fund complex with respect to any given corporate matter, including the sponsor's actively managed funds and other non-index-fund vehicles.[11] These

---

[8] Schwartz, "Stewardship Theater." 417–418.
[9] Brown, Aaron. 2023. "Time Bomb of Public Pension Funding Ticks Louder." Bloomberg. https://www.bloomberg.com/opinion/articles/2023-02-13/time-bomb-of-public-pension-funding-ticks-louder?embedded-checkout=true.
[10] See, e.g., Govindarajan, Vijay and Anup Srivastava. 2019. "We Are Nowhere Near Stakeholder Capitalism." HARV. BUS. REV. https://hbr.org/2020/01/we-are-nowhere-near-stakeholder-capitalism.
[11] For a helpful overview of how certain of the largest asset management firms centralize governance decision-making and more generally structure their investment stewardship processes, see Lund, Dorothy S. and Adriana Z. Robertson. 2023. "Giant Asset Managers, the Big Three, and Index

governance units define their general philosophy and approach to issues that commonly arise in the form of publicly available proxy voting guidelines and principles. The large asset managers stress that these guidelines are applied with discretion and that voting decisions take into account a range of issues and facts specific to the company and the individual ballot item. In practice, they rarely deviate from their guidelines. Governance units end up taking a broad brush approach in how they engage with companies, applying a top-down, sweeping view of corporate governance best practices across their portfolio of companies. Evoking again the words of law professor Dorothy Lund, they act like regulators by promulgating rules and guidelines that embody a universal conception of what companies *should do* and then applying them to the thousands of companies within their portfolios (which frequently comprise the largest companies in United States).

Centralization and generalization are an outgrowth of two dynamics in the asset management industry. One is the push to minimize expenses and the prohibitive costs and hurdles associated with either delegating decision-making authority to the thousands of portfolio managers employed at any given firm (who typically view their job as focused on the more directly financial aspects of investment advisory work), or hiring additional staff to manage the stewardship function on an individualized, case-by-basis basis (which, in light of the thousands of companies in the portfolios of today's largest asset management firms, would encompass decision-making with respect to tens of thousands of proposals in any given year). Another driver is that normatively it no longer makes sense to define the behavior of today's large asset management firms by reference to the conventional model of the undiversified, individual shareholder that engages with a limited universe of companies. The centralized model implicitly accepts this reality by avoiding the impracticalities associated with undertaking a sum-of-the-parts exercise in which the differing interests and time horizons of an asset management firm's clients—often institutional investment vehicles themselves—are weighed and balanced. Instead, the large asset managers recast the act of expressing voice as a responsibility to the ultimate "real" providers of capital—the millions of average working people whose savings and retirement assets represent the

---

Investing." USC CLASS Research Paper No. 23–13, Available at SSRN: https://ssrn.com/abstract=4406204 or http://dx.doi.org/10.2139/ssrn.4406204. See also Bebchuk, Lucian and Scott Hirst. 2019. "Index Funds and The Future of Corporate Governance: Theory, Evidence, and Policy." Columbia Law Review, Vol. 119, No. 8; Fichtner, Jan, Eelke M. Heemskerk, and Javier Garcia-Bernardo. 2017. "Hidden Power of the Big Three? Passive Index Funds, Re-Concentration of Corporate Ownership, and New Financial Risk." *Business and Politics*. Available at SSRN: https://ssrn.com/abstract=2798653 or http://dx.doi.org/10.2139/ssrn.2798653.

bulk of capital flowing through the investment advisory industry—and articulate a deeper notion of the collective interests signified by those providers of capital in terms of a generalized long-term interest in a well-performing economy. As former State Street CEO Cyrus Taraporevala has noted, "[w]e seek long-term value for *millions of ordinary investors* (emphasis added)." "We are essentially permanent capital and cannot turn the S&P 500 into the S&P 499. That means we need to take a long-term perspective on behalf of our clients."[12]

(2) While the large asset management firms have rhetorically embraced a broader-minded vision of their role as public custodians of capital, how they have actually gone about giving meaning to that vision prioritizes the perspectives and interests of a limited group of internal and external constituencies. The big asset managers' embrace of the ESG-based stakeholder model is the key example. The premise of ESG—that factors that are not traditionally viewed to have economic import can impact the long-term financial performance of a company—is uncontroversial and in principle would suggest the need to consider a wide range of matters in running a business, such as the treatment of employees, supply chain management and geopolitical risks. The fact that ESG advocacy has historically focused on a narrow band of environmental and social causes reflects an affirmative decision to prioritize a restricted category of issues. There is little evidence that ESG advocacy on climate change and gender diversity has improved corporate profitability or other metrics of shareholder value, and there are widespread disagreements about the social significance of the underlying issues and how best to address them. There may be plenty of legitimate reasons motivating advocacy on climate change and gender diversity, but it is untrue that the level of attention generated by these topics stems from a self-evidently incontrovertible and universally accepted understanding of their materiality to economic performance. Other forces are at play.[13]

---

[12] Taraporevala, Cyrus. 2018. "Index Funds Must Be Activists to Serve Investors." Financial Times. https://www.ft.com/content/4e4c119a-8c25-11e8-affd-da9960227309.

[13] See also Lund, "Asset Managers." 86 ("In particular, if internalizing externalities or reducing systematic risk was the goal, there are more direct ways of achieving it. For example, the Big Three could take a more aggressive stance toward disclosing and restricting corporate money in politics, which compromises regulatory efforts to regulate risk and externalities. Instead, the Big Three generally vote against shareholder proposals aimed at limiting corporate influence in the political process. Again, this is likely because investor activism on corporate political spending has not been broadly embraced by their clients (and corporate America in particular), in contrast to policies aiming to reduce carbon emissions and improve board diversity.") 112 ("Although empirical evidence generally suggests that increased board diversity creates shareholder value, it is not conclusive. By contrast, there are other ESG initiatives that have as strong, if not stronger, links to value creation for diversified and undiversified investors, but that have not garnered broad consensus among the business community: for

The big asset management firms do not publicly delve into the details of how they go about determining what topics they choose to prioritize, but several potential sources can be identified. One is client demand. The most significant clients of the large asset management firms (both by size and willingness to exert influence) are the public pension plans. For instance, the majority of BlackRock's AUM (over two-thirds) is in the form of pension plan assets that are managed on behalf of corporations, governments, and unions.[14] The largest of these pension plans hail from states like California and New York whose population and political leadership widely espouse Progressive, left-of-center political sensibilities that incline them to embrace causes like climate change and gender diversity that have a more liberal political valiance. These causes tend to have more cache among the types of individuals who fill investment stewardship roles at asset management firms and pension funds—elite, upper income, highly educated professionals with careers in law and compliance—than bread and butter pocketbook issues that may more directly resonate with the general public.[15] Moreover, studies have shown that elite opinion tends to exhibit more homogeneity than wider public opinion, further driving uniformity in the level of support and enthusiasm that headline ESG issues command among the largest asset managers.[16]

---

example, seeking improved conditions for workers, reducing outsized executive compensation, and improving community relations.").

[14] See Lund, "Asset Managers" (arguing that demand from clientele—particularly large pension funds and other institutional vehicles—governs choice of policies and proposals advocated by the Big Three and other large asset management firms).

[15] Pazzanese, Christina. 2017. "Gauging the Bias of Lawyers." The Harvard Gazette. https://news.harvard.edu/gazette/story/2017/08/analyst-gauges-the-political-bias-of-lawyers/#:~:text=The%20reason%20why%20is%20because,you%20look%20at%20elite%20lawyers; Lichter, Samuel Robert, and Stanley Rothman. 1983. "How Liberal Are Bureaucrats?" American Enterprise Institute. https://www.aei.org/articles/how-liberal-are-bureaucrats/#:~:text=Again%2C%20bureaucrats%20are%20somewhat%20more,more%20liberal%20than%20the%20traditionals; Weiss, Debra Cassens. 2015. "Lawyers 'Lean to the Left,' Study Says; Which Schools, Firms and Practice Areas Are Most Liberal?" ABA Journal. https://www.abajournal.com/news/article/lawyers_lean_to_the_left_study_says_which_law_schools_firms_are_practice_ar#google_vignette.

[16] As Dorothy Lund points out in a footnote in "Asset Managers": "Another way of conceptualizing this dynamic is that it represents the influence of elite political opinion on asset managers. Elites—including corporate leaders and pension fund managers—tend to form homogenous political viewpoints. See Litsa Nicolaou-Smokoviti & Burt Baldwin, Hierarchies, Attitudes, and Gender, in GENDERING ELITES: ECONOMIC AND POLITICAL LEADERSHIP IN 27 INDUSTRIALISED SOCIETIES 207, 212 (Mino Vianello & Gwen Moore eds., 2000) (finding evidence that the higher you go in corporate management hierarchy, the higher the degree of attitudinal homogeneity); see also Harold R. Kerbo & L. Richard Della Fave, The Empirical Side of the Power Elite Debate: An Assessment and Critique of Recent Research, 20 SOCIOLOGICAL Q. 5, 14–15 (1979) (describing the phenomenon of "elite unity"). Accordingly, elite demand for rules is shaped by these political views. In turn, asset managers, by publicly advertising their congruence with these political views, likely influence public opinion on these issues. Cf. James N. Druckman, Erik Peterson & Rune Slothuus, How Elite Partisan Polarization Affects Public Opinion Formation, 107 AM. POL. SCI.

Another important client constituency is millennials, who embrace mostly liberal views on social and environmental topics. As University of Virginia law professor Michal Barzuza notes in a 2020 paper, index funds and other large asset managers are "locked in a fierce contest to win the soon-to-accumulate assets of the millennial generation."[17] Based on Barzuza's research, somewhere between $12 trillion and $30 trillion will be transferred to millennials in the coming decades. Even the low end of that spectrum will mark the largest intergenerational wealth shift in history.[18]

Political considerations also likely play a role in how institutional investors go about exerting their voice. It is not uncommon for businesses to factor in broader political sentiments in their decision-making, especially in regulated industries like financial services where heightened scrutiny from the public and politicians makes companies particularly mindful of how changes in political headwinds may impact their regulatory standing.[19] While political opinion in the United States is sharply divided, historically it has been politically liberal social and environmental activist groups that have been the most assertive in lobbying and pressuring businesses, in turn shaping executive sensitivities on political issues. The asset management industry is no exception. In addition to the indirect political pressure the large asset managers face from public pension funds in large Democratic states, a slew of liberal non-governmental organizations such as the climate change activist group As You Sow have dominated the public shareholder proposal submission process and have pressured both the companies in which they hold stock—and the institutional investors who hold stock alongside them—to pay heed to their policy demands. In recent years, conservative "anti-ESG" groups have ramped up their activist efforts, but these groups remain relatively marginal actors and more importantly promote a reactive form of activism that is focused on pushing back against climate change and gender diversity initiatives promoted by liberal activists, as opposed to offering an independent

---

REV. 57, 74–75 (2013) (finding that the strength and polarization of elite positions significantly influences broader public sentiment). This process generates a feedback loop by which investors approve of and even seek out mutual funds that espouse these same political preferences." "Asset Managers." 110, fn. 170.

[17] Webber, David H., Michal Barzuza & Quinn Curtis. 2020. "Shareholder Value(s): Index Fund ESG Activism and the New Millennial Corporate Governance." Southern California Law Review. Vol. 93. https://scholarship.law.bu.edu/faculty_scholarship/976.

[18] Ibid.

[19] University of Utah Law Professor Jeff Schwartz probes this dynamic in his paper "Stewardship Theater", in which Schwartz characterizes politics—as opposed to finance—as the animating force behind the voting behavior and corporate engagement practices of the large asset management firms. Schwartz, "Stewardship Theater".

affirmative conservative agenda.[20] Although it would be a stretch to characterize politics as the driving force behind how asset managers go about exerting their voice, it is probably fair to say that political activism helps reinforce advocacy among asset managers on environmental and social issues like climate change and board diversity that already command attention and support from their institutional clients.

Finally, the failure of ESG advocacy to challenge the traditional shareholder primacy model in the domain of procedural corporate governance issues (such as how a company's board of directors should be structured and the extent to which shareholders should be permitted to influence or drive corporate decision-making) can be understood as the product of the limitations and structural incentives inherent to large asset management firms. Asset management firms view themselves as shareholders. Even with their more open-minded conception of what it means to be a universal shareholder and how best to fulfill that role, these firms accept the premise of the traditional shareholder primacy model that corporations must heed the directives of their shareholders, and support shareholder primacy-grounded reforms to the governance machinery of corporations.

(3) Although the large asset management firms centralize much of the decision-making process relating to proxy voting and engagement in independent investment stewardship groups, they somewhat deviate from that approach with respect to matters that are traditionally economic in nature or have concrete financial implications, such as a company's business and financial strategy and special situations, like proxy contests or strategic transactions that require shareholder approval. At most firms, active fund portfolio managers have a greater role in decision-making on these topics. While the Big Three investment stewardship teams continue to retain formal authority to make decisions on economic issues, they more directly engage active portfolio managers in the underlying decision-making process. At other firms, decision-making authority is formally vested in (or shared with) the relevant portfolio managers. The voting recommendations of leading proxy advisory firms—like ISS and Glass Lewis—also figure more prominently in how the large asset managers decide to vote on economic topics, even as the large

---

[20] Conservative intellectual Julius Krein has written a number of essays examining the negative orientation of conservative social activism, particularly in the context of the broader relationship between conservatives and the business world. See, e.g., Krein, Julius. 2023. "What Do Conservative Donors Want?" The Giving Review. https://philanthropydaily.com/what-do-conservative-donors-want/; 2023. "Why the Right Can't Beat ESG." Compact Magazine. https://www.compactmag.com/article/why-the-right-can-t-beat-esg/; 2022. "The Poverty of Theory: Is There Such a Thing as American Conservatism?" TLS. https://www.the-tls.co.uk/politics-by-region/north-american-politics/the-right-matthew-continetti-book-review-julius-krein/.

asset management firms have otherwise decreased their reliance on proxy advisory firms in recent years. Many of the leading "repeat player" activist hedge funds—like Elliott and Icahn—have long-standing relationships with key decision-makers at the large asset managers whom they regularly lobby to support their positions on the gamut of economic and financial topics that motivate their activist efforts.

Again, the large asset management firms do not publicly explain why they structure their decision-making processes as they do, but a likely starting point is the nature and frequency of matters that come up in the proxy voting process. The overwhelming majority of proposals that come before shareholders for a vote in any given year involve non-operational and financial topics, such as procedural corporate governance matters (e.g., whether shareholders should be permitted to call special meetings or a corporate board should be "classified") or ESG topics that carry important business ramifications but which do not delve into company-specific business and operational matters. Subject to limited exceptions, the SEC allows companies to exclude from their proxy materials shareholder proposals that relate to a company's ordinary business operations. Most proposals submitted to shareholders involve recurring topics that do not ask shareholders to bring to bear extensive knowledge of the relevant company. Both shareholders and corporate management tend to frame their perspectives with respect to proposals on corporate governance practices by invoking generalized notions of governance best practices, often justified by reference to industry and academic studies. The same applies to ESG proposals. Much of the proxy voting process involves engaging with topics that have a legal and policy flavor, and the personnel that have come to staff these investment stewardship groups come from legal and policy backgrounds, whose experience and training often involve thinking about similar types of generalized, academic questions. The head of stewardship at Vanguard was a staffer in President Obama's administration. BlackRock's is run by a former senior official from the Bank of England.[21]

In this context, company-specific financial and other business developments draw less attention from investment stewardship teams in their day-to-day work. These issues surface in the proxy voting process far less often than governance and ESG items and require a level of familiarity with the businesses of individual companies that the predominantly legal and policy-trained professionals staffing investment stewardship groups do

---

[21] Schwartz, "Stewardship Theater." 420.

not possess. By contrast, active portfolio managers have direct career incentives in the financial performance of the companies in their portfolios—as investment professionals, their job is to drive financial returns—and are more in the weeds of evaluating the regular reports and public disclosures those companies put out about their businesses. Compared to investment stewardship team personnel, who are more comfortable thinking about abstract corporate governance topics, the active fund managers both have professional motivations and the temperamental disposition to want to directly shape decision-making on economic matters. In the case of the activist hedge funds that lobby the large asset management firms, the career incentives and temperamental tendencies are even greater. ISS and Glass Lewis issue detailed voting recommendations with respect to virtually all proxy contests or strategic transactions that come for a shareholder vote, providing investment stewardship teams with ready-made material to consult and draw from in developing a view on any given special situation.

The practical result is that, despite rhetoric among many large asset management firms that they seek to promote "long-term value creation" and the "long-term economic interests" of their investors, there is little evidence that this rhetoric has translated into any change in how the large asset management firms go about engaging corporations on economic and financial issues since the supposed heyday of shareholder primacy in the 1980s and 1990s. Active managers continue to confront the same—if not greater—pressure to maximize short-term financial returns that they faced before the rise of ESG. ISS and Glass Lewis maintain close ties to the activist hedge fund industry and generally push forward an aggressive "pro-shareholder" posture in contested votes pertaining to director elections and economic matters. The relationships that certain leading activist hedge funds have developed with the big asset management firms often provide them an important advantage in proxy fights over corporate executives and boards who generally lack similarly strong relationships. "If you are an activist your job is harder if you have to convince 25 to 30 big shareholders," in the words of one banker, "your job is made easier if you only have to convince four or five managers, especially if it is the same four or five individuals you know well and talk to on a regular basis."[22] Even the Big Three index funds—whose passive orientation and established independent stewardship teams should in theory make them less supportive of hedge fund activists—do not appear to be exempt from these pressures. As we described in Chapter 7, studies demonstrate a positive association between an increase in index fund ownership and successful

---

[22] Ronald Orol. 2017. "How Index Funds Could Turbocharge Activism." TheStreet. https://www.thestreet.com/markets/how-index-funds-could-turbocharge-activism-14229514.

hedge fund activism campaigns.[23] In the context of proxy fights, the voting record of the Big Three index funds does not substantially differ from that of other large asset management firms whose active holdings comprise a greater percentage of their investment portfolios. A review of the voting record of the top five shareholders in contested annual meetings from 2020 through 2023 shows that index funds voted for the activist shareholder 43% of the time, while "growth" and "value-focused" managers—like Fidelity, T. Rowe Price, Wellington and Dimensional Fund Advisors—voted for the dissident slate 53% of the time.[24] Index funds may in certain instances be less inclined to support activists, but it would be inaccurate to characterize their voting record as orders of magnitude different from that of the major institutional investors with more substantial active portfolios.

---

[23] Appel, Ian R., Todd A. Gormley, and Donald B. Keim. 2019. "Standing on the Shoulders of Giants: The Effect of Passive Investors on Activism." Review of Financial Studies. Vol. 32, no. 7: 2720–2774. https://academic.oup.com/rfs/article-abstract/32/7/2720/5106042.

[24] This analysis is based on the author's review of contested annual meeting results from 2020 through 2023 as reported by FactSet, the business data and analytics research provider. The analysis excludes all proxy contests (1) in which all top five shareholder data was not available as of May 8, 2024; (2) proxy contests involving closed-end funds; and (3) vote-no campaigns.

10

The Post-ESG World and a Roadmap for the Future

Over the past several years, the popularity of ESG has dissipated. ESG advocacy has generated significant criticism from conservative pundits and politicians who view it as Trojan Horse for the advancement of liberal political objectives. In the first nine months of 2023, investors pulled more than $14 billion from ESG funds, with the third quarter of 2023 representing the first time more sustainable funds liquidated or removed ESG criteria from their investment practices than were added.[1] On earnings calls, mentions of ESG have declined since 2021. In the fourth quarter of 2021, 155 companies in the S&P 500 referenced ESG initiatives. In the second quarter of 2023, there were only 61 mentions.[2] Even hitherto vocal ESG advocates in the asset management community have moderated their rhetoric. In December 2022, Vanguard announced its exit from the Net Zero Asset Managers initiative "to make clear that Vanguard speaks independently on matters of importance to our investors."[3] Larry Fink, who has been at the forefront of the investment management industry's promotion of ESG, has stated that he no longer uses the term. "I don't use the word ESG any more," Fink noted in a June

---

[1] Shifflett, Shane. 2023. "Wall Street's ESG Craze Is Fading." The Wall Street Journal. https://www.wsj.com/finance/investing/esg-branding-wall-street-0a487105.

[2] Cutter, Chip, and Emily Glazer. 2024. "The Latest Dirty Word in Corporate America: ESG." The Wall Street Journal. https://www.wsj.com/business/the-latest-dirty-word-in-corporate-america-esg-9c776003.

[3] Kerber, Ross and Noor Zainab Hussain. 2022. "Vanguard Quits Net Zero Climate Effort, Citing Need for Independence." Reuters. https://www.reuters.com/business/sustainable-business/vanguard-quits-net-zero-climate-alliance-2022-12-07/.

2023 interview, "because it's been entirely weaponized … by the far left and weaponized by the far right."[4]

The concerns that helped birth the ESG movement in the wake of the 2008 financial crisis do not appear to have been addressed in any substantive way. The pressures towards financial short-termism and myopic shareholder-centric thinking are stronger than ever. The number of activist hedge fund campaigns reached a new peak in 2023, with the total board seats won by activists increasing for the third consecutive year, up 13% globally year-over-year, and a record 31% of board seats won through proxy contests, well above the prior five-year historical average of 17%.[5] Share buybacks and dividends have risen.[6] The world seems to be even further behind in the battle against climate change, with greenhouse gas emissions from fossil fuels reaching new heights in 2023.[7] Despite the progress made in enhancing director diversity over the last few decades, there is scant evidence that those measures have improved gender or race relations outside the rarified confines of the executive boardroom.

These failures call for a reassessment of the ESG paradigm, and a fresh perspective towards the essential challenges endemic to our system of institutional investor capitalism and how best to overcome them.

A Return to Shareholder Primacy?

With advocates of the ESG-based stakeholder model finding themselves on the defensive, there have been efforts, principally among political conservatives, to push the rewind button back to the 1980s and to resuscitate the spirit of Milton Friedman by "banning" ESG and requiring institutional investors to focus on maximizing financial returns without regard to environmental,

---

[4] Binnie, Isla. 2023. "BlackRock's Fink Says He's Stopped Using 'Weaponised' Term ESG." Reuters. https://www.reuters.com/business/environment/blackrocks-fink-says-hes-stopped-using-weaponised-term-esg-2023-06-26/.

[5] Lazard. 2024. "Annual Review of Shareholder Activism 2023." Lazard. https://www.lazard.com/research-insights/annual-review-of-shareholder-activism-2023/.

[6] Janus Henderson. 2023. "Global Share Buybacks Surge to a Record $1.31 Trillion Almost Equalling Dividends." Janus Henderson Group. https://www.janushenderson.com/en-us/advisor/press-releases/global-share-buybacks-surge-to-a-record-1-31-trillion-almost-equalling-dividends/; Pisani, Bob. 2024. "Good News, Bad News. Record Dividends Paid to Investors in 2023, But Buybacks Plunged." CNBC. https://www.cnbc.com/2024/01/04/good-news-bad-news-record-dividends-paid-to-investors-in-2023-but-buybacks-plunged.html.

[7] NOAA, "Record Emissions"; Jackson, "Emissions Record.".

social or other non-economic factors.[8] These efforts are ill-advised and counterproductive. The decisive lesson of the American experiment in Chicago School economics is that a single-minded fixation on short-term financial returns hurts companies and society as a whole. The idea that government can counterbalance the excesses of a stockholder value-focused regime of corporate law and governance simply through other regulatory mechanisms that manage the effects of corporate behavior ignores the basic reality that corporations can act to influence the political process as independent actors and that, in an economic system in which corporations are pushed to do whatever it takes to maximize returns to their institutional investors, the political process itself will likely be distorted to overemphasize the interests of institutional shareholders at the expense of other stakeholders.[9]

For those who view the traditional ideology of shareholder value maximization as a purer intellectual framework for ordering corporate behavior than ESG, it is important to underscore the inherently symbiotic relationship between these two philosophical frameworks. In the same way some ESG activists fail to recognize the extent to which their conception of stakeholder capitalism is defined by reference to shareholder primacy, those calling for a return to the tenets of shareholder primacy fail to appreciate that ESG is itself a product of the shareholder primacy paradigm. As conservative intellectual Julius Krein has noted, regulatory efforts to quash ESG would likely entail more, rather than less, government micromanagement of corporate behavior.[10] ESG activism on climate change has had its shortcomings, but that does not alter the fact that "major environmental catastrophes are generally bad for business and represent a risk to shareholders." While one can debate the merits of whether racial or gender diversity is an appropriate hiring criterion for a job that requires specific technical knowhow and experience, an entertainment or other consumer-facing company "can easily make a prima facie case that its management should reflect the demographics of its target audience, to better understand and serve its customers." ESG prohibitions

---

[8] In its 2023 resolution prohibiting the consideration of ESG factors in investing decisions, the Florida legislature directed state funds to make investments "based solely on pecuniary factors." (h0003er.docx (flsenate.gov)) In the same vein, in August 2022, 19 Republican state attorneys general attacked BlackRock's embrace of ESG principles in a public letter on the basis that in pushing forward an ESG agenda BlackRock was using "the hard-earned money of our states' citizens to circumvent the best possible return on investment (emphasis added)." Fink, Larry. 2022. "Blackrock Letter." Texas Attorney General. https://www.texasattorneygeneral.gov/sites/default/files/images/executive-management/BlackRock%20Letter.pdf.

[9] Strine addresses this particular argument of shareholder primacy evangelists in depth in "Stakeholder Capitalism's Greatest Challenge." 340.

[10] Krein, Julius. 2023. 'Why the Right Can't Beat ESG." Compact Magazine. https://www.compactmag.com/article/why-the-right-can-t-beat-esg/.

would necessarily require an affirmative effort by policymakers to differentiate between environmental and social factors that are and are not appropriate for companies and investors to consider as risks to shareholder value. Such efforts would increase costs to companies and investors, running counter to the central presupposition of shareholder primacy that business executives and investment managers should prioritize the maximization of financial returns. One 2022 study estimated that anti-ESG legislation in Texas could cost taxpayers up to $532 million in higher interest costs within a year by limiting the available menu of borrowing options for municipalities and other government entities. Another study projected that an Indiana bill to limit ESG investing could cut state pension returns by $6.7 billion over the next ten years. In March 2023, the Arkansas Public Employees Retirement System estimated that it could lose $30 million to $40 million a year in potential investment returns due to a similar law. The economics consultancy firm ESI conducted an expansive analysis of anti-ESG legislation in six states—Kentucky, Florida, Louisiana, Oklahoma, West Virginia, and Missouri—and concluded that taxpayers could be on the hook for up to $700 million in excess interest payments in the event restrictions on sustainable investing were implemented.[11]

The idealized conception of the undiversified individual shareholder that propels a lot of mainstream discourse about shareholder value no longer makes sense in today's world (putting aside the question of whether it ever made much sense). Asset managers today deploy a gamut of investing strategies where it is not sensible to make voting decisions based on an intensive company-by-company analysis. The prototypical investor in the first half of the twentieth century might have poured over the financial news to obtain the latest updates about the companies in which he or she had invested, but an investor in an index fund that tracks the performance of a particular market index, like the S&P 500 or the Dow Jones Industrial Average, will have little reason to closely monitor the performance of the individual companies comprising the index. It is challenging to come up with a meaningful conception of shareholder value as a rubric for making investing and voting decisions in connection with algorithmic strategies that generate returns from trends in market data and other technical factors unrelated to a company's fundamental performance. These complexities are aggravated in the context of today's large diversified asset management firms whose very structure undermines conventional notions of shareholder value.

---

[11] Frosh, Brian and Nancy Kopp. 2023. "Anti-ESG Politicians Cost Their States and Cities Billions." Bloomberg. https://www.bloomberg.com/opinion/articles/2023-07-25/anti-esg-politicians-cost-their-states-and-cities-billions.

Conversely, it is undeniable that ESG has created political blowback, undermined trust in corporate America, and enjoyed limited success in addressing the environmental and social concerns that are the focus of the movement. Attempting to restore a 1980s/1990s-style ethos of shareholder idolatry may not be the answer to today's crisis of confidence, but neither is doubling down on ESG in its current manifestation nor trying to dress up the ESG agenda under another label without facing up to the forces and structural limitations that have been responsible for its shortcomings. The public discourse would be served by a degree of humility and open-mindedness on the part of those who have been at the forefront of the ESG movement—both in terms of revisiting long-standing foundational assumptions about corporate governance that continue to inform their thinking, as well as acknowledging the extent to which their more generalized left-of-center sensibilities have shaped the substantive scope of the ESG agenda in a country whose population espouses a diversity of political opinions.

The reality that both critics and supporters of ESG must confront is that important aspects of what they find troubling in the business world and the financial markets are driven by the same root cause: the rise of asset managers as the dominant shareholders of America's corporations, and the concomitant increase in control asset managers have accumulated over corporate America. Legal and policy measures have played just as, if not a more, significant role in empowering asset managers to amass this level of influence as broader economic and technological factors. Today's configuration of relationships among corporations, institutional investors, and the ultimate providers of capital to those institutional investors is not an organic market phenomenon but instead reflects specific political decisions, and any serious effort to improve the status quo must begin with a recognition of this essential fact.

Policy Solutions

In thinking about potential reforms, it is worthwhile to stipulate an outline of first principles that should be embodied in an ideal system. One principle is accountability. Can the regular people and small businesses who represent the "flesh and blood" providers of capital to the asset management industry (borrowing from former Delaware Supreme Court Chief Justice Leo Strine's turn of phrase) effectively hold investment intermediaries to account in how they exercise the power and control associated with that capital? Accountability has a legal dimension (whether or not the providers of capital have the legal right to direct and check the behavior of institutional investors who hold custody of capital) as well as a practical dimension (whether or not the capital providers can reasonably be expected to exercise that right given the costs, benefits, and other practical considerations involved in doing so). By analogy, harkening back to Berle's analysis of the trust model of corporate law, an individual retail shareholder may have the legal ability to sue a corporate board of directors in the event of a breach of fiduciary duties, but for most individual shareholders other than the very wealthy the ordeal of pursuing a lawsuit would be prohibitively expensive, rendering it an unattractive remedy.

Another principle, especially in a system where complete accountability cannot be guaranteed, is responsiveness. Are asset managers adequately able to address the interests of their ultimate providers of capital? Responsiveness must be assessed holistically in light of all of the interests a capital provider may have with respect to a relevant matter. An employee who indirectly owns stock in a wide swath of public companies through his or her 401(k) or pension plan is not investing in a single company, but the broader economy. Those interests extend beyond the capital provider's standing as an investor in any given company. Lower- and mid-level employees who own stock in their employer may enjoy an immediate economic return on their equity holdings in the event their employer pursues a dividend or sale transaction to a third party, but it is unlikely that for most employees that return would be sufficient recompense to the extent it is financed through cost reductions that entail the termination of those employees' jobs from which they derive the bulk of their wealth and income.

Finally, it is critical to examine the bigger costs and benefits involved in pursuing any path towards reform. In economics parlance, what are the externalities of any particular configuration of rights and responsibilities that cannot be appropriately factored by focusing exclusively on the relationship between institutional investor intermediaries and their providers of capital? Corporations are social institutions, and any examination of corporate-investor relations must take into account the societal context in which those corporations and investors operate.

Pass-Through Voting

One seemingly simple change would be to implement a pass-through system in which voting power is passed from the investment manager intermediaries who are the legal owners of a company's shares to the providers of capital. Under a pure pass-through system, there should be no accountability problem given that the capital providers would have the authority to directly make voting decisions with respect to the shares in which their capital has been invested. For years, numerous academics have advocated for pass-through voting on these grounds.[12] More recently, pass-through voting has found support among anti-ESG conservatives who view it as a mechanism to dilute the power of the Big Three index funds and their influence as pro-ESG activists. In May 2022, Senate Republicans introduced the "Investor Democracy Is Expected Act," or the Index Act, which would have required passive investment fund managers that own more than 1% of a public company to collect instructions from their clients on how to vote their shares.[13] In response, asset management firms, including BlackRock and Vanguard, began to voluntarily expand pass-through voting to a wider menu of their investment offerings.[14]

The elegance of pass-through voting as a viable policy solution quickly falls apart after closer examination. As a threshold matter, it is questionable whether such a system can even be implemented in a complete form. Presumably, an asset management firm should be able to identify direct individual investors in its products with relative ease, but that exercise becomes more challenging when the investor is another institutional intermediary, like a pension fund, such that at least two layers of institutional ownership have to be pierced to reach the ultimate human provider of capital. Complex and costly steps would have to be undertaken to ensure appropriate coordination between investment intermediaries to identify and verify the number of shares indirectly held by the capital provider; to sort out different positions for different securities held within the fund's portfolio; to provide timely communications about the issues subject to the companies' proxies, including passing along corporate proxy materials; and to track and tabulate shareholder

---

[12] See, e.g., Stewart, Georgia. 2023. "How to Restore Shareholder Agency with Pass-Through Voting." CLS Blue Sky Blog. https://clsbluesky.law.columbia.edu/2023/08/11/how-to-restore-shareholder-agency-with-pass-through-voting/?amp=1; Lund, Dorothy Shapiro. 2018. "The Case against Passive Shareholder Voting." The Journal of Corporation Law. Vol. 43. https://chicagounbound.uchicago.edu/cgi/viewcontent.cgi?article=13741&context=journal_articles; Fisch, Jill E. 2021. "Mutual Fund Stewardship and the Empty Voting Problem." 16 BROOK. J. CORP FIN. & COM. L. Vol. 71. 90–92; Griffin, Caleb. 2020. "We Three Kings: Disintermediating Voting at the Index Fund Giants." 79 MD. L. REV. 954, 983; Griffith, Sean. 2020. "Opt-In Stewardship: Toward an Optimal Delegation of Mutual Fund Voting Authority." 98 TEX. L. REV. 983, 990; Weil, Dick. 2018. "Passive Investors, Don't Vote, WALL ST. J." https://www.wsj.com/articles/passive-investors-dont-vote-1520552657.

[13] Ramaswamy, Vivek and Riley Moore. 2022. "The Market Can Curtail Woke Fund Managers." Strive. https://www.strive.com/article/the_market_can_curtail_woke_fund_managers.

[14] Human, Tim. 2023. "BlackRock Expands Voting Choice Service to Largest ETF." IR Magazine. https://www.irmagazine.com/investor-perspectives/blackrock-expands-voting-choice-service-largest-etf.; Vanguard. 2023. "Vanguard to Expand Proxy Voting Choice to Additional Funds in 2024." Corporate Statement. https://corporate.vanguard.com/content/corporatesite/us/en/corp/articles/expanding-proxy-voting-choice.html.

feedback.[15] Quantitative analyses of the additional costs that would result from trying to operationalize a pass-through regime are difficult to come by, but one 2006 Investment Company Institute study that examined the costs associated with implementing a New York Stock Exchange proposal to bar brokers from voting proxies in director elections estimated that this one change alone would double the cost of a typical proxy.[16] Unsurprisingly, the major asset management firms that have voluntarily implemented pass-through programs have limited those programs to apply to a restricted universe of funds, with what frequently appears to be just a single layer of pass-through voting (leading to the same overrepresentation of key fund client views and preferences we described in Chapter 9).

Even if it were possible to overcome these challenges in an economically sensible way, a pure pass-through system would create other problems. While pass-through voting would provide for accountability in a technical sense, that accountability would have little real-world import. The vast majority of people lack the fluency in financial and business matters to make informed voting decisions. Even those who do are unlikely to have enough time and resources at hand to make educated decisions across the variety of companies in their diversified investment portfolios. An individual investor in Vanguard's total stock market index fund would have to cast tens of thousands of votes each spring for the stocks held in that fund alone.[17] A pure pass-through system would reprise the "separation of ownership and control" that characterized the relationship between corporations and shareholders in the early part of the twentieth century, where the existence of a dispersed shareholder base imposed collective action challenges that considerably diminished the practical effectiveness of the shareholder vote as a check on the behavior of corporate management.

Imposing a pass-through voting program across the board today would require prohibiting individuals and businesses from delegating the power to make proxy voting decisions to investment advisors. This feels like an unfair and economically suboptimal outcome for those who would rather not be bothered with the task of sifting through any given year's array of shareholder proposals. If society is prepared to accept the right of individuals and institutions to entrust an investment advisor to make investing decisions on their behalf, why should they not be permitted to delegate the right to cast votes as investors?

---

[15] Stevens, Paul Schott. 2018. "SEC Should Reject Complex, Costly 'Pass-Through' Proxy Voting." Investment Company Institute. https://www.ici.org/viewpoints/view_18_passthrough_voting.
[16] Ibid.
[17] Ramaswamy, "Woke Fund Managers.".

Consequently, many advocates of pass-through voting support pass-through voting in an incomplete form, either as a default that only applies to indexed or other passively managed funds (as proposed in the Index Act) or to investors who do not affirmatively elect to delegate the authority to make proxy voting decisions to an investment advisor. If implemented at scale, either of these approaches would have the likely result of amplifying the influence of actors that specifically seek to change the corporate strategy of their portfolio companies. Historically, retail shareholders tend to not participate in shareholder voting, often because they lack the time, resources, and interest to go through the exercise of casting a proxy vote. Prescribing pass-through voting as the default standard would mean that the wider population that supplies the substantial majority of capital to the asset management industry would functionally have no voice in the proxy voting process. Some academics have argued in favor of this outcome based on the view that incomplete pass-through voting would result in more "informed" shareholder voting, but the practical impact would be to magnify the voice of self-interested actors, like activist hedge funds, that have short-term incentives and financial motivations that differ from the diversified and longer-term orientation of the investing public. Since most corporate actions that are the subject of a shareholder vote turn on receiving the support of a majority or plurality of the votes present at a shareholder meeting (as opposed to the total shares outstanding), at many companies incomplete pass-through voting could result in an activist hedge fund exercising effective voting control.

Many of the challenges that afflict pass-through voting are relevant to other policy proposals aimed at curtailing the voting power of asset managers. Efforts to require asset managers to more closely tie voting to the preferences of their fund investors—such as by requiring asset managers to consult with or poll their fund investors—pose similar administrative and logistical complexities, with respect to how to engage the real-world capital providers investing through institutional intermediaries like pension funds that are the asset manager's direct clients.[18] Scaling back regulations that encourage institutional investors to vote their shares risks creating an unlevel playing field between, on the one hand, the substantial amount of public capital that is

---

[18] Coates, *The Problem of 12*. 138 (noting that investment advisors could be required to engage regularly with their investors in some structure); Schwartz, "Stewardship Theater." 400 (proposing that "asset managers should be required to poll investors on principles and to reflect these principles in their voting."). See also Fisch, Jill E. and Jeff Schwartz. 2023. "Corporate Democracy and the Intermediary Voting Dilemma." U of Penn, Inst for Law & Econ Research Paper No. 23–06, Texas Law Review, Forthcoming, University of Utah College of Law Research Paper No. 536, European Corporate Governance Institute—Law Working Paper No. 685/2023, Available at SSRN: https://ssrn.com/abstract=4360428.

invested through passive index fund providers and other large asset managers (who may be reluctant to exercise their voting power in the absence of regulation) and, on the other hand, activist hedge funds and other short-term actors that have greater motivation to participate in the proxy voting process.[19]

In light of the unworkability of pass-through voting and other similarly spirited policy measures, consideration must be given to other avenues of reform that accept the role of asset managers as corporate shareholders.[20]

Antitrust Solutions

A number of scholars have suggested antitrust solutions targeted at curbing the growing power of large asset managers, including introducing common ownership limitations to prevent the accumulation of large equity stakes in particular companies or concentrated industries.[21] These policies may help decrease the outsized influence wielded by the largest asset managers, but they would not address the essential accountability and responsiveness problems afflicting our current system. There is no evidence to believe that the internal institutional factors that drive antisocial behaviors among asset managers will change as a result of decreasing the ownership concentration of individual firms. In place of a world where a handful of institutional investors exercise control over America's corporations, such proposals would do nothing

---

[19] Fisch, "Mutual Fund Stewardship and the Empty Voting Problem." 93 (suggesting that a "more moderate reform would involve scaling down the existing regulations that force or pressure institutional investors to vote the shares of their portfolio companies.").

[20] Another "market-based solution" that has drawn attention is that of encouraging individuals to sell their proxy voting rights in the open market. In early 2024, a number of financial media outlets, including *The Wall Street Journal*, reported on the growing popularity of Shareholder Vote Exchange, a small California-based start-up that ran auctions for voting rights in shareholder meetings. The company shut down a few months later and ultimately enjoyed limited success in scaling its business model. Shareholder Vote Exchange's business targeted direct shareholders, as opposed to individuals who indirectly held stock through 401(k) and other institutional investment products, in connection with which voting rights are delegated by contract to an investment advisor. Nevertheless, if there were a mechanism for allowing investment plan participants to detach and sell their indirect voting rights, the practice would pose many of the same potential adverse social consequences flowing from the implementation of a pass-through system. In particular, both schemes would run the risk of encouraging the aggregation of voting power in activists and others that may have short-term incentives and financial motivations that differ from the diversified and longer-term orientation of the investing public. Osipovich, Alexander. 2024. "Votes for Sale! A Startup Is Letting Shareholders Sell Their Proxies." The Wall Street Journal. https://www.wsj.com/finance/stocks/buy-my-vote-a-startup-is-letting-shareholders-sell-their-proxies-122f0eb9.

[21] Posner, Eric A., Fiona M. Scott Morton, and E. Glen Weyl. 2016. "A Proposal to Limit the Anti-Competitive Power of Institutional Investors." Antitrust Law Journal. https://papers.ssrn.com/sol3/papers.cfm?abstract_id=2872754; Elhauge, Einer. 2016. "Horizontal Shareholding," 129 HARV. L. REV. 1267, 1301; Goshen, Zohar and Doron Levit. 2021. "Common Ownership and the Decline of the American Worker." (Eur. Corp. Governance Inst., Working Paper No. 584/2021) 49–58.

more than spread that power to a wider group of relatively smaller asset management firms. There would also be considerable expenses and operational hurdles associated with implementing concentration limits, which would likely be passed on to consumers and detract from the immense financial benefits that passive investing products have conferred on the wider public. Investment limits would diminish the ability of asset managers to diversify client and fund portfolios, and industry-specific limitations would be difficult to define in light of the diversity of business lines any given company may pursue through its corporate life.[22]

Disclosures

Given our disclosure-driven regulatory regime for public markets, disclosures are a common "go-to" policy lever for academics and policymakers, many of whom have proposed enhanced disclosure obligations on the part of institutional investors. These include proposals that institutional investors like index funds be required to report their voting practices on a more frequent basis (currently, the requirement is only annual) and provide detailed disclosure concerning how they go about voting fund shares.[23] There have also been proposals that activist hedge funds disclose their ownership stakes in companies on a more accelerated timeline, along with a wider range of economic and legal arrangements that may be relevant to the fund's interests in its portfolio companies.[24] On October 10, 2023, the SEC amended the rules governing beneficial ownership reporting under Section 13(d) of the Securities Exchange Act of 1934, which imposes reporting obligations on activist funds when they acquire more than 5% of a voting class of a company's equity, by accelerating the filing deadlines for initial and amended Schedules 13D and 13G beneficial ownership reports and clarifying that a person is required to disclose interests in all derivative securities (including

---

[22] BlackRock. 2017. "Index Investing and Common Ownership Theories." Yale Law School Center for the Study of Corporate Law. https://ccl.yale.edu/sites/default/files/viewpoint-index-investing-and-common-ownership-theories-eng-march.pdf.
[23] Coates, Problem of 12. 135–140.
[24] See, e.g., Strine, Leo. 2019. "Toward Fair and Sustainable Capitalism." Constance Milstein and Family Global Academic Center at NYU. https://www.law.nyu.edu/sites/default/files/Fair%20and%20Sustainable%20Capitalism%20Proposal%20-%20White%20Paper_09.26.19%20FINAL.pdf; Strine, Leo. 2020. "The Centrality of Institutional Investor Regulation to Restoring a Fair and Sustainable American Economy (U of Penn, Inst for Law & Econ Research Paper No. 20–55, Columbia Law and Economics Working Paper No. 633), Available at SSRN: https://ssrn.com/abstract=3719145 or http://dx.doi.org/10.2139/ssrn.3719145.

securities-based swaps) that use the issuer's equity security as a reference security.[25]

Enhanced disclosures have social value in the basic sense that they provide for greater transparency. They also impose costs on the disclosing parties who must expend time and resources to track the relevant information and create and disseminate the disclosures, increasing the risk of potential "information overload" for readers given the extensive information investment advisors and other SEC registrants are already required to publicly divulge. It is imperative then to determine whether or not any new proposed disclosure can be expected to be meaningful to its intended audience. By way of example, recall Berle's characterization of the value of mandatory corporate disclosures in *The Modern Corporation*. According to Berle, such disclosures were not beneficial solely by virtue of the fact that they afforded the public greater visibility into the conduct of big corporations, but because they were a prerequisite to the ability of individual shareholders to make informed and timely decisions as to whether to buy, hold, or sell securities in a world where they lacked alternative means to effectively check corporate management.

Through this lens, the overall value of heightened disclosures by institutional investors is debatable. While mandatory corporate disclosures are intended to assist shareholders in formulating investment decisions, it is hard to imagine a fund investor altering its investment decisions based on additional disclosures pertaining to institutional investor voting behavior or other corporate engagement activities. The typical real-world person whose equity holdings are limited to retirement funds parked in a 401(k) account or pension is almost certainly not going to pay close enough attention to notice the additional disclosures. Even if he or she does notice the disclosures and is able to understand their import (which is doubtful), it is difficult to envision the supplemental information being of sufficient significance that most regular people would go out of their way to modify their retirement plans, assuming they have the ability to do so. At the very least, it would be a hassle to effect a modification given how company-sponsored retirement

---

[25] Levi, Scott, Danielle Herrick and Russell Deutsch. 2023. "SEC Adopts Rule Amendments to Modernize Beneficial Ownership Reporting." White & Case LLP. https://www.whitecase.com/insight-alert/sec-adopts-rule-amendments-modernize-beneficial-ownership-reporting.

plans tend to be configured.[26] Fund investors who are investment intermediaries may be more inclined to review disclosures and take action, but again, the question arises as to the likelihood that those disclosures will motivate a change in investment strategy. The trustees of a pension fund investing in an activist hedge fund possess ample financial sophistication to understand that activist hedge funds pursue short-term strategies to drive their returns and probably decide to invest because of the hope to participate in those returns, irrespective of the broader adverse social consequences that flow from the pursuit of hedge fund activism. Would it then be reasonable to expect that the pension fund will try to alter its relationship with, or modify the behavior of, the hedge fund because of what it may learn from additional disclosures? The Big Three index funds and the other large asset management firms are currently required to disclose their voting policies and procedures, including their voting records for each calendar year. The data that they have provided has been enough to stir up an active and vibrant debate about ESG and the role of institutional investors as social activists. Would more detailed or timely disclosures really add anything meaningful to the existing mix of information?

Additional disclosure requirements can provide value in other ways. In the case of activist hedge funds, even if enhanced or accelerated disclosure obligations are not of much interest to underlying fund investors, they do make it incrementally more difficult for activist hedge funds to mount pressure campaigns and so theoretically should decrease the probability that companies will be subjected to the ravages of hedge fund activism. Because of the SEC's October 2023 amendments, it is now costlier for activist hedge funds to build their equity positions before having to go public (given the shorter disclosure deadlines); activist hedge funds have less flexibility to take advantage of derivative instruments to evade Schedule 13D reporting; and there is greater risk that activist hedge funds will be deemed to be acting as a "group" with third-party supporters, subjecting activist hedge funds to more expansive potential liability exposure under the securities laws.[27]

Despite these potential benefits, there is little reason to anticipate that in the grand scheme of things the impact of measures like the SEC's October 2023 amendments will be anything other than marginal. Mounting a pressure

---

[26] For example, 401(k) plans generally offer many different types of funds, but do not offer competing funds of the same type, making it unfeasible for 401(k) investors to simply move to a similar fund with a better return. See Pool, Veronika K., Clemens Sialm and Irina Stefanescu. 2016. "It Pays to Set the Menu: Mutual Fund Investment Options in 401(k) Plans." 71 J. FIN. 1779, 1788 ("[A]ffiliated funds are more likely to be more basic investment options (such as standard domestic equity funds or passively managed index funds), whereas unaffiliated funds are more likely to be specialized funds (such as international or sector funds)."). See also Schwartz, "Stewardship Theater." 417.

[27] Ibid.

campaign may become costlier, but there is no evidence that these added costs will materially reduce the returns activist investors hope to generate from their campaigns or otherwise reduce the incentive to engage in activism to a degree that these funds will end up running fewer campaigns. A company that has a frustrated institutional investor base will still find itself vulnerable to an activist attack. In the time that has passed since the implementation of the October 2023 amendments, the number of activist hedge fund campaigns has exceeded the number of campaigns carried out during the equivalent period of time in the preceding year.

A New Stewardship Framework

What proponents of policy solutions like pass-through voting, ownership concentration limits, and expanded disclosures share is a failure to recognize that how the relationship between the corporation and its shareholders is constituted shapes how companies are run, which is in and of itself a question of paramount social importance. A brief recap of the evolution of the corporate form and the nature of equity investing is edifying in this respect.

Corporate status is nothing more than a package of legal rights conferred by the state to one or more human beings in connection with the formation of a business. In granting that status, the state implicitly makes a judgment that the operation of the relevant business has sufficient social worthiness as to warrant the privileges and protections associated with being a corporation. Before the widespread adoption of general incorporation laws, states would only grant corporate status to businesses they expressly deemed had social value, with legislators actively molding the organizational documents of each corporation on a case-by-case basis to reflect the economic and governance arrangements they believed best served the public good and balanced the interests of the corporation's various stakeholders. By the end of the nineteenth century, most states in the United States had scrapped this approach and adopted general incorporation laws. But the passage of those laws itself reflected a determination that it was socially beneficial to facilitate the growth of businesses—particularly capital-intensive enterprises in a then rapidly industrializing America—by flexibly providing grants of corporate status so that more entrepreneurs could enjoy the benefits of limited liability together with wider discretion in managing their businesses. Both before and after general incorporation, corporations also operated subject to an extensive collection of laws intended to regulate their behavior for the benefit of particular constituencies, like workers and consumers, and the government and/or the protected classes could directly enforce compliance with those laws by taking legal action against the corporation. The emergence of the administrative state in the early twentieth century ushered in the rise of independent federal and state agencies as another mechanism for regulating corporate behavior.

Shareholders had the right to take legal action against the corporation and its directors and officers in the event the latter breached the terms of the corporation's organizational documents or violated the corporate law. This right was merely a safeguard to protect against egregious instances of misconduct—so egregious as to be illegal—and not a means to affirmatively shape business strategy. Shareholders could as a group decide to change the composition of a corporation's board of directors, but in practice, this was a defensive measure taken in response to executive mismanagement, and in light of the dispersed nature of the shareholder base, required a high bar of misconduct in order to overcome the collective action challenges of garnering the necessary level of shareholder support. The prototypical shareholder would make the decision to invest in a company because he or she fundamentally believed in the strategic vision of the company and with the hope of participating in the financial returns generated by the company as it executed its long-term vision.

As a contractual arrangement, corporate equity is a valuable instrument to both the issuer and the investor. A company can forego the periodic interest expense payments associated with shouldering debt, and shift the risk of an insolvency event onto the investor who has no recourse to the assets of the corporation if the business fails to succeed. In exchange, the investor has the right to share in the profits and value appreciation of the company—unlike a lender that is only entitled to receive a fixed payment of interest and principal—and enjoys certain protections under the law and the company's organizational documents, including the right to elect and remove directors. There have been, and continue to be, variations in certain aspects of this arrangement, but the basic construct has remained unchanged through American history, and has played a vital role in marshaling capital to entrepreneurs and facilitating the growth of the overall economy. Care and caution are warranted before inviting lawmakers to tinker too significantly with the essential contours of this arrangement.

Nevertheless, over the last half century, the political economy of capitalism has evolved in profound ways that have transformed the constellation of relationships that define the corporation and how corporate businesses are managed. Today, most capital that is invested in corporations is channeled through institutional vehicles, and in that process, the concept of equity investing has changed. The emergence of 401(k) accounts and other equity-based retirement plans sponsored by institutional investors has resulted in a dramatic increase in participation in the public equity markets among regular working individuals. Equity investing is no longer the province of a limited class of affluent individuals whose wealth largely consists of their investments, but a savings conduit for a wide swath of the general population whose economic interests outside of their role as investors are often more important to them than the interests signified by their equity investments (*e.g.*, as employees reliant on wages to pay the bills, consumers sensitive to fluctuations in the prices of goods, etc.). A considerable amount of this capital is invested on a diversified basis, such that it is more appropriate to view the typical investor as an investor in the overall economy rather than a single company or assortment of companies that have no connection whatsoever with one another.

In intermediating this flow of capital from the public to corporate America, institutional investors have emerged as the controlling shareholders of the vast majority of America's public companies. Unlike the prototypical Berlean investor, the largest asset managers—who are the custodians of the bulk of this capital and whose actions substantially drive shareholder voting outcomes—represent truly universal owners, and the ability to assert voice as an investor has emerged as their only practical lever of influence. These firms centralize the authority to engage with individual companies and make voting decisions in governance units that act on behalf of the entire fund complex with respect to any given corporate matter. A litany of incentives and other limitations have shaped the way this power is exerted, which has not fully caught up with the more essential changes in how public capital is sourced and the nature of the various interests of the providers of that capital. With the centralization of the voting decision-making process at the world's largest asset managers, it is incontrovertible that shareholder voting is no longer a straightforward investment exercise based on a bottom-ups analysis of a limited universe of companies. A separation of ownership from ownership has emerged, but perhaps more importantly, that separation has birthed a new conception of voting and control that is disconnected from traditional notions of investing. Efforts to describe the voting behavior of the large asset managers by reference to "systematic" risk or other diversified investing concepts may seem more appropriate than the traditional model of the individual undiversified investor, but even these updated investment frameworks have limited explanatory capacity for the reasons laid out in Chapter 9. The exercise of shareholder voice has in all practical respects assumed the form of a regulatory power, carried out on the basis of a generalized view of what

10 The Post-ESG World and a Roadmap for the Future   147

is "good" for corporate America as a whole, and then applied to America's public companies across the board.

The question becomes as follows: Given the reality of how today's asset management firms exert influence in our public markets, what is the most appropriate framework within which to describe that reality and then to theorize how that influence *should be* exerted? Rather than try to shoehorn our understanding of asset manager power into a stylized investment decision-making framework that does not reflect the reality of how that power is exercised, why not take it for what it is and react accordingly? Now that this power has transmogrified into a political power, is it sensible to attempt to undo that transmogrification with all the attendant costs that may come from that exercise? Or should we start our examination with a frank recognition of the state of the world as it is today?

11

A New Stewardship Framework

Two important observations can be drawn from accepting the reality of how asset managers go about wielding their influence as shareholders, the assortment of factors that mold their behavior, and the nature of the interests at stake.

First, it is not self-evident that the power vested in the hands of the largest asset management firms should be exclusively conceived of as a prerogative of institutions acting in their narrow capacity as shareholders or investment intermediaries. Instead, this power, which flows from the role of asset managers as custodians of *public capital*, should be forthrightly thought of as a political power, and the question of how and to what ends this power should be exercised ought to be examined as part of an open discussion about the type of economy and society we wish to live in, taking into account the wide variety of considerations informing any discussion on matters of public interest.

Second, the core premise of our democratic system is that political questions ought to be settled in one form or another by the general public. Today, that democratic system includes administrative agencies that carry responsibility for promulgating, enforcing, and adjudicating regulations pertaining to particular policy areas, but those agencies are overseen by individuals and institutions that are subject to direct democratic accountability. There is no reason why the question of how asset management firms in corporate America should exert influence, with all the interests and concerns implicated by that question, should not be made subject to some form of the same democratic processes.

Taking these observations to their logical conclusion would suggest that government should have a greater role in regulating the proxy voting power of large asset management firms. The most heavy-handed form of regulation would be to entrust the government with the power to decide how the votes associated with the shareholdings of the large asset managers are cast.[1] A department could be established within a federal agency—like the SEC and/or the Department of Labor—that would operate like an investment stewardship group within one of the large asset management firms. The department could promulgate a general set of voting principles and standards to guide its decision-making processes and utilize notice-and-comment rulemaking procedures to solicit public input as it formulates those rules. In turn, the department would make voting decisions based on a case-by-case application of the principles and standards to the specific facts and circumstances relevant to any given situation. Following any voting determination, certain stakeholders—company management, shareholders, employees—could be permitted to request that the agency explain its rationale for any particular voting decision, which the agency would be required to publicly release in order to add an additional layer of public oversight.

At first glance, it may seem that this type of direct regulation would necessitate a radical expansion of the federal bureaucracy. This need not be the case. There are existing federal agencies that could fill this role. The SEC is the agency most naturally suited to define voting policy given its mandate to regulate securities markets and its staff's experience with and knowledge of corporate and securities law matters. The Department of Labor could also play a part given its status as the primary enforcer of the Employee Retirement Income Security Act of 1974 (ERISA), which establishes minimum standards for pension plans in private industry, including the standards that govern how investment managers exercise the voting rights associated with any pension plan assets that they manage. Of course, additional investments would have to be made to ensure that the relevant agencies are equipped to take on the new mandate, but there is no reason to think that such outlays would be in the realm of the extraordinary. For example, assuming conservatively that the SEC could not dedicate any existing staff to administer the voting decision-making function, and that each new employee onboarded by the agency could on average oversee no more than, say, ten companies, that would imply a required increase of less than four hundred new employees

---

[1] Much of the analysis below draws from the author's article for American Affairs entitled "The New Power Brokers: Index Funds and the Public Interest", published in 2020: https://americanaffairsjournal.org/2020/11/the-new-power-brokers-index-funds-and-the-public-interest/.

based on the current number of U.S. public companies. This would amount to less than a ten percent increase in the SEC's current staffing levels while also representing over eight times the number of employees that the largest index fund firm in the world, BlackRock, currently has dedicated to stewardship activities for its entire portfolio of companies.[2] Direct government engagement in the proxy voting process could arguably translate into *reduced* compliance costs for large asset managers who would no longer require a full-scale investment stewardship team and an army of compliance professionals to manage and oversee the voting decision-making function.

An alternative, more hands-off policy construct would be for government to function as an intermediating body among the panoply of voices that have an interest in the proper functioning of America's public companies, and to use that position to help steer asset management firms towards a more constructive form of corporate engagement. A federal agency—again, like the SEC or the Department of Labor—could work in hand with stakeholders via notice-and-comment rulemaking or other regulatory processes to establish a framework of standards that large asset managers would be encouraged to reflect in their voting determinations. Superficially such a framework would resemble the investment stewardship principles that have been adopted by financial regulatory bodies in countries like the United Kingdom and Japan, although the latter typically only set out very high-level philosophical principles and do not dive into the substance of the litany of matters decided by shareholder vote.

Whether government assumes a more or less heavy-handed role in overseeing how the largest asset management firms express their voice, regulatory mechanisms offer important advantages relative to the status quo in ensuring that the expression of that voice reflects the interests of the asset management industry's ultimate capital providers. The last decade has revealed that, despite the fanfare surrounding the rise of ESG activism, an array of limitations has made it challenging for asset managers to spearhead a genuine, New Deal-style stakeholder capitalism revival. In contrast, for all of their imperfections and inefficiencies, regulatory procedures and processes are designed to channel input from a broad range of stakeholders. Agency rulemaking processes provide the public at large—not just a small group of wealthy individuals and institutions—the opportunity to mold the formulation of agency rules and decisions. Political representatives are subject to periodic election cycles that enable the public to effect a change in policy course, given that the

---

[2] Employee figures based on SEC Fiscal Year 2022 Agency Report (https://www.sec.gov/files/sec-2022-agency-financial-report.pdf); BlackRock's 2023 Investment Stewardship Annual Report (https://www.blackrock.com/corporate/literature/publication/annual-stewardship-report-2023-summary.pdf).

individuals leading federal agencies are often political appointees. To be sure, some of the largest investment managers have instituted programs in recent years to solicit feedback from their fund investors, but these efforts have been limited in nature and focus on giving voice to major institutional clients, like pension funds, whose behavior is shaped by many of the same factors driving the behavior of professional asset managers. Regulatory processes have a wider reach that allows for fuller engagement with the perspectives of the real flesh and blood capital providers to the asset management industry and in the process can help check the influence of pernicious actors in our capital markets like activist hedge funds.

Explicit involvement on the part of regulators in how institutional investors make voting decisions has the potential of fostering a healthier political discourse about the role and responsibilities of big corporations in American society. Traditional political conservatives, who are often loathe to embrace expanded government power, must accept that the influence that institutional investors have accumulated over the last century does not reflect the natural workings of the free market, but is the product of an amalgamation of legal, economic, and technological developments. The question is not so much whether government should have a role in shaping the behavior of asset managers but what that role should look like. From this vantage point, political conservatives should welcome greater regulatory engagement. Directly acknowledging the inherently political nature of the role asset managers play in our economy—whether it pertains to ESG or other matters—provides conservatives an opening to put forward an affirmative policy vision that reflects their economic and political preferences. Today's shareholder-centered discourse masks the ideological character of the ESG discourse and corners conservatives into supporting an idealized view of shareholder primacy that ignores both their substantive policy concerns and the reality of today's political economy of capitalism. Although conservatives might worry about the politically liberal inclinations of federal bureaucrats, at least they can be removed and replaced following a successful election cycle, unlike the personnel who staff asset manager investment stewardship teams.

Formal regulatory processes that empower the public to shape the voting decisions of asset managers can also serve as a release valve through which public feeling about big business can be directed away from more disruptive corporate reform efforts. According to a Gallup poll, a combined 43% of Americans today express "very little" or "no" confidence in big business, the worst percentage recorded in the 48-year history of the poll, with the previous lows recorded in 2007 and 2009, around the time of the Great Financial

Crisis.[3] In recent years, much of that anxiety has found expression in the rise of a new antitrust movement that views rising market concentration in the U.S. economy as the central economic problem of our time and calls on regulators to reverse the trend by taking aggressive action to break up large companies. While the new Brandeisians have advocated sensible changes in a few discrete policy domains, the movement's fixation on eliminating "bigness" has limited its constructive capacity in ways that echo the experiences of the original Brandeisians in mid-twentieth -century America. As was the case then, the companies that drive the nation's economic engine today require size and scale to operate. Large corporations (defined by the Small Business Administration as firms employing at least 500 workers) are significantly more productive than small firms, resulting in lower prices for consumers and higher wages for workers. Large companies provide more benefits to their workers and invest more in training their workers as well as research and development than smaller firms. The rise of internet businesses whose size and reach are attributable to network effects raises even greater questions as to the advisability of Brandeisian policy solutions in the technology context. There is little evidence that breaking up a company like Facebook or Twitter would lead to an explosion of smaller-scale social media start-ups, or drive users to leave bigger platforms with established communities.[4] By focusing attention on how America's public companies should operate, enhanced regulatory engagement in the proxy voting landscape can help reroute public angst away from a one-dimensional, campaign to destroy the "curse of bigness" towards a more positive-minded effort to reform corporate behavior.

* * *

Despite the arguments favoring a greater role for government in the regulation of asset manager voting behavior, direct regulation of asset manager proxy voting power would represent a significant change in how we regulate our financial markets, one that warrants careful and thorough deliberation before putting theory into practice. In the words of John Coates, financial capitalism and financial institutions like asset managers do not present so much "a problem if that implies a solution to be found", but "a deep conflict

---

[3] Gallup. 2024. "Big Business." Gallup. https://news.gallup.com/poll/5248/big-business.aspx.
[4] Atkinson, Robert D. and Michael Lind. 2018. Big Is Beautiful: Debunking the Myth of Small Business. MIT Press. See also Robert D. Atkinson, "The Emergence of Anti-Corporate Progressivism", American Compass (August 25, 2021) (https://americancompass.org/the-commons/the-emergence-of-anti-corporate-progressivism/) and Michael Lind, "Antitrust or Countervailing Power?", American Compass (December 21, 2020) (https://americancompass.org/the-commons/antitrust-or-countervailing-power/).

between economics and politics, with the right response being public… oversight and management of private activity" without compromising the many financial and social benefits that the asset management industry produces by virtue of centralization and economies of scale.[5] Moreover, it would be naïve to expect that garnering sufficient political support for enhanced regulation of this sort would be a straightforward feat in today's political climate. Corporate boards may not be enamored with the excessive influence wielded by today's largest asset management firms, but it is difficult to imagine them being any more enthusiastic about government bureaucrats taking on that role. As countless social and cultural commentators have pointed out throughout the history of the United States, many Americans—across partisan lines—tend to be temperamentally averse towards government regulation relative to their counterparts in Europe and elsewhere where the concept of individualism and limited government is less closely intertwined with one's sense of national identity. The instinctual suspicion that many conservatives possess towards efforts to expand government regulation also presents a formidable political obstacle, notwithstanding the philosophical reasons why conservatives should be inclined to welcome enhanced regulation in the domain of proxy voting.

In the absence of subjecting the voting decision-making and corporate engagement processes of the large asset managers to direct democratic accountability, the question becomes what measures can asset managers take to improve their responsiveness to the interests of their providers of capital. Defining how asset managers can better perform their role as custodians of public capital, in terms of the actual substance of their voting decisions, is the critical problem that any effort to reform our current system must tackle—whether implemented through regulatory reform or the volitional efforts of industry actors.[6] The experiences of the last half century of institutional investor capitalism offer a number of important lessons as to how to operationalize this principle:

(1) Issues pertaining to the long-term economic health of companies and their role as constructive economic actors in society should take a front and center place in the voting decision-making and corporate engagement processes of large asset management firms. In the spirit of the business planning and stakeholder theorists of the post-New Deal Era, investment stewardship groups should carefully examine how business decisions impact the

---

[5] Coates, The Problem of 12. 142.
[6] See Strine, "Stewardship 2021: The Centrality of Institutional Investor Regulation to Restoring a Fair and Sustainable American Economy." 24 (institutional investors should be required to consider the investment objectives and horizons of their ultimate beneficiaries). See also Strine, "Toward Fair and Sustainable Capitalism." 15.

overall health of the corporation and the interests of its various constituencies. Recognizing that their flesh and blood capital providers are diversified investors in the overall economy, large asset management firms should candidly assess any given corporate practice or initiative in the context of its wider potential economic and social consequences, rather than through a stylized shareholder value maximization framework more appropriate for the undiversified individual investor of yore. In some cases, this may require an examination of "firm-specific" risks and opportunities, and in other cases, systematic issues that apply across the asset manager's investment portfolio. With respect to companies that require significant capital expenditures (like infrastructure or energy businesses) or research and development investments (such as technology or life sciences businesses), asset managers should encourage appropriate outlays for those purposes and intensively scrutinize proposals to reallocate cash to finance short-term returns to shareholders in the form of dividends or stock repurchases. Due consideration should be given to companies that emphasize a deliberate approach towards driving profitability, even if that means a tepid growth strategy relative to companies that turbocharge returns through serial acquisition activity that may not provide for as stable a foundation for a business' long-term wellbeing. Companies that maintain a lean overhead structure through perennially low wages and a flippant approach towards layoffs should not receive credit compared to businesses that adopt a thoughtful human capital management strategy that results in greater expense outlays but enables the preservation of a cohesive, experienced workforce that can produce higher-quality products and better service customers. Supply chain management—an area where the COVID-19 pandemic revealed the risks of offshoring and breaking up supply chains in an effort to lower costs and drive short-term returns to shareholders—is another domain where long-term thinking and foresight should be encouraged.[7] Re-orienting investment stewardship groups to consider economic matters requires personnel with the right expertise to appropriately factor in those matters in their analyses. Rather than exclusively staffing investment stewardship groups with legal and compliance specialists who lean on active fund managers and proxy advisors for guidance on economic issues, the large asset management firms should hire individuals with real-world business experience to help devise and implement their corporate engagement efforts.

---

[7] The law firm Wachtell, Lipton, Rosen & Katz put out a memorandum on this topic in the wake of the COVID-19 pandemic. Silk, David M. and Sabastian Niles. 2020. "The Other 'S' in ESG: Building a Sustainable and Resilient Supply Chain." https://corpgov.law.harvard.edu/2020/08/14/the-other-s-in-esg-building-a-sustainable-and-resilient-supply-chain/.

(2) Unlike the classical model of the individual shareholder, the regular working people who supply the substantial majority of capital flowing through the public equity markets have meaningful economic interests outside of their role as investors that are frequently more important to them than the interests signified by their equity investments (e.g., as employees reliant on wages to pay the bills, consumers sensitive to fluctuations in the prices of goods, etc.) Shareholder behavior that encourages companies to act in ways that give precedence to the interests of short-term financial investors can materially harm these interests. In formulating their engagement strategy, asset management firms should consider how corporate behavior holistically impacts the range of economic interests relevant to their beneficiaries, rather than single-mindedly focusing on the interests those beneficiaries have in any given public company as shareholders. The recent history of climate change activism is instructive. Institutional investors should not view emissions as a problem endemic to individual companies, but instead as a general social predicament, and ought to avoid pressure tactics that push companies to offload emission-producing businesses and assets to less environmentally conscious actors. In the same spirit, asset management firms should reject activist efforts to characterize climate change as a one-dimensional environmental challenge that does not implicate other important considerations relevant to their diversified investor base. The ultimate beneficiaries of asset managers include energy consumers and workers in industries whose prospects are intertwined with the health of the energy sector. Pushing energy companies to do whatever it takes to reduce emissions, without adequately giving weight to second and third-order effects (via higher energy prices and a depressed labor market), is likely to have a net negative impact on the economy and the overall wellbeing of those beneficiaries.

(3) While anti-ESG efforts to draw a neat line between economic topics and non-economic social and environmental concerns are unproductive, it is worthwhile for asset managers to exhibit caution when engaging with subjects that have obvious partisan overtones. In the words of Adolf Berle, whether a "public consensus" exists with respect to any given issue should be a critical factor that institutional investors consider in deciding what opinions to embrace and the vigor with which they assert those opinions. Attention to public opinion has an important accountability function in ensuring that the perspectives promoted by asset managers do not dramatically run counter to those espoused by their wider community of beneficiaries. It also allows asset managers to better understand what issues matter to the public (not just vociferous social activist groups) and may otherwise be overlooked by the relatively well-to-do, highly-educated professionals who run today's investment

firms. Climate change may be an existential crisis in the eyes of many corporate governance experts, but polling data consistently shows that the wider population does not share the same level of angst. Similarly, fighting climate change may seem like a straightforward exercise in cutting emissions until one reckons with the impacts on jobs and energy security among the general population, particularly lower and middle income households who disproportionately bear the impact of higher energy prices. These facts should make asset management firms pause before devoting so much time and resources to the topic (and deciding how they go about doing so) over other bread and butter pocket issues that have wider resonance with the public.

There are indications that some of these ideas are finding their way into the proxy voting and corporate engagement activities of the major global asset management firms. In January 2024, the *Financial Times* reported that BlackRock had been stressing "financial resilience" over traditional ESG themes in its meetings with executive management teams, asking companies to speak to their plans for managing concrete business and macroeconomic risks, like high interest rates.[8] The rise of artificial intelligence in particular has emerged as an important issue in corporate governance and institutional investor discourse, generating intense discussion among legal practitioners and industry participants as to the appropriate governance and disclosure practices that corporations should adopt with respect to their use of AI.[9] Asset managers have also started shifting away from supporting climate change activist efforts that simply focus on pressuring energy companies to cut back emissions towards more forward-looking measures, such as directing capital towards infrastructure projects intended to speed the transition from fossil fuels.[10] In his 2024 letter to investors, Larry Fink omitted any mention of ESG—consistent with his comment the year prior about no longer using the term—and called for "energy pragmatism" in balancing the need for

---

[8] Levine, Matt. 2024. "Coinbase Trades Beanie Babies." Bloomberg. https://www.bloomberg.com/opinion/articles/2024-01-18/coinbase-trades-beanie-babies; Khalaf, Roula. 2024. "BlackRock stresses financial strength over ESG in company calls." Financial Times. https://www.ft.com/content/b7c04084-68ee-4512-833b-0bba4f608a36.

[9] See, e.g., Hong, Richard. 2024. "AI and Corporate Securities Disclosures." American Bar Association. https://www.americanbar.org/groups/litigation/resources/newsletters/corporate-counsel/spring2024-artificial-intelligence-corporate-securities-disclosures/; Levi, Stuart and Meredith Slawe and Priya Matadar. 2024. "Data Collection & Management, Professional Perspective—How Companies Should Be Thinking About Disclosing AI Usage to Consumers." Bloomberg Law—Practical Guidance. https://www.bloomberglaw.com/external/document/XDEBUU4K000000/data-collection-management-professional-perspective-how-companie; Katz, David A. and Laura A. McIntosh. 2024. "AI Disclosure and Governance in the Spotlight." New York Law Journal. https://www.law.com/newyorklawjournal/2024/05/22/ai-disclosure-and-governance-in-the-spotlight/?slreturn=20240623205530.

[10] Pitcher, Jack, and Amrith Ramkumar. 2024. "Step Aside, ESG. BlackRock Is Doing 'Transition Investing' Now." The Wall Street Journal. https://www.wsj.com/finance/investing/step-aside-esg-blackrock-is-doing-transition-investing-now-59df3908.

companies to meet global energy demands while also pursuing longer-term investments in clean energy alternatives.[11] Meanwhile, institutional investor support for shareholder proposals that parrot ESG activist positions on hot-button political issues has declined. Just 3% of the 257 resolutions submitted by shareholders in 2023 on environmental and social issues won majority support, down from 14% in 2022 and 21% in 2021.[12]

Other public policy and activist groups have also started to adjust their advocacy efforts in response to the changed dynamics of today's capital markets. Most notably, The Shareholder Commons—a non-profit organization founded by a former managing partner of one of Delaware's leading corporate law firms—has made it its mission statement to help diversified shareholders "reprioritize their activism" by addressing "social and environment issues from the perspective of shareholders who diversify their investments to optimize risk and return."[13] Rather than view shareholder interests through the traditional lens of an investor's interest in a particular company, the Shareholder Commons calls on companies to take a portfolio view of their shareholder's interests based on their interests as diversified investors. As of the date of this book's publication, it is uncertain whether these endeavors have produced change in corporate behavior. Importantly, these efforts have thus far predominantly involved filing lawsuits and lobbying shareholder proposals at companies without similarly pushing their asset manager shareholders to update their model of decision-making with respect to corporate engagement and proxy voting. Given that there is no explicit basis in state statutory or common law—which defines the parameters of corporate board fiduciary duties—for conceiving of corporate fiduciary duties by specific reference to the interests of diversified investors, corporate boards have been able to successfully push back on this type of shareholder activism. But at the very least the emergence of organizations like the Shareholder Commons signals the beginning of an effort to boldly rethink conventional notions of how investor–corporate relations should be structured that is promising.

---

[11] Fink, Larry. 2024. "Larry Fink's 2024 Annual Chairman's Letter to Investors." BlackRock. https://www.blackrock.com/us/individual/about-us/larry-fink-annual-chairmans-letter?gad_source=1&gclid=CjwKCAjw5ImwBhBtEiwAFHDZx-22qsYou2VszibidE-kQbMZO2MzalFdiIEHZW6huX319jieVA_-UhoCpVkQAvD_BwE&gclsrc=aw.ds.

[12] Bryan, Kenza. 2024. "A 'catastrophic' decline in support for shareholder activism: Support for ESG resolutions plunges among the biggest asset managers." Financial Times | Moral Money: Anti-ESG Investing. https://www.ft.com/content/a54eef2c-337b-4758-a279-c737c89ffed9.

[13] The Shareholder Commons. 2024. "About—Mission and Vision." https://theshareholdercommons.com/about/#our-team.

Ultimately, enhancing the responsiveness of asset managers to the needs of their real-world providers of capital requires a comprehensive reassessment of the ideas and assumptions that have conventionally driven the decision-making processes of institutional investors. Berle concluded *The Modern Corporation* by noting that the rise of the modern corporation in early twentieth-century America "has brought a concentration of economic power which can compete on equal terms with the modern state—economic power versus political power, each strong in its own field."[14] A similar comment can be made today about the rise of asset managers. The emergence of a healthier relationship between today's asset managers and corporations hinges on an appreciation of the inherently *political character* of the power that asset managers have accumulated. Whether or not that appreciation can come to form solely through the voluntary actions of market actors, or will require more direct action by regulators, remains to be seen.

---

[14] Berle, The Modern Corporation, 313.

Index

A

activist hedge funds vi, 3, 4, 10, 11, 46, 47, 51, 52, 64, 93, 95, 103, 105, 106, 108, 111, 114, 115, 127, 128, 139, 141, 143, 152
algorithmic trading 48
anti-ESG 5, 91, 134, 137, 156, 158
antitrust 32, 34–36, 91, 140, 153

B

Berle, Adolf 6, 17, 23–25, 30, 37, 156
Big Three viii, ix, 1, 5, 9, 50, 78–80, 85–88, 94, 95, 121, 126, 128, 129, 137, 143
BlackRock viii, 1, 50, 78–80, 88, 91, 124, 132, 133, 137, 141, 151, 157, 158
Brandeis, Louis 24, 25, 31
Business Roundtable v, vi, 60, 71, 79

C

Chicago School 8, 55–57, 59, 67, 75, 133
classified 92, 127
climate change vi, 1, 4, 5, 9, 10, 29, 30, 75, 78, 83, 85, 86, 88–90, 111, 112, 116, 123, 124, 132, 133, 156, 157
corporate law viii, 7, 8, 19, 25, 26, 28, 29, 53, 57, 60, 65, 70, 73, 136, 141, 145, 158

D

Delaware vi, 7, 19, 28, 29, 49, 54, 158

E

energy industry 10, 11, 105, 106, 110, 114–116
Engine No.1 1–5
Enron 57, 69
ERISA 40, 41, 59, 84, 150

ESG ix, 2, 4, 9–11, 29, 30, 76–80, 84–94, 99, 111–115, 117, 123, 125–128, 131–135, 137, 143, 151, 152, 157, 158
Exxon 1, 2, 4, 5, 106

F

Fink, Larry 78, 131, 157, 158
Friedman, Milton 55, 60, 67, 132

G

Galbraith, John Kenneth 36, 73
gender diversity 9, 10, 30, 85–89, 123, 124, 133
Glass Lewis 64, 126, 128
Great Financial Crisis 4, 9, 10, 69, 75, 92, 97, 99, 153

H

High-frequency Trading 49

I

index funds viii, ix, 5, 39, 42, 50, 51, 54, 78, 95, 119, 123, 128, 129, 137, 141, 143
investment stewardship v, vi, 64, 85, 124, 126–128, 150–152, 154, 155
investor activism 45
ISS 64, 126, 128

J

Jensen, Michael 56

L

Larry Fink 79
Lund, Dorothy 88, 122

M

mandatory disclosures 5, 7, 29
Martin, Roger 69
Monks, Robert 59, 64

N

New Deal 4–7, 9, 10, 33, 36, 37, 39, 44, 67, 73–75, 90, 154

O

Obama, Barack 75, 83, 84, 111

P

pass through 136–140
Posner, Richard 56
Preston, Lee 72
private equity 8, 43, 44, 46, 47, 51, 52, 58, 63, 100, 102–104
private markets vii, 10, 99, 100, 103
proxy advisory firms 59, 64, 93, 126, 127

S

SEC vi, 29, 34, 42, 44, 48, 58, 59, 85, 88, 93, 101, 127, 138, 141–144, 150, 151
shareholder activism 43, 106, 158
shareholder primacy 5, 8, 11, 55–62, 65, 67, 68, 70, 75, 76, 78, 86, 92, 126, 128, 133, 134, 152
short-termism 4, 10, 11, 61, 62, 64, 70, 92, 97, 115, 132
stakeholder capitalism vi, 4, 9, 29, 71–73, 75, 76, 79, 133, 151
State Street viii, 1, 50, 78, 79, 87, 123
Stout, Lynn 70
Strine, Leo 7, 49, 135
SWOT 74

T

takeovers 56, 57

The Modern Corporation 6, 7, 24, 26, 28–30, 32, 33, 45, 50, 55, 72, 73, 99, 142, 159

Trump, Donald 83, 84, 88

V

Vanguard viii, 1, 42, 50, 76, 78, 79, 85, 131, 137, 138

9783031647321